21世纪英语专业系列教材

美国诗歌选读

Selected Readings in American Poetry

陶 洁 主编

编者 陶 洁　刘树森　张世耘　陈法春
　　　林 斌　李 晋　金衡山　崔鲜泉

北京大学出版社
PEKING UNIVERSITY PRESS

图书在版编目(CIP)数据

美国诗歌选读 / 陶洁主编. —北京：北京大学出版社，2008.9
(21世纪英语专业系列教材)
ISBN 978-7-301-13843-4

Ⅰ.美… Ⅱ.陶… Ⅲ.①英语-阅读教程-高等学校-教材 ②英语-诗歌-文学欣赏 Ⅳ.H319.4:I

中国版本图书馆 CIP 数据核字(2008)第 067937 号

书　　　　名：	美国诗歌选读
著作责任者：	陶　洁　主编
组稿编辑：	张　冰
责任编辑：	刘　强
标准书号：	ISBN 978-7-301-13843-4/I·2044
出版发行：	北京大学出版社
地　　　址：	北京市海淀区成府路 205 号　100871
网　　　址：	http://www.pup.cn
电　　　话：	邮购部 62752015　发行部 62750672　编辑部 62767347　出版部 62754962
电子邮箱：	landwok@163.com
印　刷　者：	北京飞达印刷有限责任公司
经　销　者：	新华书店
	787 毫米×1092 毫米　16 开本　17.5 印张　405 千字
	2008 年 9 月第 1 版　2008 年 9 月第 1 次印刷
定　　　价：	32.00 元

未经许可，不得以任何方式复制或抄袭本书之部分或全部内容。
版权所有，侵权必究　举报电话：010-62752024
　　　　　　　　　　　电子邮箱：fd@pup.pku.edu.cn

《21世纪英语专业系列教材》编写委员会

(以姓氏笔画排序)

王守仁　王克非　申　丹
刘意青　李　力　胡壮麟
桂诗春　梅德明　程朝翔

总 序

　　北京大学出版社自 2005 年以来已出版《语言与应用语言学知识系列读本》多种,为了配合第十一个五年计划,现又策划陆续出版《21 世纪英语专业系列教材》。这个重大举措势必受到英语专业广大教师和学生的欢迎。

　　作为英语教师,最让人揪心的莫过于听人说英语不是一个专业,只是一个工具。说这些话的领导和教师的用心是好的,为英语专业的毕业生将来找工作着想,因此要为英语专业的学生多多开设诸如新闻、法律、国际商务、经济、旅游等其他专业的课程。但事与愿违,英语专业的教师们很快发现,学生投入英语学习的时间少了,掌握英语专业课程知识甚微,即使对四个技能的掌握也并不比大学英语学生高明多少,而那个所谓的第二专业在有关专家的眼中只是学到些皮毛而已。

　　英语专业的路在何方?有没有其他路可走?这是需要我们英语专业教师思索的问题。中央领导关于创新是一个民族的灵魂和要培养创新人才等的指示精神,让我们在层层迷雾中找到了航向。显然,培养学生具有自主学习能力和能进行创造性思维是我们更为重要的战略目标,使英语专业的人才更能适应 21 世纪的需要,迎接 21 世纪的挑战。

　　如今,北京大学出版社外语部的领导和编辑同志们,也从教材出版的视角探索英语专业的教材问题,从而为贯彻英语专业教学大纲做些有益的工作,为教师们开设大纲中所规定的必修、选修课程提供各种教材。"21 世纪英语专业系列教材"是普通高等教育"十一五"国家级规划教材和国家"十一五"重点出版规划项目《面向新世纪的立体化网络化英语学科建设丛书》的重要组成部分。这套系列教材要体现新世纪英语教学的自主化、协作化、模块化和超文本化,结合外语教材的具体情况,既要解决语言、教学内容、教学方法和教育技术的时代化,也要坚持弘扬以爱国主义为核心的民族精神。因此,今天北京大学出版社在大力提倡专业英语教学改革的基础上,编辑出版各种英语专业技能、英语专业知识和相关专业知识课程的教材,以培养具有创新性思维的和具有实际工作能力的学生,充分体现了时代精神。

　　北京大学出版社的远见卓识,也反映了英语专业广大师生盼望已久的心愿。由北京大学等全国几十所院校具体组织力量,积极编写相关教材。这就是说，这套教材是由一些高等院校有水平有经验的第一线教师们制定编写大纲，反复讨论，特别是考虑到在不同层次、不同背景学校之间取得平衡，避免了先前的教材或偏难或偏易的弊病。与此同时，一批知名专家教授参与策划和教材审定工作，保证了教材质量。

当然，这套系列教材出版只是初步实现了出版社和编者们的预期目标。为了获得更大效果，希望使用本系列教材的教师和同学不吝指教，及时将意见反馈给我们，使教材更加完善。

航道已经开通，我们有决心乘风破浪，奋勇前进！

胡壮麟
北京大学蓝旗营

前言

美国文学中,包括早期的殖民文学,诗歌是发展得比较早的。1620年第一批清教徒抵达新大陆,1650年安妮·勃莱特斯特里特(Anne Bradstreet,约 1612—1672)的诗集《近来在美洲出现的第十个缪斯》就在英国出版并且受到大洋两岸读者的欢迎。虽然她的诗歌在形式技巧方面表现出英国诗歌的影响,但内容却完全不同,涉及清教主义的政治和宗教,反映殖民者在美洲大陆艰苦创业的生活和心态。此后200年,美国很少出版女诗人的作品,甚至勃莱特斯特里特的诗歌也逐渐为人忘却,但当女性主义者在20世纪把她"重新发现"时,评论家不得不承认她的作品,尤其那些描写个人经历和家庭生活的抒情诗歌仍然有其特色和欣赏价值。

殖民时期另一位值得关注的诗人是菲利斯·惠特莱(Phyllis Wheatley,1761—1784)。她在非洲出生,7岁时被掳,被迫成为波士顿一个商人的奴隶。但她天资聪颖,15岁就发表诗歌并获得好评。1773年她出版第一部诗集,标题《关于各种题材——宗教和道德方面的诗歌》说明她的写作反映新英格兰地区的文化和清教思想,尽管她的手法技巧仍然模仿英国诗歌。然而她关于被迫为奴的《从非洲到美洲》却是十分典型的美国题材。使她成为美国黑人文学的创始人。她还是第一个出版诗集、第一个以写作维持生计的美国黑人女诗人。

18世纪殖民者忙于为独立而奋斗,诗歌方面的建树不是很大,无论在音韵格律还是修辞用典方面都没有摆脱英国诗歌的影响,但他们开始强调以美洲大陆为题材。随着独立革命的成功和美利坚合众国的建立,美国诗歌和美国文学进入了新时期。政治家丹尼尔·韦伯斯特(Daniel Webster,1782—1852)强调美国在军事上取得胜利,在文学艺术方面也必定不会落后于他人。爱默生(Ralph Waldo Emerson,1803—1882)号召美国人民相信自己,割断对英国和旧世界的依赖,走自己的路,创建崭新的国家和文学。他身体力行创建超验主义俱乐部,撰写文章宣传人的灵魂和直觉意识是宇宙中的"超灵"(相当于上帝)的一部分,因此人也有神性,应该得到尊重。上帝在自然界显现,人可以通过自然了解上帝从而了解自己,由于个人与上帝相通,因此人应该也必须相信自己。诗歌的作用正是为了表现自我并且反映真理。爱默生在自己的诗歌创作中从题材内容到音步韵律都进行试验,努力使诗歌摆脱传统的束缚。他并不是最出色的诗人,但他在推动美国浪漫主义诗歌和文学的发展方面却起着不可磨灭的作用。在他的肯定与鼓励下,惠特曼(Walt Whitman,1818—1892)独辟蹊径成为真正富有美国特色的一代大师。另一位美国诗人埃米莉·狄金森(又译:迪金森)(Emily Dickinson,1830—1886)未必完全同意爱默生的超验主义自然观,但他的理论却促使她对自然、上帝与自我和生死等问题进行更为深入的思考,创作了近2000首匠心独具的优秀作品。

美国诗歌选读

美国诗歌从一开始就具有多样性和反叛性的特点。这两者在19世纪浪漫主义诗歌表现得更为突出。所谓多样性，不仅仅指诗人是由各种民族和不同种族组成，更重要的是他们在诗歌的风格技巧和主题内容等方面都各具特色，极少雷同。在当时的诗歌中心新英格兰地区既有力求创新、以大自然为主要歌颂对象的爱默生、梭罗(Henry David Thoreau, 1817—1862)等超验主义诗人，也有亨利·朗费罗(Henry Wadworth Longfellow, 1807—1882)、詹姆斯·罗素·洛厄尔(James Russell Lowell, 1819—1891)等"婆罗门"诗人。他们出身名门望族，本人常常在欧洲接受教育，后来成为大学教授或知名学者，他们崇尚高雅，坚持以欧洲文化为中心的"斯文传统"，当然在诗歌写作方面仍然遵循保守的欧洲传统。他们蔑视大胆革新的惠特曼，认为他的诗歌粗俗下流。约翰·格林里夫·惠蒂亚(John Greenleaf Whittier, 1807—1892)甚至把惠特曼送他的《草叶集》扔到火炉里烧毁。然而，这些"婆罗门"诗人虽然有共同的诗歌主张，他们的作品并不雷同。惠蒂亚表现新英格兰地区农民的生活；詹姆斯·罗素·洛厄尔的诗歌多半抨击社会和政治问题，以机智和讽刺见长。至于最著名的朗费罗，他的诗歌描绘美国的风土人情和历史传统，他的《海华莎之歌》是第一首歌颂美洲大陆土著居民印第安人的史诗。

另一位认同欧洲传统的诗人是爱伦·坡(Edgar Allan Poe, 1809—1849)。但他似乎更喜欢充满异国情调的背景、遥远的年代、梦魇般的气氛、阴暗的心理和美人之死。他十分重视节奏、音韵、象征手段以及情节结构和手法技巧所产生的效果。他是第一个对国外，尤其是法国诗人产生巨大影响的美国诗人，可惜他在当时的美国诗歌界不受重视，被称为"叮当诗人"。

即便是两位最富有革新精神的惠特曼和埃米莉·狄金森都大相径庭。前者的诗篇气势磅礴，包罗万象，后者小巧玲珑，从日常生活的一点一滴入手，以小见大。前者抛弃传统的诗歌韵律规则和诗歌语言，后者虽然也采用日常口语但在诗节、韵律等要素方面却遵循古老的赞美诗的传统。两位诗人的为人也很不一样。惠特曼为了宣传自己可以匿名写赞美评论。狄金森却只要求亲友的欣赏，并不追求名利，生前发表的诗歌竟不到10首。

美国诗歌的另一个特性——反叛——在19世纪也体现得很突出。爱默生率先号召新型诗人跟英国传统彻底决裂，以美国为题材创建崭新的富有美国特色的新诗歌。他在惠特曼的诗歌中看到了希望，因此，他给惠特曼写信说，"在你伟大事业开始的时候，我向你致意。"惠特曼不负所望，写出歌颂个人和自我的民主诗歌。他糅合演讲术、新闻报道和歌剧等各种技巧，用散文式的日常口语成功地创造了充满重复、排列、长句、头韵等富有音律节奏感的自由体诗歌。惠特曼开创了美国诗歌试验革新之先风，对20世纪，甚至当今美国和世界诗歌都有深刻影响。

埃米莉·狄金森在创新方面的成就不次于惠特曼。虽然她经常采用4行一节并且押韵的传统的赞美诗形式，但她使用不正规押韵、突兀的中断、甚至奇怪的破折号或大写字母等手法使她的诗歌具有莫测高深的神秘色彩。她无视一切语法规则，把名词等同于动词，不可数名词变成可数名词，但这一切又显得十分自然贴切。她的意象和比喻别出心裁，加上她简练而精确的刻画常常产生出乎异常的效果。她对生与死、爱情和苦难、上帝和神灵等问题所抱的怀疑而又执著探讨的精神使她超越了她的时代，成为20世纪现代主义诗歌的先驱。

可惜,无论传统派或革新派都没有强大的诗人群体,美国诗歌在世界诗坛并没有什么影响。直到1872年,英国评论家威廉·罗赛蒂(William Michael Rossetti,1848—1919)编辑出版了《美国诗歌选》,并且把书献给了惠特曼,对他做出很高的评价,美国诗歌才开始走出国门,引起了外界的注意。

1912年是美国诗歌史上的一个重要年代。这一年,女诗人哈利特·门罗(Harriet Monroe,1860—1936)创办小杂志《诗刊》,为有志于革新诗歌的诗人提供出版园地,开始了又一次反叛运动——现代主义诗歌运动。在庞德(Ezra Pound,1885—1972)的推荐下,《诗刊》后来发表了艾略特的《普罗弗洛克的情歌》以及日后成为大家的弗洛斯特(又译:弗罗斯特)(Robert Frost,1874—1963)、华莱士·史蒂文斯(Wallace Stevens,1879—1955)和芝加哥诗人林赛(Vachel Lindsay,1879—1931)、埃德加·李·马斯特斯(Edgar Lee Masters,1869—1950)等人的早期作品。也在1912年,庞德和英国诗人休姆(T.E. Hulme,1883—1917)等提出意象派诗歌的三条原则:用精确的语言直接描绘主观或客观的事物;使用简练的语言,取消一切无助于表达的词语;节奏依附于音乐性词语的顺序而不是按照节拍来安排。庞德的主张得到艾米·洛厄尔(Amy Lowell,1874—1925)、希尔达·杜利特(Hilda Doolittle,1886—1961)、威廉·卡洛斯·威廉斯(William Carlos Williams,1883—1963)等诗人的支持。1914年庞德编辑出版意象派诗人的诗集,扩大了新诗运动的影响。

作为新诗运动的领袖,庞德不仅要求美国作家日新月异,形成新的"文艺复兴"和文学"大觉醒"并且为试验革新提出各种理论主张和原则,介绍英国、法国和其他任何地方的诗歌信息。他大力推荐艾略特、弗洛斯特等人的作品,甚至帮助艾略特修改他的《荒原》。另一方面,他身体力行把自己的理论原则运用到自己的创作中,例如,视觉独特而个性鲜明的意象诗歌《地铁车站》;充满非线性叙述、拼贴式碎片、无关联意象等手法和表现异化、批判社会等现代派诗歌特色的《休·塞尔温·莫伯利》。当然还有被一些评论家称为"现代派诗歌巨作"而内容庞杂,从诗歌理论到道德哲学以至名人评价、经济政策,几乎无所不包的《诗章》。虽然他在第二次世界大战期间支持意大利法西斯分子,在他们的电台上发表广播讲话,攻击美国和犹太人,战后美国法院判他犯有叛国罪行。但他对英美现代诗歌发展所做的贡献还是值得肯定的。艾略特是又一位住在英国的新诗运动主要人物,他的《荒原》运用"想象力的逻辑",抛弃一般诗歌中的过渡、概括、论述等手法,借用大量的欧洲文学典故、神话、历史、暗示和联想,运用多种语言,以不连贯的结构、多变的语言、有节奏的自由体,构成一部思想和情调和谐一致的诗篇,一时成为诗人们模仿的典范。但是扎根美国生活的诗人并不完全接受艾略特的诗歌理论。威廉斯就曾说过:"《荒原》的发表好像爆炸了一个原子弹,把我们的世界给毁灭了。"威廉斯既摒弃诗歌传统,又反对艾略特大量运用博学典故、过分强调修辞的主张。他的诗歌如《佩特森》(Paterson)等深受惠特曼的影响,朴素简洁、不拘形式,摆脱传统韵律的束缚。

那时期的美国诗人不仅学习20世纪的流派还深受19世纪法国象征派诗人、17世纪英国玄学派诗人,以及中国、印度等世界文化,当然还有19世纪本国诗人如惠特曼、狄金森等人的影响。他们的诗歌可以说是百花齐放,诗人们有意识地对诗歌的传统风格、表现形式和技巧进行革新,纷纷寻找十分个性化的语言和手法来表现自己对社会、世界、人生的看法。例如,许多诗人用自由诗体而不大喜欢格律音步严谨的传统诗体,弗洛斯特虽然表面上采用传统形式,但他并不完全遵守固定的模式。在语言方面,诗人们反对传统的高雅诗歌语言,采用日常生活的口语。当然,诗人们也各不相同,威廉斯的自由诗体跟艾略特和庞德的风格就大不一样。威廉斯更强调视觉效果,而艾略特则看重音步和节奏的音乐性。他们都主张用口语,但弗洛斯特采用新英格兰地区农民的语言,林赛和桑德堡使用中西部老百姓的语言,而艾略特的诗歌虽然有口语的味道,他却认为有些思想感情用其他风格也许能表现得更好。诗人们深切感到现代生活非常复杂,充满了矛盾和冲突,他们的诗歌就是要表现这种不协调。于是,他们大量采用幽默与反讽。桑德堡和林赛依靠西部幽默,在高度夸大中达到挖苦的目的,弗洛斯特则突出新英格兰地区不露感情的冷漠式的讽刺,而艾略特、威廉斯和斯蒂文斯等人的反讽就更为含蓄和深沉。诗人们还常常提出自己的文学主张。他们的理论,如庞德对意象派诗歌的定义等理论、艾略特的"客观对应物"、"感受的分化"、"想象力的逻辑"、"作家不能脱离传统但要像催化剂那样使传统起变化"以及威廉斯的"不表现观念,只描写事物"和斯蒂文斯关于客观现实和想象力的关系等理论不仅在当时起作用还对后来的诗歌有很大的影响。

　　这时期百花齐放,流派纷呈,充分体现美国诗歌多样化的特点。在中西部有坚持惠特曼的传统、反映劳动人民思想感情的芝加哥诗人。林赛有意识地吸收民歌和爵士音乐的成分,使诗歌更具有美国特色。马斯特斯采用短小精悍、自由韵体和日常口语的诗歌反映小城镇平庸保守的生活给人带来的磨难。桑德堡(Carl Sandburg, 1878—1967)既继承惠特曼的传统,诗歌接近散文,没有格律韵脚和规则重音,也没有复杂的形象或比喻,他还吸收民间歌谣、民间谚语的优良传统,语言朴素而幽默。另一位中西部诗人哈特·克莱恩(Hart Crane, 1899—1932),早年追随艾略特,后来接受惠特曼和桑德堡的影响。长诗《桥》描写20世纪的机器文明和"美国神话",既模仿艾略特,又有惠特曼的影响。在新英格兰地区主要有弗洛斯特和罗宾逊(Edward Arlington Robinson, 1869—1935)。他们受到新诗歌运动的感染,但并不全盘接受它的原则和主张。弗洛斯特基本上采用传统的诗歌形式,但排斥其中矫揉造作等消极因素。他的诗歌简洁朴素、易于上口,然而朴素中寓有深意,往往从自然景色、凡人俗事开始,以深刻的哲理思想结束。1922年4月,美国南方田纳西州的范德比尔特大学开始出版一本以研究和发表诗歌为主的《逃亡者》杂志,宣告又一个诗人群体的诞生和"南方文艺复兴"的开始。该杂志主编为诗人、批评家艾伦·泰特(Allen Tate, 1899—1979)参与编辑的有包括"新批评"理论的创始人约翰·克鲁·兰瑟姆(John Crowe Ransom, 1888—1974)、美国第一个桂冠诗人和唯一在诗歌和小说两方面都获得普利策奖的罗伯特·潘·沃伦(Robert Penn Warren, 1950—1989)等人。他们提倡南方的乡土文化传统和古典美学思想,赞赏英国的玄学派诗人,强调诗歌创作是一门艺术,因此十方注重音韵节奏等诗歌形式、和反讽、隐喻等手法技巧。1925年杂志停刊,1928年,唐纳德·戴维逊(Donald Davidson, 1893—1968)编辑出版了《逃亡者:诗选》。此后,逃亡者诗人发展成为批判工业化和资本主义、主张维护和复兴南方农业经济及传统生活方式的"重农学派"。尽管人员变化并不大,尽管他们的政治主张和创作原则都趋于保守,但由于他们都是有成就的诗人和学者,后来又多半当了大学教授和杂志主编,他们的文学主张和批评理论在年轻人中有很大的影响。例如,罗伯特·洛威尔(Robert Lowell, 1917—1977)为了追随兰瑟姆和泰特,宁可放弃哈佛的学业到南方的肯庸学院上学。

第一次世界大战以后还涌现出一批女诗人,除了热心意象派诗歌的艾米·洛威尔和希尔达·杜利特以外还有居住在法国但对现代主义文学运动起很大影响的格特鲁特·斯泰因(Gertrude Stein, 1874—1946)、既写诗歌又写诗剧的埃德娜·圣文森特·米莱(Edna St. Vincent Millay, 1892—1950)、本人因一本《诗选》(1951)而同时获得三项大奖并在担任《日晷》杂志编辑发现提携年轻诗人的玛丽安·莫尔(Marianne Moore, 1887—1972)和她的年轻朋友伊丽莎白·毕晓普(Elizabeth Bishop, 1911—1979)等。

这时期的多样性还表现在诗人种族的多元化。在纽约哈莱姆黑人居住区的黑人音乐家、诗人和小说家纷纷用各种形式表现他们作为黑人的自豪和信心以及黑人文化的尊严,形成著名的"哈莱姆文艺复兴"。在诗歌方面最著名的是兰斯顿·休斯(Langston Hughes, 1902—1967)。他的贡献在于他把黑人的布鲁士、爵士等音乐节奏和手法运用到诗歌中。他有很明确的写作目的——为黑人申诉和呼吁。他用幽默的手法讽刺白人对黑人的偏见,控诉他们的种族压迫,满怀同情地叙说黑人的痛苦与无奈以及他们奋斗反抗的决心。休斯在写诗的同时还从事创作小说和戏剧。由于他一生都为自己的人民而写作,他被称为"黑人的桂冠诗人"。"哈莱姆文艺复兴"中还有两位诗人——贡体·卡伦(Countee Cullen, 1903—1946)和吉恩·图墨(Jean Toomer, 1894—1967)。他们两人的黑人意识都没有休斯强烈。卡伦排斥现代主义诗歌的新手法,坚持雪莱、济慈的抒情诗传统。图墨的《甘蔗》并非都是诗歌,其中还有小说和散文,被认为是第一部黑人作家采用十分先进的现代主义手法反映黑人生活和种族歧视的重要作品。可惜此后,图墨刻意同黑人文学保持距离,很少发表以种族为主题的作品。

在这个美国文学史上第二次文艺复兴的时期里,出现了大量日后被认为是经典的诗集,例如,桑德堡的《芝加哥诗集》(1916)、《人民,是的》(1936);华莱士·史蒂文斯的《在基韦斯特形成的秩序观念》(1934)、《带蓝吉他的人》(1937);威廉·卡洛斯·威廉斯的《春天及其他》(1923);弗洛斯特的《西去的溪流》(1929)、《诗选》(1930)和《又一片牧场》(1936);哈特·克莱恩的《桥》(1930);约翰·克鲁·兰瑟姆的《寒战与发烧》(1924);兰斯顿·休斯的《疲惫的布鲁士》(1926);图墨的《甘蔗》(1923);女诗人莫尔的《诗选》(1935)和毕晓普的《北与南》(1946)等。当然还有艾略特的《荒原》(1922)、《圣灰星期三》(1930)和《四个四重奏》(1945)以及庞德的《休·塞尔温·莫伯利》(1920)和《诗章》(1915—1970)等。

1929年美国股市崩溃,加上干旱等天灾,美国陷入严重的经济危机。人们为生存而挣扎,无暇顾及历来被认为是高雅艺术的诗歌。然而1934年美国诗人学会的成立对支持诗人和发展与普及诗歌起了很大的影响。一位在欧洲长大的美国人玛丽·布洛克夫人(Mrs. Marie Bullock, 1911—1986)回到美国发现这里不像法国等欧洲国家那样重视诗歌和诗人,她在朋友的帮助下成立了美国诗人学会,目的在于"帮助诗人"和"培养大众对诗歌的兴趣"。学会成立以来一直为实现这两个目的而努力,建立了7个大奖、200多个学院诗歌奖、资助出版诗歌的基金、倡导先在纽约、华盛顿后来普及到全国大城市的诗歌朗读和讨论活动、1996年又确定每年4月为诗歌月、1997又建立诗人网(poets.org),提供500多位诗人的信息和2000多首诗歌,访问人数每月超过 100 万,是美国最受欢迎的网页之一。几乎所有有一定名望的诗人都曾在某个时期得到过这个学会的帮助。70 多年来,学会始终不渝地坚持当年的两个宗旨,不仅成功而且日益兴旺。这在物欲横流的美国实在是非常难能可贵的。

第二次世界大战后,美国以头号强国的面目出现于世界。作为在大战中获益最大而损失最小的国家,战后美国进入了空前的繁荣、发达和扩张的时期并充满信心地致力于发展社会、经济、科技和提高人民生活水平等问题。但随着冷战与麦卡锡主义的加剧,美国作家开始反思美国价值的真实内涵、考虑个人是否应该顺应时势和社会的规范。50 年代作家普遍批评郊区中产阶级对物质生活的追求和企业、公司对人的个性的压抑。在诗歌方面,影响最大的著作可能是艾伦·金斯堡的长诗《嚎叫》(1956)。他和杰克·凯鲁亚克(Jack Kerouac, 1922—1969)、威廉·巴勒斯(William S. Burroughs, 1914—1997)、劳伦斯·佛林盖逖(Lawrence Ferlinghetti, 1919—)等人形成了声势浩大的反文化的"垮掉一代"①。他们抽大麻,过放荡不羁的生活,以持不同政见的文化战士自居,通过诗歌和小说来揭露中产阶级的美国和官方政治,冲击传统的观念、习俗,甚至生活方式。他们的出现受到欢迎也引起恐惧和攻击。经过几乎半个世纪的争论,现在的共识是,"垮掉一代"的诗人和作家在嬉笑怒骂的后面是严肃的对生存危机的关注,他们企图通过嘲弄调侃来颠覆已有的秩序,惊醒读者,解放受各种压抑,包括性压抑的年轻人,使他们考虑如何建立新秩序和重建一个新的美国。

"垮掉一代"作家更大的贡献在于对文体的试验和改革。金斯堡直抒胸臆而又激情澎湃的长句一反艾略特的非个性诗歌理论,冲破新批评派为诗歌规定的种种束缚,掀起一场新诗歌革命。当时已经成名的老诗人威廉斯把金斯堡给他的信件收入长诗《佩特森》。1955 年,罗伯特·洛厄尔——一位紧跟新批评规范的诗人在西海岸听了金斯堡和加里·斯奈德(Gary Snyder, 1930—)吟诵(有时甚至在爵士乐的伴奏下)他们的尚未发表的诗歌——《嚎叫》和《神话与文本》大受震撼,开始改变诗风,采用个人化的话语,反映个人的情感与心态,开创了自白派诗歌,并且在年轻人中间造就了一批诸如西尔维亚·普拉斯(Sylvia Plath, 1932—1963)和安·塞克斯顿(Anne Sexton, 1928—1974)等自白派诗人。

洛厄尔的年龄介乎艾略特等老一代诗人和金斯堡等年轻诗人之间,因此,他的转变表明美国诗歌不再有一个占主导地位的派别或中心。50 年代以后,美国诗歌越来越多元化。当时老一代诗人,尤其是从前的"逃亡"派诗人如艾伦·泰特、罗伯特·潘·沃伦等仍然在写作。但他们的诗风并非一成不变。威廉·卡洛斯·威廉斯 1948 年以后出版的《佩特森》跟他早期的作品就并不完全一样。例如,他在这首长达五卷、以一个城市为背景、描写时代变迁的史诗中加入新闻报道和别人给他的信件的摘要。沃伦 1966 年以前的诗歌都受艾略特的影响,但从 60 年代末开始,他的风格有了明显的个性化的改变。

---

① "the beat generation"在中文里常常译为"垮掉的一代",但创造这个名称的凯鲁亚克在 1959 年的《垮掉的一代的起源》中称,"'beat'一词原意为贫穷、穷愁潦倒、过流浪生活、悲哀的、在地铁睡觉的。由于此词正在成为一个正式的名词,它正在被扩展到包括那些不在地铁睡觉但有一种新的姿态、或新的态度(我只能描绘为)一种新的**道德态度**。'垮掉的一代'已经成为在美国在生活方式方面的一场革命的口号或标签。"见 A. 罗伯特·李编《垮掉的一代作家》,伦敦:柏拉图出版社,1996,第一页。但"beat"一词还相当于诗歌或音乐的"节奏",从社会学、心理学意义上说,它有"被打垮、被异化、被边缘化"的含义,代表从边缘看社会,拒绝社会的规范与行为准则的一种态度;由于这些诗人或作家相信禅宗佛教,它又有"纯真、福祉"等意思。

当时还有一些诗歌跟某个学校、城市或诗人名字联系在一起。如居住在旧金山地区的加里·斯奈德、肯尼斯·雷克斯罗斯(Kenneth Rexroth, 1905—1982)等人形成的旧金山派。他们后来认同纽约的金斯堡等人而形成"垮掉一代"诗人。在北卡罗莱纳州黑山学院任教的查尔斯·奥尔森(Charles Olsen, 1910—1970)、罗伯特·克里莱(Robert Creeley, 1926—2005)、罗伯特·邓肯(Robert Duncan, 1919—1988)等人是"黑山派"诗歌的中心人物。他们跟"垮掉一代"诗人一样,反对传统的诗歌形式,提倡"放射诗",认为诗人通过诗歌把诗人的"能"传递给读者,诗歌的内容是诗人的"感悟",而一个"感悟"要快速而直接地紧跟着下一个"感悟"形式是内容的延伸,诗歌以诗行为基础,而诗行是开放式的,取决于呼吸和言辞的长短。

另一个比较著名的诗人群体是纽约派,包括约翰·阿什贝里(John Asbbery, 1927—   )、弗兰克·奥哈拉(Frank O'Hara, 1926—1966)、肯尼思·柯契(Kenneth Koch, 1925—   )等。他们大多是哈佛大学的先后同学,在纽约担任博物馆负责人、艺术评论家或跟画家们合作。他们受超现实主义和先锋艺术的影响,诗歌的语言简洁明快,意象生动鲜明。他们不赞成自白派诗歌,也不主张用诗歌来表现政治或道德问题。他们的诗歌诙谐幽默,但内涵深邃,比较难懂。

1950年代中期"垮掉一代"诗人金斯堡所开始的反传统潮流,随着60年代的民权运动、反越南战争运动以及女权运动而不断发展壮大,并且走进了公共领域,跟政治、跟群众发生密切的联系。到了70年代,庞德、洛威尔、毕晓普、詹姆斯·赖特(James Wright, 1927—1980)等在诗坛很有影响的诗人纷纷去世,另外一些70岁左右的诗人如罗伯特·潘·沃伦以及比他们年轻的艾伦·金斯堡、詹姆斯·梅里尔(James Merrill, 1926—1995)和加里·斯奈德等还在写作,有些诗人如沃伦还不断有新作发表。但从总体来说,这时期为更为年轻的诗人提供了成功的机会。80年代以后,年轻人的天地更广阔了。他们有意识地冲破老一代的框框,开始了自觉的反叛。这些年轻的诗人虽然继续老一代诗人对社会、对历史和对弱势群体的关注,也继续对自我本质的反思,但他们同前辈们还是有所不同的。他们不再急迫地对失去宗教信仰或科学技术及工业进步的消极影响感到忧虑,他们对诗人和诗歌的作用也有不同的看法。查尔斯·赖特(Charles Wright, 1935—   )主张诗歌不必反映现实也不会给人以精神梦想。另一位诗人约翰·阿什贝里则认为诗歌无需言志。

70年代以后,美国诗歌没有出现像艾略特那样的权威,也没有像新批评那样起领导作用的理论或像黑山学院那样的中心。它只有分散的派别,众多而不是单一的诗歌团体,或者是由于思想意识的一致,如女性主义、同性恋、少数族裔,或者是由于地理上的接近,如纽约派、艾奥瓦城超现实主义等。20世纪最后30年的一大特色是诗歌朗诵成风,无论是在校园还是在书店,甚至在酒吧间和咖啡馆,到处都有诗歌朗诵会。朗诵者甚至可以不是诗人,即便是家庭妇女都可以上去朗读自己的或自己喜爱的诗歌。尽管这种做法也许降低了诗歌的质量,但却促使诗歌回归现实主义。

在这方面,1997—2000年的"桂冠诗人"罗伯特·平斯基起了很大的作用。平斯基主张诗歌应该回归传统,回归普通人。他在《美国诗歌在美国生活中的地位是什么?》里认为艾略特的文章和为人说明他把诗歌看成是属于有闲阶级的。而美国应该欢迎诗歌大众化的局面。他认为艺术的形式取决于媒介,而诗歌的媒介"不是词,甚至不是行,甚至不是声音",而是来自"个人的身体","诗歌是为说和听而写的……它是比演戏更亲切的个人的形式……体现了一种特别的、对相当于个人演说的艺术的需求"。不仅如此,诗歌无论如何内省都要求有一个读者,也就必然斡旋于读者的内心意识和他人的外部世界。① 因此,在他当桂冠诗人期间,他大力提倡和推广一个"喜爱的诗歌项目",并为之建立专门的网页。他还认为诗歌应该有理性,在艺术的世界里表现客观世界。他不赞成内省反思式的诗歌,也不喜欢现代主义的不连贯性。他认为任何题材,大至美国小到网球,都值得思考,都可以进入诗歌。他写的诗语气平和,态度略带讽刺,目的在于教诲。例如,他的长诗《解释美国》,标题就让人知道诗的主题和通过理性分析进行解释的方式。副标题《给女儿的诗》说明这是封信,是他对女儿的独白。"我要告诉你一些关于我们国家的事情/或者我对它的看法:解释它/如果不是对你,那就是对我思想中的你……",好像他在谈话,在跟人分享信息或观点,在进行交流,用完全个人化的话语讨论重大的问题。

作为主流的现实主义诗歌走的是中间道路。根据评论家布雷斯林(James E. B. Breslin, 1936—1996)的看法,这类"自传性的、意象取自自然或家庭生活的抒情短诗……的左岸是持不同意见的'语言诗人';其右岸是新形式主义"②。后者看重诗歌形式,重新采用音步和押韵等传统手法和16世纪法国的19行的维拉内拉诗、六节诗、十四行诗以及由隔行同韵的四行诗节组成的传统甚至古老的诗歌形式。1989年,在《逆流》杂志一篇谈诗歌的论文中,作者把新形式主义及新叙事诗歌合在一起,称之为"扩展诗歌"。其创建人迪克·艾伦(Dick Allen, 1939—)认为,"扩展诗歌"博采各家之长而不是排斥性的。它吸收"垮掉一代"诗歌对社会、文化、政治、宗教和听众的重视但抛弃其自恋成分,采用新超现实主义的一些手法但摈弃其达达主义的方面。"扩展诗歌是非自白或自传式的","它是一种叙述性的、戏剧性的、有时候是抒情的诗歌,表现对自我以外的外部世界以及自我跟这个外部世界的种种关系的、非自白性的观察、思索和感情……看重的是为广大非先锋派听众所接受的非自传性成分和更有普遍意义的主题与题材……采用的常常是传统的韵律和音步并糅入自然的讲话模式"③。另一位诗人R.S.格温(R. S. Gwynn, 1948—)指出,新叙事诗歌和新形式主义诗歌的出现是年轻诗人对60年代"垮掉一代"、自白派、深层意象派等诗歌的反动。他们转向更老的如罗宾逊、弗洛斯特和哈代等诗人,以他们为样本,甚至"通过恢复更早期的形式和体裁来对抗现代主义"。他认为,当时年轻诗人只有两条出路,"语言诗人企图在混乱与主观方面走得更远,完全排斥听众;新叙事诗歌和新形式主义诗歌则回到一个更能让人接受的观点,主张听众是不可缺少的。……他们不过是响应听众关于诗歌的形式应该可以听得见、其叙述的方式内容应该可以听得懂的要求"④。

70年代以来,语言诗歌一直是美国诗歌界的一支重要力量。它最能吸引人的地方恐怕在

---

① 罗伯特·平斯基:《美国诗歌在美国生活中的地位是什么?》,《美国诗歌评论》,1996年,第25卷,第2期,第23—14页。
② 《哥伦比亚美国文学史》(英文版),第1100页。
③ 迪克·艾伦:《克服依赖技巧的习惯:新扩展诗歌的兴起》,《扩张诗歌与音乐在线》(EP&M Online)。
④ R.S.格温为《新扩展诗歌》写的"序言",转引自《扩张诗歌与音乐在线》,1999年。

于诗人们把"语言诗歌"这几个字的英语字母"language poetry"中间都加上等号,变成了"L=A=N=G=U=A=G=E P=O=E=T=R=Y"。语言诗歌跟垮掉派和黑山派的区别在于金斯堡和奥尔森都强调以诗人的呼吸作为诗行长短的衡量标准,他们的注意力都放在诗歌本身,认为诗歌是在说话的诗人的产物。但语言诗人不同意这种看法,认为这是坚持陈旧的浪漫主义的做法。他们强调语言,认为语言是一种体制,在诗人之前就已经存在,而且对诗歌有一定的要求,诗人的作用就是要去左右这些要求,而不被它们所控制,诗人不再是说话的个体,而是话语的操纵者。因此,他们的诗歌不是像《嚎叫》那样的一气呵成的长句,而是没有关联的碎片。他们用随手拈来的语言写诗。语言诗歌并不仅仅是一个让人们重新对语言感兴趣的运动,而是要大家注意语言的结构和代码,"以质疑主流诗歌的许多为常人接受的假设来建构自己的理论框架。他们并不把诗歌视为创造和表现所谓真实的声音和人格的表演场所,而是认为诗歌的主要原料是语言,是语言产生经验……",他们"重视语言运作,轻视表现人生经验"。[①]诗人们认为语言也是有政治性的,因此他们要破坏语言以发动他们对英语内在的社会与政治结构的反抗性的攻击。

在讨论70年代以来的美国诗歌时,女性诗歌已经是一个不可回避的话题。女性诗歌运动的领袖人物艾德里安娜·里奇(Adrienne Rich, 1929—)创作生涯的变化很典型地反映了第二次世界大战以后美国诗歌摆脱主流社会的影响走向政治的公共领域的变迁。里奇在读大学时希望自己跟男人一样出色,追随男性诗歌传统,模仿奥登(W. H. Auden, 1872—1957)、洛威尔和弗洛斯特等男性诗人,使用传统的诗歌形式和音韵格律。1951年,她的诗集《一个世界的变化》受到奥登的注意,被收入"耶鲁年轻诗人丛书",但奥登的前言对她的评价并不很高,甚至说她的眼光和想像力还比较平凡。1953年里奇结婚以后很快有了三个孩子,终日为家务所困扰,无暇创作。她在努力做传统意义上的贤妻良母的同时也为没有时间思考与写作而痛苦。终于在50年代末期,她开始直接描写自己作为女人的经历,1963年出版的《一个儿媳妇的快照》是她创作生涯的转折点,她开始运用松散的个人化的语言和自由诗体描写关于束缚、反抗、逃避等情感问题。尽管她后来认为该诗集中的诗歌还太看重典故,文学味道还太重,甚至不敢采用第一人称,但它们还是真切地反映了被束缚在家庭圈子里的女人的痛苦和愤怒。60年代以后里奇积极投身席卷美国的民权、反战等政治运动,尤其是妇女运动,从而在更广阔的社会政治运动中抒发她对个人冲突、文化压抑和性别歧视等问题的看法。在《改变的意志:1968—1970的诗歌》(1971年)中,她公开表示她担心她所用的语言不是她自己的语言,而是父权社会的又一个产物。这种认识促使她抛弃传统的诗歌形式与叙述方式。她强调,"重新审视——这种回顾的行为,这种以新的眼光看待事物的行为,这种从一个新的批评角度进入一个旧文本的行为——对于妇女来说不仅是文化史上的一个章节:它是一种生存行为。"[②]她反对诗歌应该与诗人生活保持距离的看法,决心从女人的身体和经历出发,公开直接地以女人的身份写作。她在手法上也开始采用当代的节奏和意象,甚至借鉴电影的

---

① 张子清:《20世纪美国诗歌史》,吉林教育出版社,1995年,第834—835页。
② 阿德里安·里奇:《当我们死者苏醒的时候:写作作为重新审视》,引自《论谎言、秘密与沉默:1966—1978散文选》,诺顿出版公司,1979年,第35页。

拼贴和跳跃剪辑等技巧。她的《潜入残骸1971—1972年的诗歌》被认为是妇女运动的诗歌宣言。那些充满激情和愤怒的诗歌如《在黑暗中醒来》、《努力跟一个男人说话》等可以说是在为整个一代女性诉说，使她们看到自己是有力量对付社会的压力的。里奇在她此后的诗集里表明自己的政治立场和诗歌想像力，探讨各种文化、历史和种族的妇女的经历，论述有关口头特权、男性暴力和同性恋等问题。她还关心如何建立多元化的、多族裔的女性主义理论和强调多样性与不同意见的诗歌。由于里奇在妇女运动和女性诗歌中的作用，当今的女性主义作品选和当代诗集无不收入她的作品，介绍她的诗作和观点。

女诗人们各自有自己的风格，属于不同的流派。到了90年代，即便在曾经以男性诗人为主的扩展诗歌领域里，也已经出现相当数量的女诗人，其中甚至有国家级的桂冠诗人丽塔·多弗(Rita Dove, 1952—)和康涅狄克州桂冠诗人玛丽琳·纳尔逊(Marilyn Nelson, 1946—)。评论家琳·凯勒在《扩展的形式：近来妇女创作的长诗》(1997年)中指出，越来越多的女诗人采用史诗、戏剧式叙述甚至不连贯叙述等过去男诗人常用的诗歌形式，因为它们可以利用不同的角度、感情和声音，采用歌曲、日记、信件、故事、回忆、传记、自传等不同的写法，是探讨妇女在历史和文化中地位的理想的形式。而且长诗的各种文体，无论自由诗体的史诗、连续的正规的十四行诗还是互不连贯的高度试验性的拼贴诗句都使它适合于反映各种各样的女性主义观点和当代政治。这些诗歌既是女权运动的产物但又反映并影响了女权运动。① 然而，即便她们属于同一类型，她们还是各不相同。如林·赫京尼恩(Lyn Hejinian, 1941—)与苏珊·豪(Susan Howe, 1937—)都是重视试验创新的女诗人，但前者看重叙述，更强调"理解"，注意使读者能够理解她的诗歌，曾把对前列宁格勒的访问写成一首长达3780行的叙事诗《奥克索塔：一本俄罗斯的短小说》(1991)，而且是模仿普希金的《叶甫盖尼·奥涅金》的形式，14行为一诗节，全书分为八个部分。苏珊·豪则更注重以语言为基础的试验。她甚至对诗歌的排版印刷都进行试验，她的诗行可以倒着写或侧着写，要求读者把它们看成既是文本也是图画。她还故意混淆文体类别，如她的《我的埃米丽·狄金森》很难说是诗歌还是散文，是在评论还是在抒发个人感受。

跟女性诗歌一样，少数族裔诗歌也在70年代以后大大发展，其中黑人诗歌，尤其是黑人女诗人的兴起更为引人注目。70年代在黑人艺术运动高潮时出现了一批以诗歌为中心的黑人小出版社，许多诗人有了发表园地。另一方面，60年代就功成名就的阿米里·巴拉卡(Amiri Baraka, 1934—)、格温朵琳·布鲁克斯(Gwendolyn Brooks, 1917—2000)等诗人到一切有听众的地方朗诵诗歌，把诗歌送到群众中去。玛雅·安吉洛(Maya Angelou, 1928—)曾受克林顿总统的邀请，在他的就职典礼上朗诵诗歌《地平线升起了》。但她的《我将仍然升起》带有鲜明的女性和黑人意识，深受几代年轻的黑人读者的喜爱，也开创了黑人女作家的写作新时代：

"你可以在写历史时把我贬得低

---

① 琳·凯勒：《扩展的形式：近来妇女创作的长诗》，转引自凯思琳·布朗：《诗歌、女性主义与公共领域》，《当代文学》1998年第4期，第644—668页。

前 言

用你那愤愤不平的、扭曲的谎言,

你可以把我踩到泥土里

然而,像那尘土一样,我将仍然升起

……

把恐怖与恐惧的黑夜留在后面

我升起

进入一个清澈美丽的破晓

我升起

带着祖先给的礼物

我是奴隶的梦想与希望

我升起

我升起

我升起。"

  1994—1995年,丽塔·多弗成为美国第一个黑人女性也是最年轻的桂冠诗人。她的诗风比较含蓄严谨,注意诗的形式和比喻、意象等技巧手法。然而,她的《街角的黄房子》(1980)虽然没有大声疾呼,虽然主要描写一个黑人姑娘在成长过程中的欢乐与痛苦,但在批判蓄奴制方面仍然十分有力。但即便都是黑人诗人,他们在风格上跟大时代一样也是多元化的。例如老诗人奥德莱·洛德(Audre Lorde, 1934—1992)就十分注意运用非洲的神话。此外,值得注意的是,黑人诗人不再局限于抗议种族歧视或感叹生活之艰难,他们还歌颂自己的文化,描述一种尽管有不公正但仍欢乐的生活。正如查尔斯·约翰逊所说,"随着黑人妇女的社会机会的增加,她们的虚构世界也将扩大,她们的(文学)题材、主题、形式和体裁也将随之发展,而且将跟她们的诗与歌的能力一样,无限宽广。"① 她们证明诗歌可以既有政治性、既起教诲作用,但又是艺术。例如乔伊纳·科德兹(Jayne Cortez, 1936—)以自由体诗来描述处在家庭、阶级、肉体、精神和道德自我中的黑人女性。

  其他少数族裔诗人,如拉丁美洲裔、印第安裔和亚裔诗人也都在80年代有新的发展,他们的诗开始进入各种美国文学选集。这些诗歌还没有黑人诗歌那么成熟,探索得比较多的还是诗人的身份与文化归属的问题。如母亲是波多黎各人、父亲是犹太人而自己12岁才到美国的奥罗拉·莱文斯·莫拉尔斯(Aurora Levins Morales, 1954—)的《美洲的孩子》(1986)就充分表现对身份归属的敏感:"……我是一个美国波多黎各犹太人,/是我从来不知道的纽约少数民族聚居区的产物""……/ 我是新的。历史产生了我。我的第一语言是西班牙英语。/我在十字路口出生。"另一方面,他们的双重身份带来的双重意识也使他们有更加丰富的生活素材,可以在诗歌中充分表现两种文化的冲突与互相作用。华裔诗人玛丽莲·金(Marilyn Chin, 1955—)的诗歌常常谈到她的双重身份,她既渴望跟主流社会融合又害怕失去古老的中国文化。在《我怎么得到那个名字》中,她愤怒地描绘了他父亲来到美国,为美国文化与

---

① 查尔斯·约翰逊:《存在与种族:1970年以来的黑人写作》,布鲁明顿:印第安纳大学出版社,1988年,第118页。

价值观念所引诱,把她的名字"梅琳"改成了大明星玛丽莲·梦露的"玛丽莲",使她"成为一个不听话的粉红色娃娃/有了一个因白酒和药物而变得臃肿的/悲剧性的女人的名字"。日裔诗人加勒特·本乡(又译:"洪果")(Garrett Hongo, 1951—)说,他对种族、家庭的根基、文化归属等渊源的寻找给了他写诗的动力。他要在混乱的时代和环境里发掘与发扬文化的和道德的价值,在混乱的生活中产生一些能反映传统知识、精神价值和个人经历的诗歌。墨西哥裔诗人加里·索托(Gary Soto, 1952—)也在诗歌里描写跟墨西哥的千丝万缕的联系。他在《历史》(1977)一诗中描写了祖母为生存而进行的挣扎,并说明祖母的历史就是墨西哥流动工人的历史,也就是他们的家庭包括诗人自己家庭的历史。他还在《破晓》、《田野之诗》等诗歌中表现在单调的苦活中,在痛苦与恐惧中仍然有值得回忆的欢快时刻。

总之,今天的美国诗坛也许没有巨匠,但各种不同的流派和各种不同族裔的诗人却使20世纪后期的诗歌变得十分丰富多采,充分体现了多元化的传统。

第一单元 ·· 1

Anne Dudley Bradstreet (1612—1672) 安妮·达德利·布拉德斯特里特 ······ 1
To My Dear and Loving Husband ·· 2
Verses upon the Burning of our House, July 18th, 1666 ·························· 3
The Prologue ·· 5

第二单元 ·· 10

Ralph Waldo Emerson (1803—1882) 拉尔夫·华尔多·爱默生 ············· 10
THE RHODORA: ON BEING ASKED, WHENCE IS THE
FLOWER? ··· 11
Brahma ··· 12
The Snow-Storm ··· 14

第三单元 ·· 17

Henry Wadsworth Longfellow (1807—1882) 亨利·沃兹沃斯·朗费罗 ······ 17
A Psalm of Life ·· 18
The Rainy Day ··· 20
Hiawatha's Childhood ·· 21

第四单元 ·· 25

Edgar Allan Poe (1809—1849) 埃德加·艾伦·坡 ······························· 25
Alone ··· 26
Annabel Lee ·· 27
The Raven ··· 29

第五单元 ·· 35

Walt Whitman (1819—1892) 沃尔特·惠特曼 ···································· 35

One's-Self I Sing 36
To the Garden, the World 38
Once I Pass'd through a Populous City 39
I Saw in Louisiana a Live-Oak Growing 40
Out of the Cradle Endlessly Rocking 41

第六单元 51
Emily Dickinson (1830—1886) 埃米莉·狄金森 51

第七单元 60
Ezra Loomis Pound (1885—1972) 艾兹拉·鲁密思·庞德 60
In A Station of the Metro 61
A Girl 62
A Pact 63
Canto XLIX 63

第八单元 67
Thomas Stearns Eliot (1888—1965) 托马斯·斯特恩司·艾略特 67
Mr. Eliot's Sunday Morning Service 68
The Burial of the Dead 70
The Hollow Men 75

第九单元 82
Robert Frost (1874—1963) 罗伯特·弗洛斯特 82
The Tuft of Flowers 83
Mending Wall 86
Stopping by Woods on a Snowy Evening 89
The Death Of The Hired Man 90

第十单元 100
Wallace Stevens (1879—1955) 华莱士·史蒂文斯 100
Anecdote of the Jar 101
Thirteen Ways of Looking at a Blackbird 102
The Idea of Order at Key West 106
The Course of a Particular 110

第十一单元 113
William Carlos Williams (1883—1963) 威廉·卡洛斯·威廉斯 113

  The Young Housewife ·········· 114
  The Red Wheelbarrow ·········· 115
  Nantucket ·········· 116
  Silence ·········· 117
  Landscape with the Fall of Icarus ·········· 118

第十二单元 ·········· 121
  Langston Hughes (1902—1967) 兰斯顿·休斯 ·········· 121
  The Weary Blues ·········· 122
  Let America be America again ·········· 124
  Madam and the Phone Bill ·········· 128

第十三单元 ·········· 132
  E. E. Cummings (1894—1962) E. E.肯明斯 ·········· 132
  Thy fingers make early flowers of ·········· 133
  Your little voice Over the wires came leaping ·········· 134
  My sweet old etcetera ·········· 136
  Anyone lived in a pretty how town ·········· 137

第十四单元 ·········· 141
  Elizabeth Bishop (1911—1979) 伊丽莎白·毕晓普 ·········· 141
  The Fish ·········· 142
  Sestina ·········· 145
  The Armadillo ·········· 148

第十五单元 ·········· 152
  Randall Jarrell (1914—1965) 兰德尔·贾雷尔 ·········· 152
  A Lullaby ·········· 153
  Next Day ·········· 154

第十六单元 ·········· 158
  Robert Lowell (1917—1977) 罗伯特·洛威尔 ·········· 158
  The Quaker Graveyard in Nantucket ·········· 159
  Skunk Hour ·········· 166
  For the Union Dead ·········· 169

第十七单元 ·········· 174
  Gwendolyn Brooks (1917—2000) 格温朵琳·布鲁克斯 ·········· 174

We Real Cool	175
Kitchenette building	176
My dreams, my works, must wait till after hell	178

第十八单元 ········· 180
Allen Ginsberg (1926—1997) 艾伦·金斯堡 ········· 180
Howl	181
America	185

第十九单元 ········· 190
John Ashbery (1927—) 约翰·阿什贝利 ········· 190
What Is Poetry	191
And Ut Pictura Poesis Is Her Name	193
Paradoxes and Oxymorons	195
Novelty Love Trot	197

第二十单元 ········· 201
Adrienne Rich (1929—) 艾德里安娜·里奇 ········· 201
Aunt Jennifer's Tigers	202
Orion	204
Diving into the Wreck	207
Transit	211

第二十一单元 ········· 215
Gary Snyder (1930—) 加里·斯奈德 ········· 215
Mid-August at Sourdough Mountain Lookout	216
Riprap	217
Pine Tree Tops	219
Clambering Up Cold Mountain Path	220
Three Deer One Coyote Running in the Snow	220

第二十二单元 ········· 222
Sylvia Plath (1932—1963) 西尔维亚·普拉斯 ········· 222
Daddy	223
Lady Lazarus	227
Words	231

第二十三单元 ·· 234

N. Scott Momaday (1934—) 斯科特·莫马戴 ·································· 234

New World ·· 235
The Horse That Died of Shame ·· 236

第二十四单元 ·· 239

Robert Pinsky (1940—) 罗伯特·平斯基 ·· 239

To Television ·· 240
The Figured Wheel ··· 242
ABC ·· 245

第二十五单元 ·· 247

Gary Soto (1952—) 加里·索托 ·· 247

Mexicans Begin Jogging ·· 248
How Things Work ·· 249
Saturday at the Canal ··· 251

目 次

第一单元

Anne Dudley Bradstreet (1612—1672)
安妮·达德利·布拉德斯特里特

作者简介

安妮·达德利·布拉德斯特里特,诗人。生于英国诺桑普顿郡,父亲早年在军队服役,后任林肯郡克林顿伯爵的管家,家境殷实。因自幼患有风湿症,常年卧床,但聪慧好学,受到良好的家教,加之有机会随父亲出入伯爵府邸,接触各种藏书,因此通晓古希腊语、拉丁语、希伯来语、法语和英语等多种语言,阅读广泛。1628年与西蒙·布拉德斯特里特结婚,1630年与父母和丈夫举家远渡重洋,航行三个多月,迁徙到美国马萨诸塞湾,成为当地的第一批移民者。马萨诸塞湾满目蛮荒,但也充满了发展的生机,她的父亲与丈夫都旋即成为当地的显赫人物,她的丈夫曾经两度担任马萨诸塞总督。布拉德斯特里特的身体也逐渐康复,生育了八个子女。

相夫教子之余,布拉德斯特里特开始写诗,记载生活经历和感受,宣泄情感,憧憬未来,目的是自娱自乐。按照当时的习俗,她的诗都是在家庭成员和亲朋好友之中传阅。然而她的姐夫伍德布里奇将她的15首诗汇集为一册,未经允许便带回英国印刷出版,题名为《新近在美洲出现的第十位缪斯》(*The Tenth Muse Lately Sprung Up in America*)。其中的大部分诗歌作于1830年至1842年之间,内容与风格都矫揉造作,显然是模仿法国加尔文派诗人杜·巴达斯的习作。布拉德斯特里对此并不满意,立志创新,由此成为她诗歌创作的一个转折点,拓宽了视野和想象力。1667年约翰·哈维·埃黎思协助出版了一个修订本,增加了一些诗歌。布拉德斯特里特因患肺结核1672年去世,她最重要的诗集于1678年由约翰·福斯特刊行,取名为《汇集非凡智慧与才学的若干诗篇》(*Several Poems Compiled with Great Variety of Wit and Learning*),几乎收入其全部诗作。

美国诗歌选读

To My Dear and Loving Husband

If ever two were one, then surely we.
If ever man were loved by wife, then thee①;
If ever wife was happy in a man,
Compare with me, ye② women, if you can.
I prize thy③ love more than whole mines of gold
Or all the riches that the East④ doth hold.
My love is such that rivers cannot quench⑤,
Nor ought but love from thee, give recompense⑥.
Thy love is such I can no way repay,
The heavens reward thee manifold⑦, I pray.
Then while we live, in love let's so persevere⑧
That when we live no more, we may live ever.

作为美国殖民地时期的第一位诗人,布拉德斯特里特的诗歌在题材、诗体形式、修辞手法、叙事技巧等方面都具有当时社会较为典型的特征,例如格律工整,主题往往兼容宗教思想、自然感悟以及对永恒价值的憧憬和吟诵。然而另一方面,她作为一个女诗人,其诗歌又具有不同于当时以男诗人的创作为主体的诗歌风尚,显示出女性所特有的深邃情感、细腻观察、清新而隽永的意象、对家庭和当时社会现实的思考与对未来的梦想,以及有关女诗人的使命与创作空间。

就题材而言,家庭、爱情与日常生活在她的诗歌中占有重要一席,《致我亲爱的丈夫》(To My Dear and Loving Husband)与《赋诗于1666年7月18日私宅被焚》(Verses upon the Burning of Our House, July 18th, 1666)两首诗便是其中的佳作。前者以简朴的语言与清新的意象淋漓尽致地宣泄了她与丈夫之间纯真而炙热的爱情,并企盼他们的

---

① thee:[古英语](thou 的宾格),你,汝。
② ye:[古英语]你,你们。
③ thy:[古英语](thou 的所有格)你的。
④ the East:17 世纪欧洲殖民者来到美洲大陆后最早选择定居的地方,现为美国东部,即阿勒格尼山以东及梅森-狄克森南北分界线以北的地域。
⑤ quench:熄灭;扑灭;抑制(欲望)。
⑥ recompense:补偿;赔偿;酬报。
⑦ manifold:大量地。
⑧ persevere:坚持,坚忍。

爱情能够天长地久。诗的开篇从第一行到第三行采用了三个由"如果"引导的叠加假设问句，以及各自简短而肯定的答复，节奏铿锵有力，感情炙热，旋即将诗人对于自己与丈夫之间爱情的满足与优越感跃然纸上，凸现了在当时马萨诸塞湾拓荒创业的艰苦生活中爱情的价值观对于个人和家庭的生存和发展具有中流砥柱一般的重要作用。诗的第四行则是具有想象力的对比，将爱情与财富放在心灵的天平上衡量。在诗人的眼中，丈夫的爱胜过全部金矿的价值，甚至胜过美国东部所有的财富；而她对丈夫的爱更为强烈，纵使海枯石烂都无法改变。类似"美国东部所有的财富"等新鲜的意象，由此开始进入美国诗歌，但对于其真正的意蕴，现代读者只能凭借想象而品味，而对于当时身处其境的诗人则是一种刻骨铭心的感受。如果说，诗人对爱情的吟咏是从世俗的角度出发，而结尾的四行诗则融入清教有关来世的信仰，以强调爱情的永恒与高尚，体现了当时殖民者思想文化的特征。

Verses upon the Burning of our House, July 18th, 1666

In silent night when rest I took,
For sorrow near I did not look,
I waken'd was with thund'ring① noise
And piteous② shrieks of dreadful voice.
That fearful sound of "fire" and "fire,"
Let no man know is my Desire.
I starting up, the light did spy③,
And to my God my heart did cry
To straighten me in my Distress
And not to leave me succourless④.
Then coming out, behold a space
The flame consume my dwelling place.
And when I could no longer look,
I blest his grace that gave and took,
That laid my goods now in the dust.
Yea, so it was, and so 'twas just.

---

① thund'ring：即 thundering，雷鸣般的；巨大的；此处因诗行音节的缘故而变体，以减少一个音节。
② piteous：凄惨的；令人可怜的。
③ spy：看见；发现。
④ succourless：无助的。

It was his own; it was not mine.
Far be it that I should repine①,
He might of all justly bereft②
But yet sufficient for us left.
When by the Ruins oft I past
My sorrowing eyes aside did cast
And here and there the places spy
Where oft③ I sate and long did lie.
Here stood that Trunk, and there that chest,
There lay that store I counted best,
My pleasant things in ashes lie
And them behold no more shall I.
Under the roof no guest shall sit,
Nor at thy Table eat a bit.
No pleasant talk shall 'ere be told
Nor things recounted done of old.
No Candle 'ere shall shine in Thee,
Nor bridegroom's voice 'ere heard shall bee.
In silence ever shalt④ thou lie.
Adieu⑤, Adieu, All's Vanity.
Then straight I 'gin my heart to chide⑥:
And did thy wealth on earth abide,
Didst⑦ fix thy hope on mouldring⑧ dust,
The arm of flesh didst make thy trust?
Raise up thy thoughts above the sky
That dunghill⑨ mists away may fly.
Thou hast⑩ a house on high erect
Fram'd by that mighty Architect,

---

① repine：抱怨；发牢骚。
② bereft：(bereave 的过去式和过去分词，)夺去；使丧失。
③ oft：时常；经常。
④ shalt：[古英语]shall 的第二人称单数陈述语气现在时，主语为 thou 时使用。
⑤ Adieu：再见；告别。
⑥ chide：责备；叱责。
⑦ Didst：[古英语]do 的第二人称单数过去式，与 thou 一起使用。
⑧ mouldring：崩溃的。
⑨ dunghill：脏物；污秽。
⑩ hast：[古英语]have 的第二人称单数现在式，与 thou 连用。

With glory richly furnished
Stands permanent, though this be fled.
It's purchased and paid for too
By him who hath① enough to do.
A price so vast as is unknown,
Yet by his gift is made thine② own.
There's wealth enough; I need no more.
Farewell, my pelf③; farewell, my store.
The world no longer let me love;
My hope and Treasure lies above.

《赋诗于1666年7月18日私宅被焚》则呈现出另外一种心态和叙事风格,以一种处惊不变的平静心情叙说诗人一家的住宅不幸失火而化为灰烬的劫难。全诗由54行构成,不分段落,一气呵成。作为一个年过五旬的妻子、母亲和祖母,诗人面对不幸的灾难,身心所承担的责任与困难之重是他人无法想象的,但她丝毫没有怨天尤人,没有诅咒,甚至没有像清教徒惯常那样反身自责。诗人泰然直面突如其来的悲剧,沉静地叙述火灾发生的全部过程以及所造成的家庭毁灭这一巨大灾难,以及无比失望的心情。在结尾的两行诗中,诗人的结论是,残酷的现实让她绝望,只能把希望寄托在天堂,虽然言简意赅,但感人至深。这种客观而沉静的叙述及其所折射出来的淡定大度的情怀,正是此诗的价值与魅力所在。诗中所衬托出来的女诗人的形象,是一个具有超凡阅历与能力的智者,在无法想象的艰难困苦面前能够沉着冷静,举重若轻,直面残酷的现实。这里所展示的经历和性格正是17世纪的拓荒者在美国生存与创业的真实写照。值得一提的是,《致我亲爱的丈夫》采用的是押尾韵的抑扬格五音步双行体,《赋诗于1666年7月18日私宅被焚》则使用了押尾韵的抑扬格四音步双行体,显示出诗人具有驾驭两种诗体的能力。前者更富有抑扬顿挫的节奏感和抒情特征,后者则有助于强化急凑而凝重的叙事风格。

The Prologue

1

To sing of Wars, of Captains, and of Kings,

---

① hath: [古英语]have 的第三人称单数现在式。
② thine: [古英语]thou 的物主代词,你的东西;你的(用于元音或 h 之前)。
③ pelf: 财富;财物。

Of Cities founded, Common-wealths① begun,
For my mean② Pen are too superior things:
Or how they all, or each their dates have run
Let Poets and historians set these forth,
My obscure③ lines shall not so dim④ their worth.

2

But when my wond'ring eyes and envious heart
Great Bartas⑤ sugared⑥ lines do but read o'er,
Fool I do grudge⑦ the Muses did not part⑧
'Twixt⑨ him and me that over-fluent⑩ store;
A Bartas can do what a Bartas will
But simple I according to my skill.

3

From Schoolboy's tongue no Rhetoric⑪ we expect,
Nor yet a sweet Consort⑫ from broken strings,
Nor perfect beauty where's a main defect;
My foolish, broken, blemished⑬ Muse so sings,
And this to mend, alas, no Art is able,
'Cause⑭ Nature made it so irreparable.

4

Nor can I, like that fluent sweet-tongued Greek⑮

---

① commonwealth：公众福利；也指美国部分州，如马萨诸塞、宾夕法尼亚和弗吉尼亚等。
② mean：低级的；微不足道的。此处是自谦的表示。
③ obscure：不引人注目的；微贱的；偏僻的；隐匿的。
④ dim：模糊的；迟钝的；愚笨的。Obscure 与 dim 两个同义词并用，具有自谦和讽喻的双重含义。
⑤ Great Bartas：指法国诗人杜·巴达斯(Guilliame du Bartas，1544—1590)，他的诗歌措辞典雅，擅长使用典故和古典意象。布拉德斯特里特对杜·巴达斯推崇备至，《新近在美洲出现的第十位缪斯》大体上是模仿其诗风的习作。
⑥ sugared：吸引人的；含糖的。
⑦ grudge：吝啬；忌恨；抱怨。
⑧ part：分离；分开。
⑨ Twixt：多用于诗歌中，相当于 between，在……之间。
⑩ over-fluent store：丰富的宝藏。
⑪ rhetoric：华丽的文辞。
⑫ consort：协调；和谐。
⑬ blemished：有瑕疵的；不完美的。
⑭ 'Cause：即 because，此处为了音节的缘故而缩写。
⑮ sweat tongued Greek：指古希腊演说家狄摩西尼(Demosthenes，公元前 384—前 322)。传说他为了克服口吃，成为口齿伶俐的演说家，数年口含卵石，面向波涛汹涌的大海苦练演说技巧，终于如愿以偿。

Who lisped at first, in future times speak plain.
By Art he gladly found what he did seek,
A full requital① of his striving pain.
Art can do much, but this maxim's② most sure:
A weak or wounded brain admits no cure.

5

I am obnoxious③ to each carping④ tongue
Who says my hand a needle better fits,
A poet's pen all scorn I should thus wrong,
For such despite⑤ they cast on female wits.
If what I do prove well, it won't advance,
They'll say it's stol'n, or else it was by chance.

6

But sure the antique Greeks were far more mild
Else of our Sex, why feigned⑥ they those nine⑦
And poesy⑧ made Calliope's⑨ own child?
So 'mongst⑩ the rest they placed the Arts divine.
But this weak knot⑪ they will full soon untie,
The Greeks did nought⑫ but play the fools and lie.

7

Let Greeks be Greeks, and Women what they are.
Men have precedency⑬ and still excel,

---

① requital：报答；补偿；回报。
② maxim：格言；箴言。
③ obnoxious：顺从的；奉承的；应受谴责的；可憎的；易受伤害的。该词具有多重含意，诗人显然并非将其局限于某一种定义，而是取其丰富的意蕴，令人玩味。
④ carping：吹毛求疵的；苛刻的。
⑤ despite：轻视；轻蔑；恶意。
⑥ feigned：伪装的；捏造的；想象的。
⑦ those nine：指古希腊中掌管艺术与科学的九位缪斯。
⑧ poesy：诗歌；作诗法。
⑨ Calliope：卡拉阿培，古希腊中九位缪斯之首，司掌诗史。按照古希腊的传统，诗史专属于男诗人，因此此处有影射的意味。
⑩ 'mongst：即 amongst，此处为了音节的缘故而缩写，在……之中。
⑪ knot：难题；纠缠。
⑫ naught：无；零；无价值的东西。
⑬ precedency：意同 precedence，领先；优先。

It is but vain unjustly to wage war.
Men can do best, and women know it well.
Preeminence① in all and each is yours;
Yet grant some small acknowledgement of ours.

8

And oh ye high flown quills② that soar the skies,
And ever with your prey③ still catch your praise,
If e'er you deign④ these lowly lines your eyes,
Give thyme or Parsley⑤ wreath, I ask no Bays⑥;
This mean and unrefined⑦ ore of mine
Will make your glist'ring gold but more to shine.

作品赏析　　《序言》(*The Prologue*)则代表了布拉德斯特里特所关注的另外一类题材,即有关宗教、哲理、诗歌创作理念等内容较为抽象的社会问题。这首诗最显著的特征是在美国文学史上首次明确提出了美国女诗人的概念、女诗人身份的合法性、女诗人应有的创作空间,以及诗歌创作理念。因此,可以说是"第十位缪斯"名副其实的创作宣言。诗在结构上共由八节构成,格律采用抑扬格五音步,尾韵为 ababcc。这种工整而错落有序的叙事结构与内容上的铺陈和推理有机地融为一体,加之遣词平易,没有浮华晦涩的字眼,风格恬谧,清澈如水,强化了诗的说服力和感染力。布拉德斯特里特的历史视野开阔,纵论古今,不卑不亢,始终以一种谦逊的口吻陈述自己的思想和观点,但对于女性诗人的权力与地位等核心问题则是斩钉截铁,以理服人,显示出非凡的见识、勇气和信心。例如在诗的第七节,诗人铿锵宣布:

让希腊人当希腊人,让女人拥有身份。
男人出类拔萃,令女人望其项背,
不必为此不平,挑起无谓的是非。
男人能力绝伦,女人坦然钦佩。
你们卓越无比,人人堪称精锐,
但必须包容女人的才智与地位。

---

① Preeminence:出类拔萃;卓越。
② quills:羽毛笔,由羽毛的羽干制成的书写笔;此处以其转喻诗人。
③ prey:被捕食的动物;捕获;掠夺品。
④ deign:赐予;屈尊;俯就。
⑤ thyme or parsley:指用作食用香料的麝香草和香芹。
⑥ bays:桂冠;月桂树。古希腊惯于将月桂树叶编织的桂冠戴在成就非凡的诗人头上。月桂是一种有毒的植物,因此此处使用桂冠的意象有讽刺的意味。
⑦ mean and unrefined ore:微不足道而未提炼的矿石,诗人对自己诗才自谦的表述。

如果将此诗与《沉思录》(Meditations)和《肉与灵》(The Flesh and the Spirit)等诗篇汇集在一起，便能够比较完整地展示布拉德斯特里特所思考的此类主题框架。

思考题

1. How do you characterize Bradstreet's feelings about her married life as represented in her poems such as "To My Dear and Loving Husband"?
2. What fresh images can you find in the three poems that help visualize Bradstreet's emotions?
3. If "Verses upon the Burning of Our House, July 18th, 1666" is a case in point, can you comment on how the 17th century Puritan thought affected Bradstreet?

推荐作品

1. *A Letter to Her Husband, Absent Upon Public Employment*
2. *The Flesh and the Spirit*
3. *The Vanity of All Worldly Things*
4. *Before the Birth of One of Her Children*

参考书目

1. Eaton, Sara. "Anne Bradstreet's 'Personal' Protestant Poetics". *Women's Writing*. 4.1 (1997): 57—71.
2. Rosenmeier, Rosamond. "Anne Bradstreet Revisited". *Twayne's United States Authors Series*. Vol. 580. Boston: Twayne, 1991.
3. Walker, Cheryl. "Anne Bradstreet: A Woman Poet". *Critical Essays on Anne Bradstreet*. Eds. Pattie Cowell and Ann Stanford. *Critical Essays on American Literature*. Boston: Hall, 1983. 254—261.

第二单元

Ralph Waldo Emerson (1803—1882)
拉尔夫·华尔多·爱默生

作者简介

爱默生出生在教会家庭,祖上有九代人担任教士职位。1820年在哈佛大学求学期间撰写了大量日记,为日后出版的散文集及诗歌集积累了宝贵素材。大学毕业后,爱默生成为惟一理教教士,终因反对沿袭圣餐仪式而于1832年辞去教职。他认为,要做一个合格的教士,就有必要脱离教会。为减轻丧妻之痛,缓解传统宗教观的消极影响,他游历欧洲,与英国浪漫主义作家和思想家华兹华斯、柯尔律治、卡莱尔等人交流思想,受到强烈感染,促成他提出超验主义哲学思想。1835年定居康科德村,积极投入演讲以及义务布道,其间与《小妇人》作者的父亲阿尔柯特、女权主义者玛格丽特·福勒、霍桑以及梭罗等人经常讨论哲学问题,此类聚会被称为"超验主义俱乐部",他们还出版了颇具影响力的文艺刊物《日晷》(The Dial)。1836年问世的《论自然》(Nature)奠定了他作为美国超验主义思想代表的基础。他明确指出人与自然之间存在神秘的联系,任何人都可以通过直觉感悟自然。第二年在哈佛大学联谊会上的讲演《论美国学者》(The American Scholar)被看作是美国思想的独立宣言。1841年的《超验主义者》(The Transcendentalist)演说阐释了物质派("materialist")与理想派即超验主义("idealist")两种思维模式。同年出版了《散文集》第一集(Essays: First Series),囊括《论历史》(History)、《论自助》(Self-Reliance)、《论超灵》(The Over-Soul)等。三年后出版的《散文集》第二集(Essays: Second Series)包括《论诗人》(The Poet)、《论体验》(Experience)、《论自然》(Nature)等。

爱默生的文笔自然流畅,语言朴实优美。他一生创作了许多优美的诗歌,如《北美杜鹃花》(The Rhodora)、《暴风雪》(The Snow-Storm)、《婆罗贺摩》(Brahma)等收在《五月天》(May-Day, 1867)以及《诗歌选编》(Selected Poems, 1876)中。爱默生以他独特的创新精神和深邃的哲学思想影响了众多美国作家和诗人,如梭罗、惠特曼、狄金森等,极大地推动了19世纪美国文学的发展。

THE RHODORA:
ON BEING ASKED, WHENCE① IS THE FLOWER?

In May, when sea-winds pierced our solitudes,
I found the fresh Rhodora in the woods,
Spreading its leafless blooms in a damp nook,
To please the desert and the sluggish brook.
The purple petals, fallen in the pool,
Made the black water with their beauty gay;
Here might the red-bird come his plumes to cool,
And court the flower that cheapens his array.
Rhodora! if the sages ask thee why
This charm is wasted on the earth and sky,
Tell them, dear, that, if eyes were made for seeing,
Then Beauty is its own excuse for being②:
Why thou wert there, O rival of the rose!
I never thought to ask, I never knew:
But, in my simple ignorance, suppose
The self-same Power that brought me there brought you.

　　这首诗节奏明快，抒发了"我"对北美杜鹃花的赞美之情，字里行间隐含着对人与自然的思考，从内容到格律都体现出诗人的超验主义思想。在《论自然》中，爱默生这样写道："田野和森林所带来的最大的乐趣在于揭示人与植物间的神秘联系。""我"的愉悦感不仅源自杜鹃花的美丽与高贵，而且来自"我"与花的和谐关系。爱默生深信，宇宙是人类灵魂的外在体现，人类可以通过直觉体验宇宙的奥妙，而诗人所代表的就是美。"我"眼中的杜鹃花是美的化身，无论灿烂的羽翎，还是芬芳的玫瑰，都无法与它媲美。那么，本应居住天堂的花朵何以安身在人间？面对假想中圣人的质疑，"我"用简单的假设，纯朴的语言，再次将象征感悟的"眼睛"——心灵的窗户——与象征美的杜鹃花相结合，引出这一哲理：美丽不需要任何理由。

　　严格的五步抑扬格衬托出人与自然和谐这一主题。前四行采用双行压韵 **aabb**，暗示

---

① whence：与 where 意思相同，多用于文学作品。
② Beauty is its own excuse for being：杜鹃花的美丽就是它存在的理由。

美国诗歌选读

自然与人对自然的体验同时并存,互相协调,相互影响,诗人完全沉浸在自然的感召中,预示"我"的孤独将因杜鹃花的出现而消散。第二行以短元音结尾,与第一行最后一个长元音音节形成对照,消沉抑郁的心境豁然开朗,自然的力量由此可见。第三、四行以清辅音收尾,与前两行末尾的浊辅音形成对比,愈加显示自然景观的神奇。第五至八行的韵律为 cdcd,不仅歌颂了杜鹃花所象征的轻快,而且借助花鸟的动静结合描绘出杜鹃花的超凡脱俗。第九至十二行再次出现双行压韵 eeff,巧妙地引出对唯理性思维模式的质疑,同时流露出"我"对直觉的推崇。最后四行的韵律为 ghgh,点明该诗的主旨:人与自然应保持和谐关系。

思考题

1. What is the significance of the line "ON BEING ASKED, WHENCE IS THE FLOWER?"
2. How do you interpret the "self-same Power"?
3. Emerson wrote in *Nature* that "Nothing is quite beautiful alone; nothing but is beautiful in the whole." Does this have any bearing on the poem?

Brahma①

If the red slayer② think he slays,
Or if the slain think he is slain,
They know not well the subtle ways
I keep, and pass, and turn again.

Far or forgot to me is near;
Shadow and sunlight are the same;
The vanished gods to me appear;
And one to me are shame and fame.

They reckon ill who leave me out;

---

① Brahma:印度教中的创造之神梵天,与破坏之神湿婆(Shiva)和保护之神毗瑟孥(Vishnu)构成印度教中三主神。
② slayer:死神(Death)。

When me they fly, I am the wings;
I am the doubter and the doubt,
And I the hymn the Brahmin① sings.

The strong gods② pine for my abode,
And pine in vain the sacred Seven③,
But thou, meek lover of the good!
Find me, and turn thy back on heaven.

作品赏析

《婆罗贺摩》原名《灵魂之歌》("The Song of the Soul"),全诗以印度教中的众神之神梵天的口吻显示印度宗教的神秘、神圣以及超越二元对立的特性,体现出印度教对爱默生的影响。第一节导入毁灭生命者以及失去生命者的意识,引出梵天的奇妙,同时也揭示其完整性、统一性及永恒性。第二节与第三节中,分别出现四对相互对立的物质,通过梵天的自我陈述,流露出其包容性与哲理性。任何矛盾都可得到化解,这也是其神圣及神秘所在。作为众神向往的神,梵天并不排斥他神的努力,但这种努力是否成功取决于其对行善的追求。梵我合一的理想境界只有通过超越人间的利益争端,放弃名利,才有可能达到。全诗前十四行诗句陈述梵天对人生的感悟,似乎使梵我合一显得不可企及,但最后两行画龙点睛:实现梵我合一、超然解脱的关键在于人的谦卑以及对真善美的领悟与实践。

全诗为工整对称的隔行押韵,不仅凸显出梵天主神与众不同,也象征其和谐统一性。尤其给人以启示的是,最后一节中第二行出现的"Seven"标志印度教的神圣及气势,在他的衬托下,第四行出现的象征基督教的"heaven"则显得渺小,也恰恰印证了行善者的皈依行为。诚然,爱默生并未单一地接受某派别的宗教思想,不过他对印度教的部分吸收极大地丰富了他的艺术创作思想。

思考题

1. Are there any similarities or differences between "the vanished gods" and "the strong gods"?
2. How do you relate "the meek lover of the good" to the "red slayer" and "the slain"?
3. What might be "the subtle ways" that Brahma keeps, passes and turns again?

---

① Brahmin:高雅人士。
② strong gods:指印度宗教中的众神之神,天神、火神、死神或审判神等。
③ Seven:古印度歌唱圣歌的七个人。

The Snow-Storm

Announced by all the trumpets of the sky,
Arrives the snow, and, driving o'er the fields,
Seems nowhere to alight: the whited air
Hides hills and woods, the river, and the heaven,
And veils the farmhouse at the garden's end.
The sled and traveler stopped, the courier's feet
Delayed, all friends shut out, the housemates sit
Around the radiant fireplace, enclosed
In a tumultuous privacy of storm.

Come see the north wind's masonry.
Out of an unseen quarry evermore
Furnished with tile, the fierce artificer
Curves his white bastions with projected roof
Round every windward stake, or tree, or door.
Speeding, the myriad-handed, his wild work
So fanciful, so savage, nought① cares he
For number or proportion. Mockingly,
On coop or kennel he hangs Parian② wreaths;
A swan-like form invests the hidden thorn;
Fills up the farmer's lane from wall to wall,
Maugre③ the farmer's sighs; and, at the gate,
A tapering turret overtops the work.
And when his hours are numbered, and the world
Is all his own, retiring, as he were not,
Leaves, when the sun appears, astonished Art
To mimic in slow structures, stone by stone,

---

① nought: 与 naught 同,没有什么。
② Parian: (似帕罗斯岛白大理石的)伯利安瓷的。
③ maugre: 不管。

Built in an age, the mad wind's night-work,
The frolic architecture of the snow.

这首诗赞美了大自然的创造性及震撼力,展示了诗人对大自然的热爱与向往。暴风雪的降临犹如上苍的艺术演出,人间万物都需驻足观赏这一气势磅礴的节目。自然的力量势如破竹,自然空间无限延伸,白雪皑皑的世界里,人类的生存空间显得格外狭窄。寒冬的使者——暴风雪让人类领略到它的力量,感受到自然的不可征服性,同时也使人类体会到家的温馨。人类的生活节奏不断加速,然而人们彼此间却缺乏沟通,产生隔阂;大自然让人意识到他的有限性,帮助人们放慢步伐,彼此靠近,在炉火旁促膝谈心,探讨生活的意义。第一节的前四行均以象征自然界的词汇——"天空"、"田野"、"空气"、"天上"结尾,接下去的四行均以标志人类生活的"(花园)末端"、"(信差)脚步"、"(家庭成员)坐"、"被困"这些词结尾,而最后一行的最后一个词"暴风雪"与前四行的自然词汇遥相呼应,牢牢围住那些象征人类生活的词语,生动形象地展现出无所不及的自然力量以及人类的相对渺小。

第二节转而描写北风的气势,进一步渲染了大自然浑然天成的主题,突出人工的局限性。该节以祈使句开始,邀请读者欣赏北风的雕刻艺术。北风的杰作不加任何人工因素,就连其雕刻材料也很神秘,"看不见的采石场"。它速度猛烈,想象力丰富。在狂风与暴雪的合作下,人间得以出现独特的美景。人工艺术无法超越精湛的自然艺术,人类的智慧在自然面前相形见绌。同时,超验主义思想所强调的直觉体验与其所反对的理性思考在该诗也有所体现。诗人用"充满想象力的"、"疯狂的"等词,展示自然的自由潇洒,而用"模仿"、"缓慢的"等词比喻人工的拘谨与呆板。

这首诗的韵律基本为五步抑扬格,但每行却没有规律的韵脚,这种写法既体现出大自然的自然节奏,又暗示大自然的不可预测性。爱默生的这首诗影响了诸如朗费罗("Snow-Flakes")、惠蒂尔、弗洛斯特("Stopping by Woods on a Snow Evening")等美国诗人,其中惠蒂尔还将爱默生这首诗的前九行作为他的"Snow-Bound"一诗的引言。

思考题

1. What poetic devices are adopted to illustrate the power of the snowstorm?
2. Do you agree that nature is a superior artist? Why?
3. Read Robert Frost's "Stopping by Woods on a Snow Evening" and explain what similarities or differences you can detect.

美国诗歌选读

推荐作品

1. *Nature*
2. *The American Scholar*
3. *The Poet*
4. *The Humble-Bee*
5. *Walden*
6. *Concord Hymn*
7. *The Sphinx*
8. *Merlin's Song*

参考书目

1. Buell, Lawrence. *Emerson.* Cambridge: Belknap Press of Harvard UP, 2003.
2. Porte, Joel, and Saundra Morris, eds. *Emerson's Prose and Poetry.* New York: Norton, 2001.
3. Porte, Joel, and Saundra Morris, eds. *Ralph Waldo Emerson*. Cambridge: Cambridge UP, 1999.

第三单元

Henry Wadsworth Longfellow (1807—1882)
亨利·沃兹沃斯·朗费罗

作者简介

亨利·沃兹沃斯·朗费罗,诗人、小说家、剧作家、翻译家。生于缅因州波特兰市,父亲为律师,并曾任议员。朗费罗自幼聪慧过人,三岁上学,六岁能够流利阅读和写作,并在母亲帮助下广泛阅读欧洲经典文学作品。他居住的波特兰,作为一个港口都市,比内地城镇拥有更为开阔的视野、繁荣的经济和多元的文化,朗费罗自幼耳濡目染,颇受影响。他13岁开始写作并发表诗歌,1820年发表的第一首诗《洛弗尔家池塘之争》(The Battle of Lovell's Pond)从一个儿童的视角描写战争带来的灾难。尽管父亲希望他继承父业,成为律师,朗费罗则心仪文学创作与治学授业。1826年至1829年,朗费罗游历意大利、西班牙、法国、德国、英国等国家,参观大学,拜访教育界和文学界名流,学习了古希腊语、瑞典语等数种北欧语言,并翻译了贺拉斯的作品,深受欧洲传统文化的影响。

在哈佛大学任教期间,朗费罗开始了活跃创作的阶段。1839年出版第一部小说《许珀里翁》(Hyperion),并发表第一部诗集《夜之声》(Voices of the Night),后者问世后旋即赢得广泛赞誉。1840年发表三幕剧本《西班牙学生》(The Spanish Student),并在霍桑的启发和鼓励下开始构思《伊万杰琳》(Evangeline),后者1847年出版后好评如潮。1854年,他辞职后专事创作,同年出版其最富盛名的史诗《海华沙之歌》(The Song of Hiawatha),在美国文学史上首次将印地安人的历史作为文学题材描写,标志着对印地安人及其遗产的承认和认同。1858年出版长篇叙事诗《迈尔斯·斯坦狄斯的求婚》(The Courtship of Miles Standish),其题材与《伊万杰琳》相呼应,讲述了普利茅斯早期殖民地时期一个悲惨的爱情故事。1861年,续弦弗朗西丝·阿普而顿因火灾去世后,朗费罗心灰意懒,无意创作,以翻译但丁的《神曲》等文学作品排遣心中的郁闷。朗费罗1882年去世,伦敦威斯敏斯特教堂的诗人之角为其竖立了一尊大理石雕像。

美国 诗歌选读

A Psalm of Life
WHAT THE HEART OF THE YOUNG MAN SAID TO THE PSALMIST①.

Tell me not, in mournful numbers②,
Life is but an empty dream!
For the soul is dead that slumbers③,
And things are not what they seem.

Life is real! Life is earnest!
And the grave is not its goal;
Dust thou art, to dust returnest④,
Was not spoken of the soul.

Not enjoyment, and not sorrow,
Is our destined end or way;
But to act, that each to-morrow
Find us farther than to-day.

Art is long, and Time is fleeting⑤,
And our hearts, though stout and brave,
Still, like muffled⑥ drums, are beating
Funeral marches to the grave.

In the world's broad field of battle,
In the bivouac⑦ of Life,
Be not like dumb, driven cattle!

---

① psalmist：赞美诗作者。
② number：韵律；韵文；乐曲。
③ slumber：睡眠；安睡。
④ returnest：即 return；因该诗的尾韵结构为 abab，此处的 return 须与此节第一行中的 earnest 押韵，故采用古英语中作为第二人称一般动词后缀的"-est(或 -st)"。
⑤ fleeting：飞逝的；短暂的。
⑥ muffled：被裹住的；沉闷的。
⑦ bivouac：露营；露营地；露宿。

Be a hero in the strife!

Trust no Future, howe'er pleasant!
Let the dead Past bury its dead!
Act,—act in the living Present!
Heart within, and God o'erhead!

Lives of great men all remind us
We can make our lives sublime①,
And, departing, leave behind us
Footprints on the sands of time;—

Footprints, that perhaps another,
Sailing o'er life's solemn main,
A forlorn② and shipwrecked brother,
Seeing, shall take heart③ again.

Let us, then, be up and doing,
With a heart for any fate;
Still achieving, still pursuing,
Learn to labor and to wait.

朗费罗作为诗人的别致之处,主要在于他始终坚持自己的创作原则:崇尚简朴的艺术,乐观地直面现实和未来,尊重各种传统,赞美永恒的价值观,诸如善良、正直、勇敢、自信、乐观、友爱、家庭为人与社会之本,以及崇敬自然等等,而不追求任何虚幻、激进、偏激,甚至极端的创作内容与形式。他的诗歌一般都具有两个显著特征,一是题材世代相传,妇孺皆知;二是诗文简朴易懂。他善于使用简单而娓娓动听的传统格律,辅之以美国读者熟悉的本土意象,将他的主题观念和情感愉悦地镶嵌到每一个读者的心中,引起共鸣,并珍藏在记忆中。

《人生颂》(A Psalm of Life)的艺术价值与魅力不在于诗歌的主题,而在于诗人没有以居高临下的智者身份规劝或者训导读者,没有引经据典,没有涉及宗教信仰与为人处世的原则,而是将诗的核心聚焦在最能体现人类生命力与希望的年轻人身上。诗人独辟蹊径,以"年轻人的心"作为叙事者,向素来被奉为智者和人类代言人的"赞美诗作者"敞

---

① sublime:崇高;庄严。
② forlorn:可怜的;被遗弃的;绝望的。
③ take heart:鼓起勇气;打起精神。

美国诗歌选读

开心扉,以淳朴直白的词汇和妇孺熟悉的歌谣体赞美自信、乐观与珍爱生命等人类永恒的价值观。古今中外,永恒的价值观和简朴的风格都是诗歌走向大众与永恒的通行证。《人生颂》中的肺腑之言琅琅上口,过目难忘,对于年幼清纯的少男少女和青年而言,犹如人生历程中的火炬,指点迷津,开启心智,涤荡心灵;对于经历了世态炎凉的中年乃至暮年读者来说,也仍然是把握人生命运的一个重要精神支柱。

The Rainy Day

The day is cold, and dark, and dreary
It rains, and the wind is never weary;
The vine still clings to the mouldering① wall,
But at every gust② the dead leaves fall,
And the day is dark and dreary.

My life is cold, and dark, and dreary;
It rains, and the wind is never weary;
My thoughts still cling to the mouldering Past,
But the hopes of youth fall thick in the blast③,
And the days are dark and dreary.

Be still, sad heart! and cease repining;
Behind the clouds is the sun still shining;
Thy fate is the common fate of all,
Into each life some rain must fall,
Some days must be dark and dreary.

《雨天》(The Rainy Day)则以描写大自然秋雨中的即景入手,第一节记叙了诗人在黑夜中从容淡定地观察雨水冲刷陈旧的墙壁,枯藤上的败叶随风飘落,此情此景,使一种自然而然的凄凉情怀扑面而来。在第二节中诗人有感而发,由物及人,将人生比作天地自然,并非永远是

---

① mouldering:腐朽的;破损的。
② gust:阵风。
③ blast:强风;疾风;攻击。

四季如春,日明月朗,而是有季节更迭,有阴晴之别,有快乐幸福之时,也有困难沮丧之日。诗将自然与人和谐地融为一体,主旨简单易懂,作为诗中的主要意象的雨司空见惯,与人生的起伏阴晴比喻也十分贴切,而且诗句容易记诵,具有永恒的启迪和感染力。

Hiawatha's Childhood

From Chapter III, Hiawatha

Downward through the evening twilight,
In the days that are forgotten,
In the unremembered ages,
From the full moon fell Nokomis①,
Fell the beautiful Nokomis,
She a wife, but not a mother.

She was sporting with her women,
Swinging in a swing of grape-vines,
When her rival the rejected,
Full of jealousy and hatred,
Cut the leafy swing asunder②,
Cut in twain the twisted grape-vines,
And Nokomis fell affrighted③
Downward through the evening twilight,
On the Muskoday, the meadow,
On the prairie full of blossoms.
"See! a star falls!" said the people;
"From the sky a star is falling!"

There among the ferns④ and mosses,
There among the prairie lilies,

---

① Nokomis:《海华沙之歌》中主人公海华沙的外祖母,印地安人神话中的大地之神,世间有生命的万物都是她养育的。她的名字的含意即祖母,显示她掌管自然、丰产、生长与生命。
② asunder:拆为碎片;被分开。
③ affrighted:惊恐万状的;惊吓的。
④ ferns:蕨类植物或羊齿植物,粗大,有根、茎、复叶,但无花,无子管。

On the Muskoday, the meadow,
In the moonlight and the starlight,
Fair Nokomis bore a daughter.
And she called her name Wenonah,
As the first-born of her daughters.
And the daughter of Nokomis
Grew up like the prairie lilies,
Grew a tall and slender maiden,
With the beauty of the moonlight,
With the beauty of the starlight.

And Nokomis warned her often,
Saying oft, and oft repeating,
"O, beware of Mudjekeewis[①],
Of the West-Wind, Mudjekeewis;
Listen not to what he tells you;
Lie not down upon the meadow,
Stoop not down among the lilies,
Lest the West-Wind come and harm you!"

But she heeded not the warning,
Heeded not those words of wisdom,
And the West-Wind came at evening,
Walking lightly o'er the prairie,
Whispering to the leaves and blossoms,
Bending low the flowers and grasses,
Found the beautiful Wenonah,
Lying there among the lilies,
Wooed her with his words of sweetness,
Wooed her with his soft caresses,
Till she bore a son in sorrow,
Bore a son of love and sorrow.

Thus was born my Hiawatha,
Thus was born the child of wonder;

---

① Mudjekeewis：印地安人神话中司掌西风的神，他使得清纯的少女维诺纳（Wenonah）受孕并生下海华沙之后，又将其抛弃，维诺纳因此夭折。海华沙由祖母诺克密思（Nokomis）养育长大，成为一个举世无双的猎手。

But the daughter of Nokomis,
Hiawatha's gentle mother,
In her anguish died deserted
By the West-Wind, false and faithless,
By the heartless Mudjekeewis.

　　《海华沙之歌》(The Song of Hiawatha)的创作特征是以塑造人物为核心,与《人生颂》和《雨天》等吟诵人生基本信念和价值的诗篇不同,展示了朗费罗驾驭叙事诗歌的非凡天赋与技巧。该诗是一首长篇史诗,共由23章和前言构成,此处节选的是第三章开篇的内容。诗中讲述了13世纪初叶印地安部落的英雄海华沙的传奇经历,塑造了一个有智慧和领导力、勇敢、善良的人物。在统治宇宙的大神的安排下,海华沙出生后由外祖母在深山老林中抚养成人,练就一身狩猎的好本领。他的父亲西风之神承诺,如果海华沙能够带来天下太平,就将其化人为神,封为北风之神。海华沙立志努力,在战胜玉米神和鱼王等邪恶的力量之后,深得印地安人的拥戴,成为首领,并教导臣民学会了农耕、狩猎、治病与绘画纪事等能力,由此天下太平。得知欧洲白人殖民者即将来临的消息,印地安人惶恐不安,海华沙则劝导同胞们友善地对待白人,和平相处,然后按照父亲的安排独自离去,就任北风之神。显然,故事的结尾将神话传说与美国殖民历史融为一体,显示朗费罗希望化解19世纪印地安人与欧洲殖民者之间愈演愈烈的冲突。

　　第三章叙述海华沙童年的生活经历,此处节选的六节是诗中最具有神话传奇特征的内容。海华沙的外祖母诺克密思天生丽质,聪明善良,但婚后无子,遭人陷害,命运坎坷。一天深夜伴随着一颗流星陨落,她生下自己的独生女维诺纳,但命运更加坎坷。维诺纳美若天仙,但生性叛逆,无视母亲的劝告,独自在草原徜徉时被西风之神的花言巧语所迷惑,坠入情网。维诺纳生下海华沙后,旋即被西风之神抛弃,在痛苦与悔恨中殒命。这一作品的价值与意义不仅在于首次以诗的形式再现了印地安人自强不息的历史,还在于诗人能够以言简意赅的诗文,惟妙惟肖地刻画每个人物鲜明的独特个性,例如西风之神的残忍可以从他在维诺纳临产时抛弃她这一情节中略见一斑。晚近,有评论认为朗费罗将13世纪的海华沙与17世纪以后来到美国的欧洲殖民者交织在一起,加之有些情节与芬兰史诗《英雄的国土》有雷同之处,是对历史缺乏尊重。

思考题

1. Can you make some comments on the images Longfellow prefers to use in the above three poems?
2. With a view to his themes and poetic genres, how do you explain the continued popularly of Longfellow as a 19th century American poet?
3. Tell which of the above three poems you like most and give accountable reasons.

美国诗歌选读

推荐作品

1. *Loss and Gain*
2. *Birds of Passage*
3. *Evangeline*

参考书目

1. Arvin, Newton. *Longfellow: His Life and Work*. Boston: Atlantic Monthly Press, 1962.
2. Calhoun, Charles. *Longfellow: A Rediscovered Life*. Boston: Beacon Press, 2004.
3. Wagenknecht, Edward. *Henry Wadsworth Longfellow: His Poetry and Prose*. New York: Ungar, 1986.
4. Williams, Cecil B. *Henry Wadsworth Longfellow*. Boston: Twayne Publishers, 1964.

第四单元

Edgar Allan Poe (1809—1849)
埃德加·艾伦·坡

作者简介

埃德加·艾伦·坡，1809年出生在波士顿，父母都是演员，一岁时父亲弃家离走，两年后，母亲病亡。之后被商人艾伦收养，幼年在南方度过，少年时随继父到英国上学。后回美国入读弗吉尼亚大学，虽学业优良但因酗酒、参与赌博，与继父发生矛盾，离开学校。此后在西点军校度过一段短暂的时间，由于对军事不感兴趣，他故意违反校规放纵自己，迫使学校把他除名。但他的同学资助他出版了在此期间写的诗集《诗歌：第二版》。

坡在年少时就已展露出文学天才，1827年发表第一部诗集《帖木尔》(*Tamerlane and Other Poems*)，随后陆续有诗集和小说集出版，尤其以诗歌《乌鸦》(*Raven*)和短篇小说《厄舍屋的倒塌》("The Fall of the House of Usher")，《威廉·威尔逊》(*William Wilson*)等闻名。1831年后，分别在巴尔的摩、理士满、费城、纽约等城市居住，以写作为生，并担任一些文学刊物的编辑，生活贫困潦倒，1849年10月3日他被人发现倒在巴尔的摩的街头，三天后去世。评论界对他去世的原因颇多争执。

在十九世纪美国内战前浪漫主义文学中，坡以怪诞著称，多受德国哥特文学影响；诗歌充满怪异意象，情调感伤、忧郁、阴暗，追求音律的唯美。小说注重心理探索，擅长描写人物的潜意识活动，讲究技巧和阅读效果，创作思想自成一派，是十九世纪美国文学中一位重要的文学批评家。坡同时也是西方推理和侦探小说的鼻祖，他写的《金龟》("Gold Bug")和《一封被偷的信》("The Purloined Letter")曾风靡一时，对后来推理小说的发展有过很大影响。坡生前和死后并没有受到重视。爱默生贬其为"叮当诗人"(jingle man)。但他在欧洲却大受欢迎，得到法国象征派诗人波德莱尔、马拉美等的热捧。多年后坡的地位终于在美国文学界得到确认，被认为是19世纪上半叶一位有着自己独特风格和创作思想的诗人、作家和批评家。

美国 诗歌 选读

Alone

From childhood's hour I have not been
As others were①—I have not seen
As others saw—I could not bring
My passions from a common spring②—
From the same source I have not taken
My sorrow—I could not awaken
My heart to joy at the same tone③—
And all I lov'd—I lov'd alone—
Then—in my childhood—in the dawn
Of a most stormy life—was drawn
From ev'ry depth of good and ill
The mystery which binds me still④—
From the torrent⑤, or the fountain—
From the red cliff of the mountain—
From the sun that round me roll'd⑥
In its autumn tint of gold—
From the lightning in the sky
As it pass'd me flying by—
From the thunder, and the storm—
And the cloud that took the form
(When the rest of Heaven was blue)
Of a demon in my view—

---

① From childhood's hour I have not been/As others were：我有过的童年与别人的不一样。
② spring：源泉。
③ I could not awaken/My heart to joy at the same tone：同样的乐声／却不能让我产生一样的喜悦。
④ The mystery which binds me still：依旧缠绕着我的神秘。
⑤ torrent：激流。
⑥ that round me roll'd：= that rolled around me.

　　这首诗是坡的早期作品，大约写于1830年代早期，在其死后于1875年发表。诗的题目为《孤独》，讲述了诗人经历"孤独"的过程和原因。本诗可以分成两个部分，第一部分叙述了从孩提时诗人就拥有的与众不同的地方：情感与忧伤、喜悦与爱都与他人不同——他只能孤单地爱他所爱。接着诗人话锋一转道出了个中原因，原来幼小时心灵就被一种神秘的东西占领，至今犹在。诗人并没有说明这是什么，但描述了它的来源：激流、喷泉、山崖，以及秋天的阳光和空中的霹雳、闪电和暴风，还有那魔鬼模样的云彩，这些都成为了神秘之物的渊源。诗歌到此戛然而止。这首小诗表明了坡一种特立独行的个性，诗中的意象有着典型的浪漫主义色彩，同时也传递出了怪异的情调，这与坡的写作风格是一致的。

Annabel Lee

It was many and many a year ago,
In a kingdom by the sea,
That a maiden there lived whom you may know
By the name of ANNABEL LEE;—
And this maiden she lived with no other thought
Than to love and be loved by me.

I was a child and she was a child,
In this kingdom by the sea,
But we loved with a love that was more than love—
I and my ANNABEL LEE—
With a love that the winged seraphs① of heaven
Coveted② her and me.

And this was the reason that, long ago,
In this kingdom by the sea,
A wind blew out of a cloud by night
Chilling my ANNABEL LEE;

---

① winged seraphs：插着翅膀的天使。
② covet：贪求，觊觎。

So that her highborn kinsman① came
And bore her away from me,
To shut her up in a sepulchre②
In this kingdom by the sea.

The angels, not half so happy in Heaven,
Went envying her and me:—
Yes! that was the reason (as all men know,
In this kingdom by the sea)
That the wind came out of a cloud, chilling
And killing my ANNABEL LEE.

But our love it was stronger by far than the love
Of those who were older than we—
Of many far wiser than we—
And neither the angels in Heaven above,
Nor the demons down under the sea,
Can ever dissever③ my soul from the soul
Of the beautiful ANNABEL LEE:—

For the moon never beams④ without bringing me dreams
Of the beautiful ANNABEL LEE;
And the stars never rise, but I feel the bright eyes
Of the beautiful Annabel Lee;
And so, all the night tide, I lie down by the side
Of my darling—my darling—my life and my bride,
 In her sepulchre there by the sea—
 In her tomb by the side of the sea.

---

① highborn kinsman：出身高贵的亲属。
② sepulchre：坟墓。
③ dissever：分离。
④ beam：照耀。

在很久很久以前,一对恋人住在海边。他们的爱引起了天使的嫉妒,一阵阴风刮来,吹散了恋人。女孩死了,海边多了一座新坟;但是,这并不能隔断"我"的爱恋,伴着月亮,看着星星,在海边,"我"守着我的新娘到永远。坡这首诗写出了一个凄婉的爱情故事,情真意切,读来让人唏嘘不已。爱情的忠贞是突出的主题。很多评论认为这首诗是写给坡的妻子弗杰妮雅。1835年坡26岁时与13岁表妹弗杰妮雅结婚,1847年弗杰妮雅逝世。两年后坡也撒手人寰。此诗在坡去世两天后发表,成为了他的绝唱。

这首诗摹仿歌谣,采用叙述体形式,一些句子和词重复,音韵低缓,传递出哀怨的感觉;跳行押韵,以"i:"音为韵脚,情意绵绵,切合忠贞主题。

The Raven

Once upon a midnight dreary, while I pondered weak and weary,
Over many a quaint and curious volume of forgotten lore①,
While I nodded, nearly napping, suddenly there came a tapping,
As of some one gently rapping, rapping at my chamber door.
"'Tis some visitor," I muttered, "tapping at my chamber door—
       Only this, and nothing more."

Ah, distinctly I remember it was in the bleak December,
And each separate dying ember wrought its ghost upon the floor②.
Eagerly I wished the morrow③;—vainly I had sought to borrow
From my books surcease④ of sorrow—sorrow for the lost Lenore—
For the rare and radiant maiden whom the angels named Lenore—
       Nameless here for evermore.

And the silken sad uncertain rustling of each purple curtain
Thrilled me—filled me with fantastic terrors never felt before;
So that now, to still the beating of my heart, I stood repeating

---

① lore: 知识,学问。
② each separate dying ember wrought its ghost upon the floor: 微弱的余烬在地板上投下散乱的影子。ember: 余烬。
③ morrow: 次日。
④ surcease: 停止。

美国诗歌选读

'Tis some visitor entreating entrance at my chamber door—
Some late visitor entreating entrance at my chamber door;—
                                    This it is, and nothing more,

Presently my soul grew stronger; hesitating then no longer,
"Sir," said I, "or Madam, truly your forgiveness I implore;
But the fact is I was napping, and so gently you came rapping,
And so faintly you came tapping, tapping at my chamber door,
That I scarce was sure I heard you"—here I opened wide the door;—
                                    Darkness there, and nothing more.

Deep into that darkness peering, long I stood there wondering, fearing,
Doubting, dreaming dreams no mortals ever dared to dream before
But the silence was unbroken, and the darkness gave no token①,
And the only word there spoken was the whispered word, "Lenore!"
This I whispered, and an echo murmured back the word, "Lenore!"
                                    Merely this and nothing more.

Then into the chamber turning, all my soul within me burning,
Soon again I heard a tapping somewhat louder than before.
"Surely," said I, "surely that is something at my window lattice②;
Let me see then, what thereat is, and this mystery explore—
Let my heart be still a moment and this mystery explore;—
                                    'Tis the wind and nothing more!"

Open here I flung the shutter, when, with many a flirt and flutter③,
In there stepped a stately raven of the saintly days of yore④.
Not the least obeisance⑤ made he; not a minute stopped or stayed he;
But, with mien⑥ of lord or lady, perched above my chamber door—
Perched upon a bust of Pallas⑦ just above my chamber door—
                                  Perched, and sat, and nothing more.

---

① token：迹象。
② lattice：窗台。
③ with many a flirt and flutter：震颤，飘动。注意押头韵"f"。
④ days of yore：往日时代。yore：昔日。
⑤ obeisance：敬意，尊敬。
⑥ mien：外表。
⑦ Pallas：雅典娜，希腊神话中的智慧和艺术女神。

Then this ebony bird beguiling my sad fancy into smiling,
By the grave and stern decorum of the countenance① it wore,
"Though thy crest be shorn and shaven, thou," I said, art sure no craven.
Ghastly grim and ancient raven wandering from the nightly shore—
Tell me what thy lordly name is on the Night's Plutonian shore!②
         Quoth the raven, "Nevermore."

Much I marvelled this ungainly fowl to hear discourse so plainly,
Though its answer little meaning—little relevancy bore;
For we cannot help agreeing that no living human being
Ever yet was blessed with seeing bird above his chamber door—
Bird or beast above the sculptured bust above his chamber door,
         With such name as "Nevermore."

But the raven, sitting lonely on the placid③ bust, spoke only,
That one word, as if his soul in that one word he did outpour.
Nothing further then he uttered—not a feather then he fluttered—
Till I scarcely more than muttered, "Other friends have flown before—
On the morrow will he leave me, as my hopes have flown before."
         Then the bird said, "Nevermore."

Wondering at the stillness broken by reply so aptly spoken,
"Doubtless," said I, "what it utters is its only stock and store,④
Caught from some unhappy master whom unmerciful Disaster
Followed fast and followed faster-so, when Hope he would adjure,⑤
Stern Despair returned, instead of the sweet Hope he dared adjure—
         That sad answer,'Nevermore!'"

But the raven still beguiling all my sad soul into smiling,
Straight I wheeled a cushioned seat in front of bird, and bust, and door;
Then, upon the velvet sinking, I betook myself to linking

---

① the grave and stern decorum of the countenance：严峻,庄重的面容表情。decorum：得体,countenance：面容。
② Plutonian：阴间,地府。源于希腊神话。
③ placid：宁静的。
④ stock and store：一切,所有。
⑤ adjure：祈求。

Fancy unto fancy①, thinking what this ominous bird of yore—
What this grim, ungainly, gaunt, and ominous bird of yore
          Meant in croaking "Nevermore."

This I sat engaged in guessing, but no syllable expressing
To the fowl whose fiery eyes now burned into my bosom's core;
This and more I sat divining②, with my head at ease reclining
On the cushion's velvet lining that the lamp-light gloated o'er,
But whose velvet violet lining with the lamp-light gloating o'er,
          She shall press, ah, nevermore!

Then, methought, the air grew denser, perfumed from an unseen censer③
Swung by angels whose faint foot-falls tinkled on the tufted floor.
"Wretch,"④ I cried,"thy God hath lent thee—by these angels he has sent thee
Respite⑤—respite and Nepenthe⑥ from thy memories of Lenore!
Let me quaff⑦ this kind Nepenthe and forget this lost Lenore!"
          Quoth the raven,"Nevermore."

"Prophet!" said I, "thing of evil!—prophet still, if bird or devil!—
Whether Tempter sent, or whether tempest tossed thee here ashore,
Desolate yet all undaunted, on this desert land enchanted—
On this home by Horror haunted—tell me truly, I implore—
Is there—is there Balm in Gilead?⑧—tell me—tell me, I implore!"
          Quoth the raven, "Nevermore."

"Prophet!" said I,"thing of evil!—prophet still, if bird or devil!
By that Heaven that bends above us—by that God we both adore—
Tell this soul with sorrow laden if, within the distant Aidenn,⑨
It shall clasp a sainted maiden whom the angels named Lenore—

---

① betook myself to linking/Fancy unto fancy：陷入猜想之中。
② divining：猜想。
③ perfumed from an unseen censer：弥漫着看不见的氤氲。
④ wretch：家伙。
⑤ respite：暂息。
⑥ nepenthe：(古希腊人用的)忘忧药。
⑦ quaff：痛饮。
⑧ Balm in Gilead：原出于《圣经》,指慰籍物。Gilead,《圣经》中一地名,balm：镇痛软膏。
⑨ Aidenn：坡自己想象的地名,指 Eden：伊甸园。

Clasp a rare and radiant maiden, whom the angels named Lenore?"
            Quoth the raven, "Nevermore."

"Be that word our sign of parting, bird or fiend!" I shrieked, upstarting—
"Get thee back into the tempest and the Night's Plutonian shore!
Leave no black plume as a token of that lie thy soul hath spoken!
Leave my loneliness unbroken!—quit the bust above my door!
Take thy beak from out my heart, and take thy form from off my door!"
            Quoth the raven, "Nevermore."

And the raven, never flitting, still is sitting, still is sitting
On the pallid bust of Pallas just above my chamber door;
And his eyes have all the seeming of a demon's that is dreaming,
And the lamp-light o'er him streaming throws his shadow on the floor;
And my soul from out that shadow that lies floating on the floor
            Shall be lifted—nevermore!

夜色深深,寒风袭人。"我"一边读书,一边在思念着逝去的爱人。这时,响起了敲窗的声音,原来是一只乌鸦飞到了窗台。你来自哪儿,叫什么名字?"我"于是与乌鸦展开了对话,但乌鸦似乎只会回答一个字:"永不"(nevermore)。"我"于是猜想是上苍遣它来送忘忧药,让"我"忘掉我的爱人。可是恰恰相反,这更激起"我"的思念,让"我"的思念永不停息。这是坡最负盛名的一首诗。此诗发表于1845年,引起轰动,坡也因此成为了著名诗人。在《创作的哲学》一文里,坡专门谈了此诗的创作过程。他认为诗歌的最高境界是描述一个美丽女人的死亡,而最适合叙述这个主题的则应是失去了爱人的恋人。显然,诗中的"我"正是这样一个叙述者。这首诗表达了叙述者"我"对逝去的爱人的一种深深的思念之情,忧伤之感跃然纸上。坡主张诗歌应主要诉诸情感,而越是忧郁、感伤之情则越能产生美感。乌鸦在诗中起了一种引子的作用,勾起了思念,触发了情感,并一步一步引向强烈,以至让"我"不能自己。这也是坡强调的诗歌创作的"效果作用"。此诗的技巧效果也非常明显,在很多地方用了押头韵(alliteration),节奏上采用扬抑格,八音步(首句)与(第二句)七音步相结合,造成一长一短,轻重相间,变化有致的音律效果;每一节以四音步结尾,出自乌鸦之口的nevermore一词同时也表达了"我"的思念永不停息的意思,长元音"ɔː"则更加重了这种情绪。这首诗是音律与内容完美结合的典范。

美国诗歌选读

思考题

1. For what does the poet talk about being "alone" in the poem "Alone"?
2. What gives rise to the sense of being "alone" in the poem?
3. What do you think makes "Annable Lee" one of the best known poems of Poe?
4. Can you find any elements showing that Poe wrote Annable Lee in the pattern of ballad?
5. How does the poem "Raven" demonstrate Poe's theory of "effect" in the composition of poetry?
6. What is special about the versification of "Raven"?

推荐作品

1. "To Helen"
2. "The City in the Sea"
3. "The Sleeper"
4. "To—Ulalume: A Ballad"

参考书目

1. Hayes, Kevin J. ed. *The Cambridge Companion to Edgar Allan Poe*. Shanghai: Shanghai Foreign Language Education Press, 2004.
2. Walker, IM. ed. *Edgar Allan Poe: The Critical Heritage*. London & New York: Routledge & Kegan Paul, 1986.

第五单元

Walt Whitman (1819—1892)
沃尔特·惠特曼

作者简介

沃尔特·惠特曼,诗人,散文、小说作家,出生于纽约州长岛(Long Island)的一个木匠家庭。11岁便辍学,先后曾在律师事务所、医疗诊所打工、在印刷所学徒,后来成为了职业编辑、记者。19世纪美国报刊界没有20世纪建立起来的新闻中立概念,各报刊往往由各党派支持、赞助,具有浓厚党派政治色彩。惠特曼也积极参与政治活动,他撰写的文章涉及广泛的社会、政治议题,表达自己的民主政治理念。而报刊党派政治等原因也使他数年后淡出了新闻职业。其后,他盖过房子,作过木匠,在战时医院中护理过伤员,还在政府部门当过小职员。他所结识的人更是形形色色,包括政治人物、军官、画家、雕塑家、乃至渡轮驾驶员、马车夫等。

尽管没有受到完整的学校正规教育,但当他还是个十来岁的学徒时,就已经开始了文学创作,在报刊上发表杂文和诗歌作品,依靠多年自学积累,他广泛涉猎文学、历史、哲学等领域知识,对歌剧、绘画也是情有独钟。丰富的社会生活历炼,对民众的熟悉和理解,以及对当下社会、政治议题的热情关注和参与都在他的作品中留下了相应的底色和广博的空间。他在1855年出版了《草叶集》(Leaves of Grass)第一版。作为诗集名字的"草叶"以其平凡、顽强的生命力、勃勃生机意喻普罗大众的精神和生活,也是19世纪美国民主政体中普通个体的整体形象。集子一共包括12首诗,语言自然、朴素,常常像是作者和读者之间的直接交谈,不使用押韵,也不拘泥传统格律,开创了自由诗体。英国诗人、评论家罗伯特·布坎南(Robert Williams Buchanan, 1841—1901)甚至认为,惠特曼的诗体"非常接近解决散文节奏与韵律诗歌之间真正关系问题"。惠特曼所经历的杰克逊时代是从建国早期精英政治向平民民主发展的重要时期。被称为"民主诗人"的惠特曼适逢其时。他的诗歌随处闪烁着19世纪美国民主精神所孕育和表达的"自我"张扬,以及诗人作为

美国诗歌选读

美国文化代言人的自觉意识、情感、洞悉和体验。《草叶集》经过不断扩充、修改，直到第9版"临终版"，成为包括389首诗的宏篇大作(1855年版，1856年版，1960年版，1867年版，1871年版，1876年版，1881年版，1888年版和1891年版)。可以说，诗集增改的过程应该也是诗人在美国19世纪下半叶社会动荡发展中心路历程的折射。惠特曼研究的权威学者詹姆斯·米勒(James E. Miller, Jr.)称之为"个人史诗"(the personal epic)。诗集涵盖的内容浩繁、庞杂，可以是历史、政治、战争、哲思、冥想、情爱、孤寂、哀思，也可以是任何平庸事物，甚至是被认为放荡、败坏的情感和观念。惠特曼以美国自己的语言和方式展现了19世纪美国的一幅幅心灵画卷。米勒教授称惠特曼的个人史诗形式是对美国诗歌重要"遗产"。

　　惠特曼的其他主要作品包括：中篇小说《富兰克林·伊凡斯》(*Franklin Evans*, 1842)；诗集《桴鼓集》(*Drum Taps*, 1865)；诗集《桴鼓集·续集》(*Sequel to Drum Taps*, 1865)；散文《民主展望》(*Democratic Vistas*, 1871)；诗歌散文集《十一月树枝》(*November Boughs*, 1888)。

One's-Self I Sing

One's-Self I sing—a simple, separate Person;
Yet utter the word Democratic, the word En-masse①.

Of Physiology from top to toe I sing;
Not physiognomy alone, nor brain alone, is worthy for the muse—
I say the Form complete is worthier far;
The Female equally with the male I sing.

Of Life immense in passion, pulse, and power,
Cheerful—for freest action form'd②, under the laws divine,
The Modern Man I sing.

---

① en-masse: [法文] 大量，大批 在此指全体，整体。
② form'd: formed.

作品赏析

这首诗是《草叶集》开篇第一首诗,以讴歌"自我"的方式,表达个人和时代的整体声音。诗人作为"现代人"的代言人,毫无保留地赞美独立、自主、与他人"分离"的单一个人,但同时也赞美个人置身其中的民主"整体"。诗人讴歌的个人具有与众不同的个性,不从他人那里获得"第二手"、"第三手"的知识,而是通过自己眼睛的观察和理解事物,是"靠自身,而不是间接力量"成长。对惠特曼的个人来说,没有什么能比一个人的自我更伟大,上帝也不例外。然而自主的个人并非遁出红尘的孤家寡人,而是与其他和自己有相似思想、情感的个体共同组成民主社会。惠特曼所歌颂的是以个人主义为基础的平民化民主。惠特曼本人曾积极参加政活动,尽管他对美国制度的弊端有所反省,但他始终热情讴歌美国式民主制度。同时,诗人对个人的赞美包括精神和肉体两个方面,而且在诗人眼中,无论精神或肉体都不能被贬低。用惠特曼的话说:"灵魂并不高于肉体","肉体也不高于灵魂"。传统西方主流思想和宗教将理性或灵魂置于主导地位,要求控制、甚至压抑激情或肉体欲望,而惠特曼却讴歌肉体的"神圣"性以及灵魂、肉体的整体性,这一方面挑战了当时美国的清教主义传统观念,另一方面,所有个体具有同一性的肉体和激情使人们成为人流中平等的一员,无论身份贵贱、博学或无知,是男人或是女人,都在宇宙之中占有自己一席之地,都具有同样的权利。惠特曼秉承了杰弗逊理想中的独立自主的小农共和政体思想,以及平等、自由等"神圣"自然权利的启蒙思想,而19世纪杰克逊民主时代充满活力和平等机会的美国北方社会应该成为理想共和政体和自主、自由个人的家园。如果从政治意义上看,惠特曼追求和讴歌的"现代人"的"最自由的行动"恰恰是萌芽于希腊古典政治理想,始见于近代英国宪政实践并已成为资本主义民主政治主流价值的所谓法治下的个人自由。而从伦理角度看,他所强调的自由又可以是更加广义的自然法则下的自由选择。

思考题

1. What does "one's self" stand for?
2. What does "physiology from top to toe" mean?
3. What is "the Form complete"?
4. What is "the Modern man"?

美国诗歌选读

To the Garden①, the World②

To THE garden, the world, anew ascending③,
Potent④ mates, daughters, sons, preluding,
The love, the life of their bodies, meaning and being,
Curious, here behold my resurrection, after slumber;
The revolving cycles, in their wide sweep, have brought me again,
Amorous, mature—all beautiful to me—all wondrous;
My limbs, and the quivering fire that ever plays⑤ through them,
　　　for reasons, most wondrous;
Existing, I peer and penetrate still,
Content with the present—content with the past,
By my side, or back of me, Eve following,
Or in front, and I following her just the same.

这是《亚当的子孙》组诗中的第一首诗。在惠特曼的时代,清教主义观念将性欲和男欢女爱看作罪恶,是公共话题的禁忌。而惠特曼认为,肉体是灵魂不可分割的一部分,肉体甚至"就是灵魂"。性爱出自自然,神圣完美。因此他讴歌一切性爱的自然冲动和欲望。难怪,诗中对性爱的直白表述被当时的世俗观念所不齿,甚至被指为淫秽、色情作品,包含"毫无羞耻的发作"。难怪,连十分赏识他的爱默生也曾建议他将《亚当的子孙》组诗从正在准备出版的《草叶集》第三版中删除。

所选诗中的人们重新回到了喻指伊甸园的"花园",在这里肉体的性爱生活获得"意义"和真实"存在","周而复始的循环"蕴含自然的规律性,"广阔范围"(wide sweep)将万千事物包括在内,而"所有这一切"又是如此"美丽"和"奇妙"。惠特曼重建了《圣经》的伊甸园故事,人类不再是从伊甸园坠落的罪人,而是重新上升,进入"花园"。人们不再因为性爱——他们的"肉体的生活"——而感到任何羞耻,他们从真实情感的压抑和"沉睡"中回归自然的纯真和"复苏",而性爱的自然表现才是对人性的本原。同时,惠特曼主张的男女平等也在这个花园中得以实现。

---
① the garden:在这里"花园"喻指伊甸园。
② the world:这里指人类。
③ to the garden the world anew ascending: to the garden, the world anew, ascending.
④ potent:有性能力的。
⑤ play:不断发生作用。

1. What is the significance of the word "ascending" in the poem?
2. What is the implication of the revolving cycles in their wide sweep?
3. Why does the speaker describe himself as "existing"?
4. Should one feel content with the present and the past as the speaker does in the garden? Why or why not, within the framework of Christianity?
5. What message is conveyed by the last two lines of the poem?
6. Who is Adam in the garden?

Once I Pass'd through a Populous City

Once I pass'd through a populous city, imprinting my brain,
    for future use, with its shows, architecture, customs, and traditions;
Yet now, of all that city, I remember only a woman I casually met
    there, who detain'd me for love of me;
Day by day and night by night we were together,—All else has long been
    forgotten by me;
I remember, I say, only that woman who passionately clung to me;
Again we wander—we love—we separate again;
Again she holds me by the hand—I must not go!
I see her close beside me, with silent lips, sad and tremulous.

这首诗是《亚当的子孙》组诗中的一首。惠特曼的手稿与发表后的文字有些不同，诗中的恋人原本是男性 (But now of all that city I remember only the man who wandered with me, there, for love of me... I remember, I say, only one rude and ignorant man.)显然，惠特曼这首诗原本是描述男性之间的情感的。尽管这表现出惠特曼对男女之间和男性之间情感的独特观念(参见下一首作品和作品赏析)，但这并不妨碍这首诗被公认为惠特曼的一首经典情爱诗篇。从另一个角度来看，也许如米勒教授所指出，惠特曼的《亚当的子孙》组诗是在讴歌"所有不同形式的性爱——自我性爱、同性性爱、异性性爱、普世性爱……把这些不同形式的性爱看作一个整体，在一定意义上，是同一种性爱。……[这些形式]相似多于不同。"

美国诗歌选读

思考题

1. Did the speaker of the poem try to remember the city's shows, architecture, customs, traditions?
2. What is the only thing the speaker remembers of all that city?
3. How is the relationship between the two lovers portrayed in the poem?

I Saw in Louisiana a Live-Oak Growing

I saw in Louisiana a live-oak growing,
All alone stood it, and the moss hung down from the branches;
Without any companion it grew there, uttering joyous leaves of dark green,
And its look, rude, unbending, lusty, made me think of myself;
But I wonder'd how it could utter joyous leaves, standing alone there, without its friend, its lover near—for I knew I could not,
And I broke off a twig with a certain number of leaves upon it, and twined around it a little moss,
And brought it away—and I have placed it in sight in my room;
It is not needed to remind me as of my own dear friends,
(For I believe lately I think of little else than of them;)
Yet it remains to me a curious token—it makes me think of manly love;
For all that, and though the live-oak glistens there in Louisiana, solitary, in a wide flat space,
Uttering joyous leaves all its life, without a friend, a lover, near,
I know very well I could not.

该诗是《庐笛》(Calamus)组诗中的一首诗。按照惠特曼的解释,芦笛代表"最大"、"最坚硬"的草的叶片部分。这组诗主要表现男性之间的友情、情感,或所谓"黏着性"(adhesiveness,这是当时颅像学的一个术语,指男性之间的伙伴感情)。惠特曼将其称为"男性伙伴之间的爱"(dear love of man for his comrade),并强调其政治层面的意义。从这个角度看,这样的"男性依恋"(manly attachment)乃是惠特曼心目中民主整体中个人之间的黏着力,是一种精神上的、没有性爱色彩的情感。也有一些学者将组诗中表达的男性之间的情感与惠特曼可能的个人的情感经历相联系，并因此将这些诗歌解释为同性恋情感（homoeroticism）的表现。具体到诗中，诗人对同伴的渴望和需要通过对橡树的联想得到了充分表达，橡树可以"孤独"地站立在那里，没有同伴，然而却能够成长，倾吐出欢乐的绿叶。"孤独"在诗人眼中与"欢乐"，代表希望的"深绿"叶子，"倾吐"和"成长"是那样的格格不入。尽管诗人从橡树的"粗犷"、"挺拔"、"精力充沛"的外表想到"我自己"，但诗人宣称，如果自己没有伙伴、友谊和爱人，就不能像橡树那样"倾诉"充满"欢乐"的"草叶"诗歌。的确，橡树"精力充沛"，虽然独自站立，却能"倾吐欢乐的绿叶"、繁茂地成长，既表现了爱恋和自然万物的生殖、生长的物理本性，又似乎象征了男性之间依恋的精神性。

 思考题

1. Why did the look of the oak make the speaker think of himself?
2. Is there any resemblance between the oak and the poet? If yes, what resemblance do you see?
3. Why did the speaker break off a twig and bring it home?
4. Why did the speaker say that he could not act like the oak?
5. What could be the implication of the solitary oak uttering joyous leaves?

Out of the Cradle Endlessly Rocking

Out of the cradle endlessly rocking, Out of the mocking-bird's throat, the musical shuttle, Out of the Ninth-month midnight, Over the sterile sands, and the fields beyond, where the child, leaving his bed,
wander'd alone, bare-headed, barefoot, Down from the shower'd halo, Up from the mystic play of shadows, twining and twisting as if they were alive,
Out from the patches of briers and blackberries,
From the memories of the bird that chanted to me,
From your memories, sad brother—from the fitful risings and fallings I heard,
From under that yellow half-moon, late-risen, and swollen as if with tears,

From those beginning notes of sickness and love, there in the transparent mist,
From the thousand responses of my heart, never to cease,
From the myriad thence-arous'd words,
From the word stronger and more delicious than any,
From such, as now they start, the scene revisiting,
As a flock, twittering, rising, or overhead passing,
Borne hither—ere all eludes me, hurriedly,
A man—yet by these tears a little boy again,
Throwing myself on the sand, confronting the waves,
I, chanter of pains and joys, uniter of here and hereafter,
Taking all hints to use them—but swiftly leaping beyond them,
A reminiscence sing.

Once, Paumanok①, when the snows had melted—
when the lilac-scent was in the air, and the Fifth-month grass was growing,
Up this sea-shore, in some briers,
Two guests from Alabama—two together,
And their nest, and four light-green eggs, spotted with brown,
And every day the he-bird②, to and fro, near at hand,
And every day the she-bird③, crouch'd on her nest, silent, with bright eyes,
And every day I, a curious boy, never too close, never disturbing them,
Cautiously peering, absorbing, translating.

Shine! shine! shine!
Pour down your warmth, great Sun!
While we bask—we two together.

Two together!
Winds blow South, or winds blow North,
Day come white, or night come black,
Home, or rivers and mountains from home,
Singing all time, minding no time,
While we two keep together.

---

① Paumanok：[印第安语]长岛。
② he-bird：男性的鸟。
③ she-bird：女性的鸟。

Till of a sudden,
May-be kill'd, unknown to her mate,
One forenoon① the she-bird crouch'd not on the nest,
Nor return'd that afternoon, nor the next,
Nor ever appear'd again.

And thenceforward, all summer, in the sound of the sea,
And at night, under the full of the moon, in calmer weather,
Over the hoarse surging of the sea,
Or flitting from brier to brier by day,
I saw, I heard at intervals, the remaining one, the he-bird,
The solitary guest from Alabama.

Blow! blow! blow!
Blow up, sea-winds, along Paumanok's shore!
I wait and I wait, till you blow my mate to me.

Yes, when the stars glisten'd,
All night long, on the prong of a moss-scallop'd stake,
Down, almost amid the slapping waves,
Sat the lone singer, wonderful, causing tears.

He call'd on his mate;
He pour'd forth the meanings which I, of all men, know.

Yes, my brother, I know;
The rest might not—but I have treasur'd every note;
For once, and more than once, dimly, down to the beach gliding,
Silent, avoiding the moonbeams, blending myself with the shadows,
Recalling now the obscure shapes, the echoes, the sounds and sights after their sorts,
The white arms out in the breakers tirelessly tossing,
I, with bare feet, a child, the wind wafting my hair,
Listen'd long and long.

---

① forenoon：上午。

美国 诗歌选读

Listen'd, to keep, to sing—now translating the notes,
Following you, my brother.

Soothe! soothe! soothe!
Close on its wave soothes the wave behind,
And again another behind, embracing and lapping, every one close,
But my love soothes not me, not me.

Low hangs the moon[①]*—it rose late;*
O it is lagging—O I think it is heavy with love, with love.

O madly the sea pushes, pushes upon the land,
With love—with love.

O night! do I not see my love fluttering out there among the breakers[②]*?*
What is that little black thing I see there in the white?

Loud! loud! loud!
Loud I call to you, my love!

High and clear I shoot my voice over the waves;
Surely you must know who is here, is here;
You must know who I am, my love.

Low-hanging moon!
What is that dusky spot in your brown yellow?
O it is the shape, the shape of my mate!
O moon, do not keep her from me any longer.

Land! land! O land!
Whichever way I turn, O I think you could give me my mate back again, if you only would;
For I am almost sure I see her dimly whichever way I look.

---

① Paumanok：【印第安语】长岛。
② he-bird：男性的鸟。

O rising stars! Perhaps the one I want so much will rise, will rise with some of you.

O throat! O trembling throat!
Sound clearer through the atmosphere!
Pierce the woods, the earth;
Somewhere listening to catch you, must be the one I want.

Shake out, carols!
Solitary here—the night's carols!
Carols of lonesome love! Death's carols!
Carols under that lagging, yellow, waning moon!
O, under that moon, where she droops almost down into the sea!
O reckless, despairing carols.

But soft! sink low;
Soft! let me just murmur;
And do you wait a moment, you husky-noised sea;
For somewhere I believe I heard my mate responding to me,
So faint—I must be still, be still to listen;
But not altogether still, for then she might not come immediately to me.

Hither, my love!
Here I am! Here!
With this just-sustain'd note I announce myself to you;
This gentle call is for you, my love, for you.

Do not be decoy'd elsewhere!
That is the whistle of the wind—it is not my voice;
That is the fluttering, the fluttering of the spray;
Those are the shadows of leaves.

O darkness! O in vain!
O I am very sick and sorrowful.

O brown halo in the sky, near the moon, drooping upon the sea!

美国诗歌选读

O troubled reflection in the sea!
O throat! O throbbing heart!
O all—and I singing uselessly, uselessly all the night.

Yet I murmur, murmur on!
O murmurs—you yourselves make me
continue to sing, I know not why.

O past! O life! O songs of joy!
In the air—in the woods—over fields;
Loved! loved! loved! loved! loved!
But my love no more, no more with me!
We two together no more.

The aria sinking,
All else continuing—the stars shining,
The winds blowing—the notes of the bird continuous echoing,
With angry moans the fierce old mother incessantly moaning,
On the sands of Paumanok's shore, gray and rustling;
The yellow half-moon enlarged, sagging down, drooping, the face of the sea almost touching;
The boy extatic—with his bare feet the waves, with his hair the atmosphere① dallying,
The love in the heart long pent, now loose, now at last tumultuously bursting,
The aria's meaning, the ears, the Soul, swiftly depositing,
The strange tears down the cheeks coursing,
The colloquy there—the trio—each uttering,
The undertone—the savage old mother, incessantly crying,
To the boy's Soul's questions sullenly timing—some drown'd secret hissing,
To the outsetting bard of love.

Demon or bird! (said the boy's soul,)

---

① atmosphere：这里指海风。

Is it indeed toward your mate you sing? or is it mostly to me?

For I, that was a child, my tongue's use sleeping, now I have heard you,

Now in a moment I know what I am for—I awake,

And already a thousand singers—a thousand songs, clearer, louder and more sorrowful than yours,

A thousand warbling echoes have started to life within me, Never to die.

O you singer, solitary, singing by yourself—projecting① me; O solitary me, listening—nevermore shall I cease perpetuating you;

Never more shall I escape, never more the reverberations,

Never more the cries of unsatisfied love be absent from me,

Never again leave me to be the peaceful child I was before what there, in the night,

By the sea, under the yellow and sagging moon,

The messenger there arous'd—the fire, the sweet hell within,

The unknown want, the destiny of me.

O give me the clew! (it lurks in the night here somewhere;)

O if I am to have so much, let me have more!

O a word! O what is my destination?

(I fear it is henceforth chaos;)

O how joys, dreads, convolutions, human shapes, and all shapes, spring as from graves around me!

O phantoms! you cover all the land and all the sea!

O I cannot see in the dimness whether you smile or frown upon me;

O vapor, a look, a word! O well-beloved!

O you dear women's and men's phantoms!

A word then, (for I will conquer it,)

The word final, superior to all,

Subtle, sent up—what is it?—I listen;

Are you whispering it, and have been all the time, you sea-waves?

Is that it from your liquid rims and wet sands?

---

① project: 这里指一方情感反映到另一方。

Whereto answering, the sea,
Delaying not, hurrying not,
Whisper'd me through the night, and very plainly before daybreak,
Lisp'd to me the low and delicious word DEATH,
And again Death—ever Death, Death, Death,
Hissing melodious, neither like the bird, nor like my arous'd child's heart,
But edging near, as privately for me, rustling at my feet,
Creeping thence steadily up to my ears, and laving me softly all over,
Death, Death, Death, Death, Death.

Which I do not forget,
But fuse the song of my dusky demon and brother,
That he sang to me in the moonlight on Paumanok's gray beach,
With the thousand responsive songs, at random,
My own songs, awaked from that hour;
And with them the key, the word up from the waves,
The word of the sweetest song, and all songs,
That strong and delicious word which, creeping to my feet,
The sea whisper'd me.

作品赏析

　　一个男孩在午夜时分,赤足来到海边,他和自然之间的共鸣与成长为诗人叙述者的成年男子的沉咏交织在一起。孩童宁静的心灵是小鸟鸣唱音符的最好翻译者,通过诗人的记忆,儿时自然感性与成年诗人感悟浑然天成。诗中互动的四方包括:小鸟、大海、男孩和男孩成人后的诗人。男孩倾听小鸟和大海的自然之音,将小鸟的啾鸣翻译成语言,探究灵魂的提问,而成年的诗人同时也是男孩语言的转译者和灵魂提问的探究者。感官经验通过翻译和转译而被赋予意义;男孩的感受向成年诗人的思考过渡,最终达至对生命、爱情、生离死别、死亡和重生意义的领悟。同时,"孤寂的歌手"和"孤寂的我在倾听"从个别经历转化成"一千个歌手"、"更清晰、更响亮、更哀伤"的"一千首歌"的普遍情感;感官世界的有限和暂时通过语言和诗歌转化为精神世界的无限和永恒,作为自然规律的死亡也因此达到诗化的重生。

　　诗歌的叙事结构巧妙,叙事者交替以男孩和成年诗人的身份叙述,男孩以他童贞的心灵在海边"倾听"、"翻译",叙事者转换通过男孩将自己成长中感受到的"形体"、"回响"、"声音和景象"转化成"心灵的回应"和"万千话语",而成年诗人又依靠"回忆"的连接,成了超越"今生"和"来世"的"统一者",使原始"音符"与男孩和诗人的"歌咏"之间的跨越天衣无缝。

惠特曼对意大利歌剧的着迷无疑在他的诗歌创作中留下了清晰印记。在诗歌吟咏中我们似乎可以听到咏叹调跌宕起伏的旋律和宣叙调的烘托过渡。W. S. 肯尼迪(William Sloane Kennedy, 1850—1929)认为，由于无韵诗摆脱了对语言的刻意雕琢，能够将注意力集中在思想表达上。惠特曼通过实验放弃使用旧的韵律节奏，他诗歌中的乐音出自于大的主调，欣赏它需要从声音的整体，而不是局部上入手。同时，诗中词汇句法安排产生的节奏效果也像大海的无尽浪潮般一浪追逐一浪。

评论界从不同角度对这首诗作出解读：有的批评家力图从惠特曼可能经历的个人情感挫折角度理解该诗，尽管这方面的证据似乎远非确凿、充分；也有评论家从精神分析角度揭示诗歌内容、诗人与家人情感纠葛以及无意识之间的关系；另外一些评论家则从诗歌美学形式、主题内容等方面做出分析。的确，不同的解读展现了多样的研究视角，也有助于我们更加深入了解惠特曼的诗歌。

思考题

1. Does the boy fully understand his experience on the beach?
2. Why does the speaker think that he of all men knows the meanings of the bird's singing?
3. Who is "the fierce old mother"?
4. Who are the trio, each uttering?
5. Why does the speaker now think that he awakes?
6. Why does the speaker think that the solitary singer projects him?
7. Why is the word death delicious?
8. What does the cradle represent or symbolize?

1. *Song of My Self*
2. *I Sing the Body Electric*
3. *Scented Herbage of My Breast*
4. *Whoever You Are Holding Me Now in Hand*
5. *As I Ebb'd with the Ocean of Life*
6. *Vigil Strange I Kept on the Field One Night*
7. *The Wound-Dresser*
8. *When Lilacs Last in the Dooryard Bloom'd*
9. *O Captain! My Captain!*
10. *Crossing Brooklyn Ferry*

11. *There Was a Child Went Forth*
12. *Leaves of Grass: Comprehensive Reader's Edition.* Ed. Harold W. Blodgett and Sculley Bradley. New York: New York UP, 1965.
13. 惠特曼《草叶集》，赵萝蕤译，上海：上海译文出版社，1991年版。

参考书目

1. Greenspan, Ezra, ed. *The Cambridge Companion to Walt Whitman.* New York: Cambridge UP, 1995.
2. Kaplan, Justin. *Walt Whitman: A Life.* New York: Bantam Books, 1982.
3. Miller, James E. *A Critical Guide to "Leaves of Grass".* Chicago: U of Chicago P, 1957.
4. 李野光选编《惠特曼研究》，广西：漓江出版社，1988年版。

第六单元

Emily Dickinson (1830—1886)
埃米莉·狄金森

作者简介

埃米莉·狄金森,生前默默无闻,死后被发现是一位天才女诗人,誉为美国文学史上最伟大诗人之一。1830年她出生在马萨诸塞州安姆赫斯特的一个望族之家。父亲曾是州参议员。狄金森在当地学校读书,接受过良好教育,曾在一所女子学院上过一年学。文学素养深厚,熟悉莎士比亚、密尔顿、齐慈,热爱同时代的英国的夏洛蒂姐妹和白朗宁夫人。狄金森一生主要在家中度过。30岁后很少出门,过着隐居生活,终身未嫁。狄金森写过一千七百多首诗,生前只有9首发表。1890年她的朋友编辑出版了第一部狄金森诗集,1955年三卷本狄金森诗集出版,狄金森作为一个伟大诗人开始进入人们的视野。狄金森诗短小,简洁,但寓意深刻,情感充沛,意想奇巧,极富创见。诗歌内容非常丰富,涵盖宗教、自然、爱情、时间、生活、死亡、永生等主题。

49

I never lost as much but twice.
And that was in the sod①.
Twice have I stood a beggar
Before the door of God!

---

① sod:草地。

Angels—twice descending
Reimbursed① my store—
Burglar! Banker—Father!
I am poor once more

324

Some keep the Sabbath② going to church—
I keep it, staying at Home—
With a Bobolink③ for a Chorister④—
And an Orchard, for a Dome—

Some keep the Sabbath in Surplice⑤—
I, just wear my Wings⑥—
And instead of tolling the Bell, for Church,
Our little Sexton⑦—sings.

God preaches, a noted Clergyman—
And the sermon is never long,
So instead of getting to Heaven, at last—
I'm going, all along.

241

I like a look of Agony,
Because I know it's true—
Men do not sham⑧ Convulsion⑨,
Nor simulate⑩, a Throe—

---

① reimburse：偿还。
② Sabbath：(基督教)安息日。
③ bobolink：(动物)歌雀。
④ chorister：唱诗班成员，(比喻)天使，鸟。
⑤ surplice：(教士穿)白法衣。
⑥ wings：(女童子军佩戴的)绿色翼章。
⑦ sexton：教堂司事，看管者。
⑧ sham：假装。
⑨ convulsion：惊厥。
⑩ simulate：模仿。

The eyes glaze① once—and that is Death—
Impossible to feign②
The Beads Upon the Forehead
By homely Anguish strung③.

作品赏析

这三首诗内容各不相同,但都与宗教有一定关系。第一首诗的主题是死亡,诗人泣诉道她已经有两次失去了亲人。诗人把自己比喻为一个乞丐,站在上帝的面前,是上帝派天使下来把她的亲人带走了。紧接着,诗人笔锋一转,把天使与偷盗者和银行家放在一起,他们拿走了她拥有的一切,让她成为乞丐一样的穷人。这首诗表达了诗人失去亲人的苦痛和悲伤,同时也透露了对上帝的抗争的情绪。诗中比喻出奇、大胆,显示了狄金森对传统宗教观念的怀疑和挑战。第二首诗表明了类似的对宗教的挑战姿态。安息日是到教堂崇拜上帝的日子,但诗人却有自己的选择,呆在家中,穿戴上自己喜爱的服饰,在庭院里尽情地歌唱。诗人眼里的上帝也与众不同,不是19世纪中叶在新英格兰仍然有着很多信徒的卡尔文教中那个威严的上帝,而是一个牧师,只是比较出名而已,而且布道也不长。最让人感到惊讶的是,诗人甚至不相信天堂。她要走她自己的路。与前面一首诗相比,这首诗表露了欢快、自信的情调和独立思考的勇气。第三首诗写的是"痛苦"。诗人说她喜欢痛苦的表情,因为它是真实的,没有人能够模仿,而更加无法模仿的是面临死亡时的痛苦状态:从额头上滴下的汗珠无声息地把痛苦串在了一起。诗人的这个描述让人联想到了耶稣基督被钉在十字架上的情景。耶稣的痛苦是真实的,这样的"真实"体现了耶稣的人性。这也应是狄金森在这首诗里讨论痛苦与真实关系的目的。同样,这也表明了她对待宗教的与众不同的态度。狄金森在女子学院期间曾被认为在宗教上"不可救药",原因就是因为她对传统的教义有不同的看法。这三首诗可以说在一定程度上体现了她的态度。

思考题

1. What do you think of the God image in poem 49?
2. What is the relation between "Burglar", "Banker" and "Father"?
3. What do you think enables the poet to act differently from others on Sabbath in poem 324?
4. What is the difference between the God in this poem and the God in the previous one?

---

① glaze:(眼睛)呆滞地看。
② feign:伪装。
③ By homely Anguish strung=strung by homely anguish.

5. How is the image of "agony" represented in poem 241?
6. Why does the poet feel that the look of agony is true in this poem?

303

  The Soul selects her own Society—
  Then—shuts the Door—
  To her divine Majority—
  Present no more—

  Unmoved—she notes the Chariots①—pausing—
  At her low Gate—
  Unmoved—an Emperor be kneeling
  Opon her Mat—

  I've known her—from an ample nation②—
  Choose One—
  Then—close the Valves③ of her attention—
  Like Stone—

709

  Publication—is the Auction
  Of the Mind of Man—
  Poverty—be justifying
  For so foul④ a thing

  Possibly—but We—would rather

---

① chariots：马车，战车。
② ample nation：足够多的事例。
③ valve：阀门。
④ foul：肮脏的。

From Our Garret① go
White—unto the White Creator—
Than invest—Our Snow—

Thought belong to Him who gave it—
Then—to Him Who bear
Its Corporeal illustration②—sell
The Royal Air—

In the Parcel—Be the Merchant
Of the Heavenly Grace③—
But reduce no Human Spirit
To Disgrace of Price—

  狄金森是一个有着强烈自我意识的诗人。尽管在表面上她只是一个普通的与外界没有多少联系的女性，但对独立人格的渴望却是她诗中一个时常出现的主题。这里选的两首诗可以作为代表之一。第一首诗形象地表达了诗人选择自己的生活的坚定态度。"门"成为了这首诗的核心意象，在门内，心灵有了自己的一片天地，即使天使驾着马车来访，或者是皇帝在门外下跪祈求，也不为所动。在诗的结尾，诗中的"我"肯定了心灵的做法，"我"与心灵合而为一，选择独立生活的决心更加明显。作为一个诗人，尤其是有着自己独特风格的女诗人要被社会接受势必会遭遇很多压力和困难。狄金森的态度是宁可没有读者，也不愿屈就出版她的诗歌。这便是第二首诗的内容。在诗人看来，出版毋宁是拍卖思想，没有了思想的人便是一个真正的穷人。诗人自认为自己的诗是"洁白无邪的"，就像与纯洁的造物主一样，因此她宁愿向造物主敞开自己的心灵，而不愿去做出版这样的投资。有意思的是，"投资"的对象是"雪"，而雪是会融化的，诗人表达了对为出版而作诗的鄙夷，诗人情愿过着在"阁楼"里的平常生活。能够拥有思想，同时又能亲身解释思想，这大概只有上帝能做到——上帝是恩典的出售者，但是请不要把人的精神按价出售，否则，这便是对人的侮辱。诗人再一次表达了持守自我独立精神的决心。考虑到诗人的女性身份，这两首诗表现了一种自觉的反抗的女性意识。

---

① garret：阁楼。
② corporeal illustration：身体表现。
③ grace：(上帝的)恩典。

思考题

1. What kind of "soul" does poem 303 represent?
2. Can we learn anything about the poet from reading this poem?
3. Why do you think the poet despises publication so much in poem 709?
4. What is the implied meaning of "white" in stanza two of this poem?

作品

333

The Grass so little has to do,
A Sphere of simple Green—
With only Butterflies, to brood,
And Bees, to entertain—

And stir all day to pretty tunes①
The Breezes fetch along,
And hold the Sunshine, in it's lap
And blow to everything,

And thread the Dews, all night, like Pearls,
And make itself so fine
A Duchess②, were too common
For such a noticing,

And even when it dies, to pass
In odors so divine—
As lowly spices, lain to sleep—
Or Spikenards③ perishing—

---

① And stir all day to pretty Tunes: 听着小调迎风招展。
② duchess: 贵妇人。
③ spikenards: (植物)甘松香。

And then to dwell in Sovereign Barns①,
And dream the Days away,
The Grass so little has to do,
I wish I were a Hay—

511

If you were coming in the Fall,
I'd brush the Summer by
With half a smile, and half a spurn②,
As housewives do, a Fly③.

If I could see you in a year,
I'd wind the months in balls④—
And put them each in separate Drawers,
For fear the numbers fuse—

If only Centuries, delayed,
I'd count them on my Hand,
Subtracting, till my fingers dropped
Into Van Dieman's Land.⑤

If certain, when this life was out—
That yours and mine, should be—
I'd toss it yonder, like a Rind,
And take Eternity—

But, now, uncertain of the length
Of this, that is between,
It goads me, like the Goblin Bee⑥—
That will not state—its sting⑦.

---

① barn：谷仓。
② spurn：驱赶。
③ fly：苍蝇。
④ wind the months in balls：把月份在球上面一遍一遍卷起来。
⑤ Van Dieman's Land：= Tasmania，塔斯马尼亚岛，位于澳大利亚东南边。
⑥ Goblin Bee：蜜蜂精灵。
⑦ sting：蛰，叮。

美国诗歌选读

作品赏析

　　一棵再平常不过的小草在狄金森的诗中却成为了可爱的尤物,生机盎然,活力四射;对着飞蝶和蜜蜂,翩翩起舞,和着微风,婀娜招展,白天,阳光映照;夜晚,露水滴珠。小草虽小,但高贵如公爵夫人也并一定知晓其美丽;即便变成了干草,也还有那温馨的美梦可做,引得诗人止不住说出了但愿变成干草的感叹。这首描写自然的诗,语言质朴、简单,意象生动、细致,传达了一种隽永之美,表达了诗人对自然的热爱。

　　爱人远赴他乡,"我"在默默企盼他早日归来。没有炽热的语言,只有简简单单的愿望和想象。时间不再能阻隔"我"的爱恋,从月到年到几个世纪,我都会等待,直到永远。至此,诗人在这首爱情诗中描述的情感应该说还是比较传统的,但是,很快,诗人转换了语气,道出了"我"的哀怨:不能确定爱人到底什么时候归来,让人心焦不已,更甚的是,还无法向他表达思念之情,就像是蜜蜂蛰人,但却说不出用意何在。狄金森这首诗据有些评论者猜测是写给她的朋友查尔斯·华慈维斯牧师的。后者在1855年、1860年、1880年三次拜访过狄金森。也许本诗并没有确切的对象,狄金森只是在诗中向心中的情人表达着自己的一往情深。此诗想象丰富,类比形象生动,如在第二节中,把月份卷在球上并分别放在抽屉里,以免弄乱,在第三节中诗人说即便是要等上几个世纪,她也会一点一点往前数时间,直到手指掉进塔斯马尼亚岛。何等逸思奇想!终身未嫁的狄金森内心感情其实丰富多彩,诗歌成为了表达她内心情感的主要渠道。

思考题

1. What makes the poet wish that she wanted to be a hay?
2. In Canto 6 of "Song of Myself", Whitman also writes about grass. What is the difference between Whitman and Dickinson in representation of "grass" in this case?
3. What are the poetical skills used in poem 511 to express the intense feeling of the poet?
4. What do you think the mood of this poem is?

1. poem 449: *I died for Beauty—but was scarce*
2. poem 441: *This is my letter to the world*
3. poem 986: *A narrow Fellow in the Grass*
4. poem 67: *Success is counted sweetest*
5. poem 328: *A bird came down in the Walk*
6. poem 640: *I cannot live with You*
7. poem 249: *Wild Nights—Wild Nights*

参考书目

1. Helen McNeil, *Emily Dickinson*, NY: Pantheon Books, 1986.
2. Roger Lundin, *Emily Dickinson and the Art of Belief*, UK: Cambridge, 1998.

第七单元

Ezra Loomis Pound (1885—1972)
艾兹拉·鲁密思·庞德

作者简介

艾兹拉·鲁密思·庞德,诗人、批评家、翻译家、编辑。生于爱达荷州海雷市。16岁就读于宾夕法尼亚大学,与后来同样叱咤诗坛的W.C.威廉斯为同窗,彼此影响至深。1907年在印地安那州沃巴施学院谋得教职,但因工作散漫(不守校规)数月后被解职,此后前往西班牙、意大利、英国和法国等欧洲国家考察,专事文学创作、编辑、出版等工作。1908年在欧洲出版第一部诗集《灯火熄灭之时》(*A Lume Spento*),并在此时对中国文学和日本文学产生了浓厚兴趣,开始致力于研习和翻译。1915年发表诗集《华夏》(*Cathy*),收入的17首诗是他在西方首次采用自由诗的形式翻译与改写李白等中国诗人的作品。1917年起担任颇有影响的刊物《诗歌》驻伦敦通信员,提出了意象派诗歌观念等若干以创新为本的文学理论见解,并结识和扶掖了一批才华横溢、后来成为20世纪最重要文学家的青年作家,包括乔伊斯、希尔达·杜利特尔、海明威、弗罗斯特、劳伦斯、T.S.艾略特等人。1924年移居意大利。20世纪上半叶,庞德以其文学理念与人格魅力在欧洲文学界产生了深远而广泛的影响。

庞德的人生历程并非一帆风顺。二战中,他曾一度为意大利法西斯政权效力,担任意大利英语广播节目主持人,播送赞美墨索里尼法西斯政权以及反犹太人等内容的讲话。因此,他在比萨被美军俘获,囚禁在露天笼子里,后在狱中开始构思《比萨诗章》(*Pisan Cantos*),反思欧洲蒙受的浩劫。1945年被遣送回美国,以叛国罪被捕入狱,因众多知名作家呼吁,以其精神不正常为理由未判罪,送进精神病医院栖居长达13年。其间,他得以继续进行文学创作,发表了若干重要作品,其中《比萨诗章》,即《诗章》的第71—84章,荣获1948年博林根图书奖。1958年,由于作家们再次呼吁,庞德被释放,移居意大利。1962年突发心脏病,健康每况愈下,此后一直隐居威尼斯,直至辞世。

庞德的主要诗歌作品还包括：《向塞克斯图斯·佩罗提乌斯致敬》(*Homage to Sextus Propertius*) 和《休·塞尔温·莫伯利》(*Hugh Selwyn Mauberley*, 1920)，其最重要的作品当推《诗章》(*Cantos*, 1915—1970)。该诗是由117章构成的长篇巨制，以全景式的视角描写人类的历史以及人性进步的历程。他的文学批评作品包括《罗曼斯精神》(*The Spirit of Romance*) 与《阅读入门》(*ABC of Reading*)。他还将古希腊、古罗马、法国等十种语言的各类作品翻译为英文，包括中国的《四书》，对于20世纪不同文化之间的文化交流和融合起到了重要的推进作用。一般认为，庞德作为诗人，其最佳作品并非他自己创作的诗歌，而是根据中国或者日本诗歌而翻译改写的作品。

In A Station of the Metro

The apparition① of these faces in the crowd;
Petals② on a wet, black bough.③

  庞德将自己的诗歌创作理念概括为创新为本，他的诗歌也以在主题与形式方面推陈出新而见长，其中包括按照中国古诗中使用意象的模式进行创作，旨在凸现诗中的意象，并激发读者的感受。《在地铁车站》不仅是庞德的诗歌佳作，也是公认的意象派诗歌的上乘之作。这首诗再现了诗人一天走出巴黎一个地铁车时一霎那的视觉感受：他一踏上地铁的出口，骤然看到潮水般涌动的行人中呈现出几个光彩夺目的漂亮面孔，犹如春天田野里盛开的鲜花。经过长达一年的构思和推敲，诗人写下一百余行的诗稿，并最终提炼为目前仅有两行诗的文本。诗的魅力在于以简约而含蓄的叙事风格以及平行重叠的意象使美丽的面孔与鲜花互为关联，由此使读者产生愉快的联想和对比，恰似"人面桃花相映红"，互为参照。意象派诗人颇为推崇中国古诗中叠加意象、并置意象等手法。显然，庞德领悟并出神入化地运用了中国诗歌的叙事特征，诗中没有使用一个单词，也没有使用任何连接词，但"面庞"、"树枝"、"花瓣"等代表形象的词语平行地组合在一起，自然而然烘托出一种具有中国含蓄风格的类比或暗示。

---

① apparition：意外或不平常的出现，尤其指幽灵、幻影、鬼怪等离奇的东西的出现。
② petal：花瓣。
③ 该诗的背景是巴黎一个拥挤的地铁的出入口。

A Girl

The tree has entered my hands,
The sap① has ascended my arms,
The tree has grown in my breast—
Downward,
The branches grow out of me, like arms.

Tree you are,
Moss② you are,
You are violets with wind above them.
A child—so high—you are,
And all this is folly③ to the world.

《少女》是根据李白的名诗《玉阶怨》改写而成，体现了意象派诗歌的主要特征与风范。意象派诗歌崇尚再现具有鲜明特色的、处于静态的意象，并着力渲染诗人瞬间捕捉到这些意象时的感官体验，而并不附带任何解说或评论性的内容。换言之，意象派诗歌是刻意突出意象作为诗歌艺术本源的作用，强调通过视觉捕捉具有深刻内涵的事物，回避或者淡化概念性的内容，试图借此匡正20世纪初叶美国乃至西方诗歌中理性成分过于浓重的弊病。如果与李白的原作相比较：

　　玉阶生白露，夜久侵罗袜。
　　却下水晶帘，玲珑望秋月。

不难发现，庞德改写的文本契合意象派诗歌的要旨，或者说他在此诗中寻找到了共鸣抑或启迪。李白虽以"怨"字作为诗的标题，但诗中字面不见"怨"字，反倒是夜色中冰凉的露水浸湿罗袜，水晶帘掩映孤独，秋月照射寒意，凡此种种，无一不淋漓尽致地再现了深深的"怨"情。《少女》一诗的标题剔除了原作中的"怨"字，使得主题更为含蓄，完全依赖重叠的意象构建意境，抒发情怀。

---

① sap：树液；汁液；精力；活力。
② moss：苔藓；指任何一种苔藓植物。
③ folly：荒唐事；蠢事；邪恶；危险或犯法的愚蠢行为。

A Pact

I make a pact① with you, Walt Whitman②—
I have detested you long enough.
I come to you as a grown child
Who has had a pig-headed③ father;
I am old enough now to make friends.
It was you that broke the new wood,
Now is a time for carving.
We have one sap and one root—
Let there be commerce between us.

  《合同》一诗并非强调意象以及与其相关的感觉效果,而是采用较为传统的诗歌形式表现主题思想。20世纪初叶,惠特曼在美国学术界与社会阅读大众中的地位仍旧是毁誉参半,庞德是最早领略并积极认同惠特曼的诗歌创作成就及其价值的美国诗人之一。《合同》的标题简单明了地呈现出庞德对待惠特曼的态度发生了根本性的转折,认识到自己因幼稚无知而曾经厌恶这位天才,但现在终于认识到自己的愚蠢,开始尊重其披荆斩棘般的艺术创新,并愿意以签订合同的方式与其结为朋友。"合同"所寓意的契约关系体现了庞德与惠特曼之间友好而平等的关系,预示了美国对惠特曼的态度的根本性转变。由于庞德的影响,当时的许多文学家都相继转变了对惠特曼的认识,例如英国小说家D.H.劳伦斯。换言之,《合同》实际上是为庞德所在的时代作代言,表明惠特曼已经进入美国经典作家的行列。

Canto XLIX

For the seven lakes, and by no man these verses:

---

① pact:合同;契约;协定。
② Walt Whitman:沃尔特·惠特曼,当今公认美国最伟大的诗人(1819—1892),主要作品是《草叶集》。该诗集1855年第一次出版,包括12首诗,此后不断扩充和删节,出版了六个版本,最后收入396首诗作。
③ pig-headed:顽固的;愚蠢的;固执的。该复合词中的"猪"构成一个具有贬义的意象。

美国 诗歌选读

Rain; empty river; a voyage,
Fire from frozen cloud, heavy rain in the twilight
Under the cabin roof was one lantern.
The reeds are heavy; bent;
and the bamboos speak as if weeping.

Autumn moon; hills rise about lakes
against sunset
Evening is like a curtain of cloud,
a blurr① above ripples; and through it
sharp long spikes② of the cinnamon③,
a cold tune amid reeds.
Behind hill the monk's bell
borne on the wind.
Sail passed here in April; may return in October
Boat fades in silver; slowly;
Sun blaze alone on the river.

Where wine flag catches the sunset
Sparse chimneys smoke in the cross light

Comes then snow scur④ on the river
And a world is covered with jade
Small boat floats like a lanthorn⑤,
The flowing water clots as with cold. And at San Yin⑥
they are a people of leisure.

Wild geese swoop⑦ to the sand-bar,
Clouds gather about the hole of the window
Broad water; geese line out with the autumn

---

① blurr：即 blur。庞德为了再现诗的内容，例如突出其远古的时间特征，间或在诗中模仿英国北部诺森伯兰郡古英语中的习惯，为辅音结尾的名词后缀一个同样的辅音字母，使其成为双辅音字母的名词，但读音不变。
② spikes：穗状花序；谷物等植物的穗。
③ cinnamon：樟属中几种树的芳香内皮；肉桂；肉桂树；桂皮。
④ scur：古英语词汇，意为暴风雪；暴风雨。
⑤ lanthorn：即 lantern，灯笼。
⑥ San Yin：即山阴，庞德在诗中使用罗马拼音字符音译了一些汉字，并以此构成一个创作特征。
⑦ swoop：猛扑；飞扑；出其不意地抓起或攫取。

Rooks① clatter over the fishermen's lanthorns,

A light moves on the north sky line;
where the young boys prod stones for shrimp.
In seventeen hundred came Tsing② to these hill lakes.
A light moves on the south sky line.

State by creating riches shd③. thereby get into debt?
This is infamy④; this is Geryon⑤.
This canal goes still to TenShi⑥
though the old king built it for pleasure

KEI MEN RAN KEI⑦
KIU MAN MAN KEI
JITSU GETSU KO KWA
TAN FUKU TAN KAI

Sun up; work
sundown; to rest
dig well and drink of the water
dig field; eat of the grain
Imperial power is? and to us what is it?

The fourth; the dimension of stillness.
And the power over wild beasts.

作为诗人，庞德的成就与声誉主要建立在长诗《诗章》之上。该诗共由117章构成，自出版至今一直是有争议的作品。按照庞德的构想，希望将《诗章》创作成一首恢弘的史诗，描写全人类数千年发展进化的历史，展现人性如何从部落时代的黑暗岁月走向未来的人间天堂的

---

① Rooks：白嘴鸦；秃鼻乌鸦。
② In seventeen hundred came Tsing：指1700年康熙巡歌山湖畔。
③ Infamy：丑名；声名狼藉；可耻的行为。
④ shd：即should。
⑤ Geryon：希腊神话中守卫地狱第八层的怪兽，外形是人首兽身蛇尾，因其品性成为欺骗的象征，后为大力士赫尔克里斯所杀。
⑥ TenShi：通县。参见注释6。
⑦ KEIMENRANKEI等四行：《卿云歌》的译音。该诗传为虞帝舜大宴群臣时的集体唱和之作，颂扬五帝禅让制度。诗的中文文本为："卿云烂兮，糺缦缦兮。日月光华，旦复旦兮！"

漫长的进步历程,内容包括远古的部落文明、各种宗教、权力与金钱等人类欲望人性进步所造成的阻碍。这首诗的创作和出版历时四十余年,内容包罗万象,包括古希腊、埃及、中国等国家的神话传说、中国和日本等国家的诗歌、古今政治和经济等理论,以及20世纪上半叶的各种时尚等等。此处节选的第49章,亦称为《七湖诗章》,因第一行诗提及七湖而得名。《七湖诗章》的主题源于《卿云歌》等若干首中国古诗,并通过叠加或并置的意象等手法再现了一幅宁静的大自然的画卷,渲染了人与自然和谐共存的理念。如同头三行诗所示,诗人在尽力抛弃传统诗歌惯于使用的动词,将"湖"、"雨"、"河"、"旅行"、"火"、"云"、"暮色"等集群意象浓缩于一个特定的空间,由此创造出一个主题清晰的意境,强烈激发读者的感悟。对《诗章》持批评态度的学者认为,虽然庞德声称在诗歌创作中坚持科学的客观性,但实际上他的创作则显示出非常主观武断的特征,诗中内容的质量参差不齐。

思考题

1. In comparison with the poems of Anne Bradstreet or Henry Wadsworth Longfellow, what metrical and rhythmical traits can you figure out in Pound's verses?
2. Try to find and interpret the patterns of images which Pound makes use of in *Canto* XLIX?
3. What do you think of the multilingualism of Pound's poems in the present age of globalization?

推荐作品

1. *The Garden*
2. *Portrait D Une Femme*
3. *The Picture*
4. *An Immortality*

参考书目

1. Beach, Christopher. *ABC of Influence: Ezra Pound and the Remaking of American Poetic Tradition.* Berkeley: University of California Press, 1992.
2. Brooker, Peter. *A Student's Guide to the Selected Poems of Ezra Pound.* London: Faber and Faber, 1979.
3. Hamilton, Scott. *Ezra Pound and the Symbolist Inheritance.* Princeton: Princeton UP, 1992.

第八单元

Thomas Stearns Eliot (1888—1965)
托马斯·斯特恩司·艾略特

作者简介

托马斯·斯特恩司·艾略特,诗人、剧作家、文学批评家。艾略特自幼博览群书,中学时代开始写诗。1906年考入哈佛大学,主修哲学,业余写诗,三年便完成本科学业,1910年获得硕士学位后攻读博士学位。其间曾前往法国和德国访学,转至牛津大学学习后与庞德相识。庞德欣赏艾略特的诗才,鼎力相助,艾略特决定定居伦敦,献身诗歌创作。1915年起,他先后在中学和银行工作,同时完成以研究英国哲学家F.H.布拉德利为题的博士论文,但终生没有返回哈佛大学进行论文答辩。布拉德利重精神而轻物质的思想,对年轻的艾略特影响甚大。自1915年开始,经过庞德举荐,艾略特在颇具影响的《诗刊》等刊物发表《J. 阿尔弗雷德·普鲁弗洛克的情歌》(The Love Song of J. Alfred Prufrock)和《风夜狂想曲》(Rhapsody on a Windy Night)等诗篇,表现一战时期西方社会弥漫的空虚和怯懦等危机现象,在诗坛崭露头角。1917年出版第一部诗集《普鲁弗洛克的情歌及其他观察》(Prufrock and Other Observations),在英国和美国均赢得广泛好评。1922年创办文学评论季刊《标准》,并长期担任主编。1927年加入英国籍,同时皈依英国国教。1948年,艾略特因《四个四重奏》"对现代诗歌杰出的开创性贡献"荣获诺贝尔文学奖;1965年因患肺气肿辞世。

艾略特的诗歌创作不以数量见长,但求艺术创新和肩负社会责任,主要诗歌创作时间介于1922年至1930年之间。1922年,他的代表作长诗《荒原》(The Waste Land)问世,描写一战使西方物质文明和精神文明所蒙受毁灭性的灾难,以及由此而带来的重重危机。1925年发表的《空心人》(The Hollow Man)也以上述内容为主题,刻画人类犹如"空心人"失去灵魂,堕落为行尸走肉。1930年出版的《灰星期三》(Ash Wednesday)以内心独白的形式诉说改过自新的经历,标志着艾略特试图在宗教的世界为人类寻求解脱之道。他的最后一部重要诗歌《四个四重奏》(Four Quartets)于1943年刊行,采用贝多芬的四重奏结构将英国与美国的四个具有历史意义的地点和事件交织在一起,描摹人类从精神幻灭中脱身而出,并最终在基督教信念中获得拯救。

艾略特自1930年转而侧重戏剧创作,因为他认为戏剧更能够使诗人获得更广泛的读者,更能为社会进步有所贡献。他进行了卓有成效的戏剧创作探索,创作了7部作品,试图建构一种具有现代精神和现代叙事特征的新戏剧,与他在诗歌作品中探讨的主题相呼应。他的剧作大多是喜剧或者以赎罪情节结尾的剧作,主要剧作包括《大教堂谋杀案》(Murder in the Cathedral, 1935),描写1170年大主教贝克特的死亡,颂扬其宗教献身精神;《合家团聚》(The Family Reunion, 1939)根据希腊神话故事改编而成,通过主人公的精神分裂揭示人性的神秘与脆弱。《鸡尾酒会》(The Cocktail Party, 1949)通过失败的婚姻寓意人类异化和孤独的境况;《机要秘书》(The Confidential Clerk, 1953)中的人物虽然身为贵族,但为了各自的私利,尔虞我诈,身份错乱,以喜剧的形式反映了道德缺陷严重扭曲了人性。

作为批评家,艾略特探讨了文艺理论与创作时间诸多方面的问题,倡导从基督教思想与文化,见解犀利深邃,建树良多,影响深远。主要著述包括《传统与个人才能》(Tradition and the Individual Talent, 1920)、《圣林》(The Sacred Wood: Essays on Poetry and Criticism, 1920)、《古今文集》(Essays Ancient and Modern, 1936)、《文化定义札记》(Notes Towards the Definition of Culture, 1940)《基督教社会的理念》(The Idea of a Christian Society, 1940)以及《诗的三种声音》(The Three Voices of Poetry, 1954)等。

Mr. Eliot's Sunday Morning Service

Look, look, master, here comes two religious caterpillars[①].
　　　　　　　　　　　　　　　　　　　　The Jew of Malta[②]

[①] caterpillars:蝴蝶或蛾子等各类昆虫的幼虫,因在成长过程中发生蜕变而变形,诗中用来指狡诈贪婪的人。
[②] The Jew of Malta:英国16世纪剧作家马洛(Christopher Marlowe, 1590)的作品《马耳他的犹太人》(The Jew of Malta.),T.S.艾略特在开篇引用的题词,出自剧中一个仆人之口:"Here comes two religious caterpillars"。

POLYPHILOPROGENITIVE①

The sapient② sutlers③ of the Lord
Drift across the window-panes.
In the beginning was the Word④.

In the beginning was the Word.
Superfetation⑤ of Τὸ Ἕν⑥
And at the mensual⑦ turn of time
Produced enervate⑧ Origen⑨.

A painter of the Umbrian school⑩
Designed upon a gesso⑪ ground
The nimbus⑫ of the Baptized God.
The wilderness is cracked and browned

But through the water pale and thin
Still shine the unoffending feet
And there above the painter set
The Father and the Paraclete⑬.

The sable⑭ presbyters⑮ approach
The avenue of penitence;
The young are red and pustular⑯

---

① polyphiloprogenitive：子孙满堂的；多子多孙的；生育能力极强的。
② sapient：自作聪明的；贤明的；极具智慧的。
③ sutlers：精明的商人，原指随军小贩；军中小贩。
④ In the beginning was the Word：指《圣经》中有关创世纪的内容。
⑤ superfetation：重孕；异期复孕；指一个胎儿已在子宫内时另一个胎儿的形成或生长。
⑥ Τὸ Ἕν：古希腊文，意为这／那一个(the one)。此处指耶稣基督。
⑦ mensual：每月一次的；每月的。
⑧ enervate：无力的；衰弱的。
⑨ Origen：古希腊天主教哲学家(185—254)，为抵制世俗诱惑阉割自身，以阐释《旧约》而闻名。
⑩ Umbrian school：指15世纪位于意大利中部的翁布里亚画派，以画《圣经》内容的作品闻名。
⑪ gesso ground：指用(雕刻、绘画用的)石膏制成的平面，表面平整，便于绘画。
⑫ nimbus：常以环状或晕出现的光轮，或者光环，在艺术作品中环绕在神、半神半人、圣徒或圣人如国王或皇帝的头上。
⑬ Paraclete：圣灵；圣父、圣子、圣灵构成基督教的三位一体。
⑭ sable：黑色的；穿丧服的；阴森的。
⑮ presbyters：牧师；长老；神父。
⑯ pustular：肿泡的；与脓疮有关的。

Clutching piaculative① pence.

Under the penitential gates
Sustained by staring Seraphim②
Where the souls of the devout
Burn invisible and dim.

Along the garden-wall the bees
With hairy bellies pass between
The staminate③ and pistilate④,
Blest office⑤ of the epicene⑥.

Sweeney⑦ shifts from ham to ham⑧
Stirring the water in his bath.
The masters of the subtle schools
Are controversial, polymath⑨.

The Burial of the Dead⑩
From The Waste Land

April is the cruellest month, breeding
Lilacs out of the dead land, mixing
Memory and desire, stirring
Dull roots with spring rain.
Winter kept us warm, covering
Earth in forgetful snow, feeding

---

① piaculative：有罪的；赎罪的；在基督教中，特指有罪需要捐钱行善来获得宽恕的人。
② Seraphim：seraph 的复数形式，六翼天使（九级天使中地位最高者）。
③ staminate：有雄性花蕊的。
④ pistilate：有雌性花蕊的。
⑤ office：职务；职责。
⑥ epicene：兼有两性的；中性的；无两性特征的；两性通用的。
⑦ Sweeney：艾略特在若干首诗歌中创作的人物。
⑧ ham：指大腿后部；大腿或臀部。
⑨ polymath：学识渊博的人。
⑩《死者的葬礼》节选的《荒原》一诗的第一节，该诗的正文前有艾略特的献词：献给大师庞德：
"For Ezra Pound
il miglior fabbro"
"il miglior fabbro"为意大利文，英文意为 "the better craftsman"。

A little life with dried tubers①.
Summer surprised us, coming over the Starnbergersee②
With a shower of rain; we stopped in the colonnade③,
And went on in sunlight, into the Hofgarten④,
And drank coffee, and talked for an hour.
Bin gar keine Russin, stamm' aus Litauen, echt deutsch⑤.
And when we were children, staying at the arch-duke's⑥,
My cousin's, he took me out on a sled,
And I was frightened. He said, Marie,
Marie, hold on tight. And down we went.
In the mountain, there you feel free.
I read, much of the night, and go south in the winter.

What are the roots that clutch, what branches grow
Out of this stony rubbish⑦? Son of man⑧,
You cannot say, or guess, for you know only
A heap of broken images⑨, where the sun beats,
And the dead tree gives no shelter, the cricket no relief,
And the dry stone no sound of water. Only
There is shadow under this red rock,
(Come in under the shadow⑩ of this red rock),
And I will show you something different from either

---

① tubers: 指马铃薯等植物的块茎或球根。
② Starnbergersee: 慕尼黑南部的一个湖。
③ colonnade: 柱廊;列柱;由有规则间隔排列的柱子构成的建筑结构。
④ Hofgarten: 慕尼黑的一个公园,艾略特曾访问此地。提示诗中的内容中具有诗人的回忆和已往的经历,而并非完全出于想象和经典中的概念。
⑤ Bin gar keine Russin, stamm' aus Litauen, echt deutsch: 德语,意为"我绝不是俄国人,我来自立陶宛,是地地道道的德国人。"1917年发生俄国革命之后,一些俄国人或后裔在欧洲回避自己的俄国身份,以便与布尔什维克区分开来。
⑥ arch-duke: 大公,尤指奥地利帝国具有与有主权的王子相等地位的贵族。暗指1914年奥地利王储费迪南德遭暗杀,成为第一次世界大战的导火索。此外,也指示这一节的叙事者是玛丽的贵族背景。
⑦ stony rubbish: 源自《圣经》的寓言,播种者将种子撒在路边和田野以及杂草和岩石上,撒在岩石上的种子很快就枯萎了,指诗中描写的现代文明犹如"荒原",干旱缺水,寸草不生,卵石遍野,一幅荒凉不堪的景象。
⑧ Son of Man: 埃兹凯斯(Ezekias,或 Hezekiah,公元前715—前686),犹大国王。据《圣经·旧约》记载,埃兹凯斯企图废除偶像崇拜,并恢复对耶和华的崇拜。
⑨ A heap of broken images: 指上帝允诺犹大国王埃兹凯斯捣毁其他虚假神明的偶像和形象。也提示《荒原》中的意象大多为独立的个体意象,意象之间组合没有采用传统的关联方式,因此从传统的角度看来,诗中的意象是"支离破碎"的。
⑩ shadow under this red rock: 诗人以这一意象提示某种解脱,或拯救,因为意象来自《以赛亚书》:以赛亚预言耶和华即将到来,他象征希望和拯救,如同巨石的阴影降落在贫瘠的原野。

Your shadow① at morning striding behind you
Or your shadow at evening rising to meet you;
I will show you fear in a handful of dust②.
    *Frisch weht der Wind*③
    Der Heimat zu
    Mein Irisch Kind,
    Wo weilest du?
"You gave me hyacinths first a year ago;
"They called me the hyacinth④ girl."
—Yet when we came back, late, from the Hyacinth garden,
Your arms full, and your hair wet, I could not
Speak, and my eyes failed, I was neither
Living nor dead, and I knew nothing,
Looking into the heart of light, the silence.
*Oed' und leer dos Meer*⑤.

Madame Sosostris⑥, famous clairvoyante⑦,
Had a bad cold, nevertheless
Is known to be the wisest woman in Europe,

---

① Your shadow at morning striding behind you/Or your shadow at evening rising to meet you: 提示阴影虽然从早到晚运动不止,但却是从属性的,毫无生气,与生机、生长和繁殖再生无关,由此凸现了"荒原"的本质。

② handful of dust: 指《圣经》中上帝用泥土创造人。也指英国国教举行葬礼时的仪式之一,在众人向死者的身体上投掷泥土的时候,牧师颂扬上帝,并说明是按照上帝的意愿,使原本来自泥土的死者再返回到泥土中去。

③ Frisch weht der Wind: 这一节歌源于德国作曲家瓦格纳(Richard Wagner,1813—1883)的歌剧《特里斯坦与伊索尔德》(*Tristam and Isolde*),英译文为:"The wind blow fresh / toward land of home: / My Irish child, / where do you roam?" 歌词提示浪漫的情怀或者情欲,并与悲伤和悼念的情感糅合在一起,以产生一种特殊的想象效果。艾略特在原作中对此提供的注释是:*v. Tristan und Isolde,* i, verses 5-8.

④ hyacinths: 风信子,地中海地区所产的一种球茎植物,叶片狭窄,总状花序,其花有多种颜色,通常有香味,花被呈漏斗状。在古希腊神话中,太阳神阿波罗失手误杀了自己所钟爱的美少年海厄辛瑟斯,为了表示悔恨和怀念,使其血化为风信子,永存于世。此处风信子的意象提示再生和繁荣。

⑤ Oed' und leer dos Meer: 源于德国作曲家瓦格纳的歌剧《特里斯坦与伊索尔德》,英译文为:"Waste and empty is the sea"。

⑥ Madame Sostoris: 相传为古埃及的国王;也指英国小说家赫胥黎(Aldous Huxley, 1894—1963)的小说《克罗维·耶娄》(*Crome Yellow,* 1921)中的一个人物,她神通广大,料事如神,能够占卜命运。艾略特在原作中对此提供的注释是:
"I am not familiar with the exact constitution of the Tarot pack of cards, from which I have obviously departed to suit my own convenience. The Hanged Man, a member of the traditional pack, fits my purpose in two ways: because he is associated in my mind with the Hanged God of Frazer, and because I associate him with the hooded figure in the passage of the disciples to Emmaus in Part V. The Phoenician Sailor and the Merchant appear later; also the "crowds of people," and Death by Water is executed in Part IV. The Man with Three Staves (an authentic member of the Tarot pack) I associate, quite arbitrarily, with the Fisher King himself."

⑦ clairvoyante: 女千里眼;能感知他人感情、生死的人。

With a wicked pack of cards①. Here, said she,
Is your card, the drowned Phoenician Sailor,
(Those are pearls that were his eyes②. Look!)
Here is Belladonna③, the Lady of the Rocks,
The lady of situations.
Here is the man with three staves④, and here the Wheel⑤,
And here is the one-eyed merchant⑥ and this card,
Which is blank, is something he carries on his back,
Which I am forbidden to see. I do not find
The Hanged Man⑦. Fear death by water.
I see crowds of people, walking round in a ring.
Thank you. If you see dear Mrs. Equitone⑧,
Tell her I bring the horoscope⑨ myself:
One must be so careful these days.

Unreal City⑩,
Under the brown fog of a winter dawn,
A crowd flowed over London Bridge, so many,

---

① a wicked pack of cards: 即占卜用的纸牌。
② Those are pearls that were his eyes: 源莎士比亚的剧作《暴风雨》，精灵艾尔瑞尔告诉费尔南德，他的父王阿朗索已经葬身汪洋，不复生存：

    Full fathom five thy father lies;
    Of his bones are coral made;
    Those are pearls that were his eyes:
    Nothing of him that doth fade
    But doth suffer a sea-change
    Into something rich and strange.
    Sea-nymphs hourly sing his knell.

③ Belladonna: 颠茄，欧亚大陆所产一种有毒的多年生草本植物，通常开单生的、摇摆的浅紫棕色钟状花，结有光滑的黑色浆果。
④ stave: 占卜牌中的一种签。
⑤ wheel: 指抓阄转轮(wheel of fortune)，可以此占卜生死福祸。这一意象提示人类社会发展过程中兴盛与衰亡的轮回。
⑥ one-eyed merchant: 指目光短浅、片面处事的人。
⑦ The Hanged Man: 指基督教中通过牺牲自己使他人获得拯救与再生的人，如耶稣基督。
⑧ Mrs. Equitone: 指上文提及的占卜者 Madame Sostoris 的主顾。
⑨ horoscope: 占星术；算命天宫图。
⑩ unreal city: 指社会呈现的虚假的景象与人们的幻觉。艾略特在原作的注释中提示读者参见法国诗人波德莱尔(Charles Pierre Baudelaire, 1821—1867)的诗作《七位老人》(*The Seven Old Men*)。该诗英译文起首的句子是：
    Swarming city, city full of dreams, Where the spectre in broad daylight buttonholes the passer-by.

美国诗歌选读

I had not thought death had undone so many①.
Sighs, short and infrequent, were exhaled②,
And each man fixed his eyes before his feet.
Flowed up the hill and down King William Street③,
To where Saint Mary Woolnoth④ kept the hours
With a dead sound on the final stroke of nine⑤.
There I saw one I knew, and stopped him, crying: "Stetson!⑥
"You who were with me in the ships at Mylae!⑦
"That corpse you planted last year in your garden⑧,
"Has it begun to sprout? Will it bloom this year?
"Or has the sudden frost disturbed its bed?
"Oh keep the Dog⑨ far hence, that's friend to men,
"Or with his nails he'll dig it up again!
"You! hypocrite lecteur!—mon semblable,—mon frère!"⑩

---

① I had not thought death had undone so many：艾略特在原作的注释中提示读者参阅但丁在《神曲·地狱篇》中所描写的地狱。但丁在《地狱篇》中相关描述的英文译文是：Such a long stream of people that I should have never believed that death had undone so many.

② Sighs, short and infrequent, were exhaled：艾略特在原作的注释中提示读者参阅但丁《神曲·地狱篇》，相关部分的英文译文是：Here, so far as I could tell, there was no lamentation except sighs....

③ King William Street：位于伦敦商业区的一条繁华街道。

④ Saint Mary Woolnorth：位于伦敦 King William Street 与 Lombard street 交叉口的一个教堂，紧邻艾略特任职的银行，始建于 12 世纪。教堂有报时钟，每天数次报时。

⑤ dead sound on the final stroke of nine：指 Saint Mary Woolnorth 晚九时的报时钟声。

⑥ Stetson：艾略特曾解释 Stetson 并非特指某个人，而是泛指现代城市中的商人。另外一种解释是暗指庞德，因为 stetson 指美国西部牛仔戴的宽边帽，而庞德有时戴这种帽子。

⑦ Mylae：位于意大利南部西西里岛的北部，公元前 260 年罗马人征服了早期定居在此的迦太基人，占领此地。诗中不同地点与时间的组合犹如蒙太奇，能够产生戏剧性的联想效果，提示人类社会数千年的沧桑变化。

⑧ the Dog：可参见艾略特在 "Marina" 一诗中类似的内容："Those who sharpen the tooth of the dog, meaning / Death."。也指天狼星。另可参见《圣经·圣歌》中的诗句："Deliver my soul from the sword; my darling from the power of the dog"。

⑨ corpse you planted last year in your garden：按照艾略特在原作注释中的提示，源于英国剧作家约翰·韦伯斯特（John Webster, 1580—1625）的作品《白魔》（The White Devil），一个发疯的母亲对她的儿子唱了一首挽歌，悼念她另一位被手足诛杀后埋葬的儿子。另一种解释是：在古埃及神话中，冥神奥西里斯（Osiris）被谋杀后，尸体遭分解，掩埋在四面八方，他的妻子伊希斯（Isis）是司掌生育与繁殖的自然女神，她将埋葬丈夫遗体的地点都变成了圣地，每年春天都能够长出鲜花，显示死亡与复生的轮回，以及大自然自我更新的生命力和多产的特点。

⑩ hypocrite lecteur!—mon semblable,—mon frère：按照艾略特在原作的注释中提示，源于法国诗人波德莱尔（Charles Pierre Baudelaire, 1821—1867）的作品《恶之花》（Fleurs du Mal）中的前言，英文译文是：

It's boredom! ....
You know him, reader, this dainty monster,
Hypocritical reader! my double, my brother!

The Hollow Men[①]

Mistah Kurz—he dead.

A penny for the Guy![②]

I

We are the hollow men
We are the stuffed men
Leaning together
Headpiece filled with straw. Alas!
Our dried voices, when
We whisper together
Are quiet and meaningless
As wind in dry grass
Or rats' feet over broken glass
In our dry cellar

Shape without form, shade without color,
Paralyzed force, gesture without motion;

Those who have crossed
With direct eyes, to death's other Kingdom
Remember us—if at all—not as lost
Violent souls, but only
As the hollow men
The stuffed men.

II

Eyes I dare not meet in dreams
In death's dream kingdom

---

① 诗的标题"The Hollow Man"出自英国小说家康拉德(Joseph Conrad 1857—1924)的小说《黑暗的心》(*Heart of Darkness*);题词"Mistah Kurz—he dead"也出自上述作品。黑人侍者在宣布欧洲商人 Mr. Kurtz 死亡的时候,因有地方口音,加之紧张,把"Mr."误读为"Mistah",把"He is dead"中的"is"省略了。在小说中,Mr. Kurtz 进入非洲原始部落的"黑暗的心"探险,但很快入乡随俗,因为内心空虚被原始的野蛮生活所同化。

② A penny for the Guy:指英国每年 11 月 5 日的盖伊·福克斯日(Guy Fawkes Day),纪念由盖伊·福克斯领导的阴谋失败。他 1605 年试图炸死国王和所有议会成员,以报复当时英国对罗马天主教徒日益严厉的迫害,但计划未遂,后被处死并焚烧尸体。已往每逢盖伊·福克斯日,孩子们通常手举用稻草制成的盖伊·福克斯形象在大街上游行,并向行人索要便士,以便购买烟花爆竹。

These do not appear:
There, the eyes are
Sunlight on a broken column
There, is a tree swinging
And voices are
In the wind's singing
More distant and more solemn
Than a fading star.

Let me be no nearer
In death's dream kingdom
Let me also wear
Such deliberate disguises
Rat's coat, crowskin, crossed staves[①]
In a field
Behaving as the wind behaves
No nearer—

Not that final meeting
In the twilight kingdom

III

This is the dead land
This is the cactus[②] land
Here the stone images
Are raised, here they receive
The supplication of a dead man's hand
Under the twinkle of a fading star.

Is it like this
In death's other kingdom
Waking alone
At the hour when we are
Trembling with tenderness

---

① crossed staves：指盖伊·福克斯日的用稻草制成的盖伊·福克斯形象。
② cactus：仙人掌；在美国俚语中意为沙漠。

Lips that would kiss
Form prayers to broken stone.①

IV

The eyes are not here
There are no eyes here
In this valley of dying stars
In this hollow valley
This broken jaw of our lost kingdoms

In this last of meeting places
We grope together
And avoid speech
Gathered on this beach of the tumid river②

Sightless, unless
The eyes reappear
As the perpetual star
Multifoliate rose③
Of death's twilight kingdom
The hope only
Of empty men.

V

Here we go round the prickly pear④
Prickly pear prickly pear
Here we go round the prickly pear
At five o'clock in the morning.

Between the idea

---

① Form prayers to broken stone：指人世间所有的宗教都名存实亡，毫无意义，而尚存的断垣残壁的石头只代表宗教的过去，目前的宗教如同破损的石头一样破损不堪。
② the tumid river：指古希腊神话中位于地狱的一条冥河，称为"痛苦之河"（Acheron）。但丁在《神曲·地狱篇》中也描写了"痛苦之河"。
③ Multifoliate rose：按照基督教的传统，玫瑰是耶稣基督和圣母玛利亚的象征；multifoliate 意为枝繁叶茂的。
④ prickly spear：仙人果：仙人掌属的一种仙人掌植物，长满刺毛，有平或圆筒状关节，常为艳丽黄色的花，梨状果，可食用。

And the reality
Between the motion
And the act
Falls the Shadow
    For thine① is the Kingdom

Between the conception
And the creation
Between the emotion
And the response
Falls the Shadow
    Life is very long

Between the desire
And the spasm②
Between the potency
And the existence
Between the essence
And the descent
Falls the Shadow
    For Thine is the Kingdom
For Thine is
Life is
For Thine is the

This is the way the world ends
This is the way the world ends
This is the way the world ends
Not with a bang but with a whimper③.

---

① thine：古英语中"thou"的物主代词，意为"你的东西"；你的；作为"thou"的所有格，用于首字母是元音或 h 音的名词前。
② spasm：指动作或感情的突然迸发；突发。
③ Not with a bang but with a whimper：此处的"bang"是指盖伊·福克斯日的爆竹声，提示盖伊·福克斯试图炸毁国会的计划，用暴力手段解决国家的宗教纠纷。

作品赏析

艾略特曾自白,他在政治上是保皇党,宗教上是英国天主教徒,文学上是古典主义者。他的诗歌创作也大体上体现了上述几个方面的基本特征。按照他的文艺创作理论,诗人是所在社会的代言人,其义不容辞的职责是以创新和个性化的语言展现现代文明的复杂性和现代人的复杂性。此外,他还主张,诗人创作内容的复杂性必定导致诗歌艰涩,难以解读,而诗歌永恒的价值与魅力也正是在于此。如果从上面提示的内容出发解读艾略特的诗歌,显然有助于了解和认识他的创作主题、技巧,以及相关的价值和意义。

就题材而言,艾略特的诗歌可谓是百科全书式的,涉及内容广泛,不仅包括古往今来、包罗万象的社会现象,以及个人信仰、心理与生活诸多方面的问题,而且善于在作品文本中大量使用宗教、文学等方面的典故,旁征博引,互为参照,刻画作品的主题。《艾略特先生的星期日早礼拜》(*Mr. Eliot's Sunday Morning Service*)、《荒原》(*The Waste Land*)和《空心人》(*The Hollow Men*)等三首诗都典型体现了上述特征。对于作品的主题,艾略特习惯在作品的正文之前引用经典作品中的文字或者意象,以此揭示主题,或者引导读者产生相关的联想。《艾略特先生的星期日早礼拜》中的具有明显讽刺和蔑视态度的引语,出自英国诗人马洛的《马耳他的犹太人》,实际上已经归纳了该诗的主题。在《空心人》中,艾略特引用英国小说家康拉德的小说《黑暗的心》中的内容,将小说中具有"空心人"特征的欧洲商人库兹呈现在读者目前,再辅以另外一位代表"空心人"的典型人物,即英国17世纪英国国教的叛逆者盖伊·福克斯,使读者可以从历史、宗教和想象等不同角度感受到他在诗中塑造的"空心人"的本质特征。此外,《空心人》还多次直接或间接引用但丁《神曲·地狱篇》中的诗句、场景和人物形象,使"空心人"徒有身躯、但缺乏灵魂与道德而且没有希望的本质跃然纸上。

再者,他引用的文字一般都是直接出自原作的文本,而不是借助于英文译本,《荒原》中引用的内容就超过了7种以上语言,所引各类作品多达数十部。他相信,被引用的原作所使用的语言本身就是再现历史与文化生命力的意象,也充满了艺术感染力。他将这种创作特征称为诗人以思想主体的身份在历史的遗产与大自然中寻找"客观对应物",因为他坚信并身体力行的创作原则是,作家必须拥有历史责任感,不仅不能脱离历史上沉淀下来的各种传统遗产,还必须通过自己的创作去丰富传统,使人类摆脱困难和危机。

作为艾略特的代表作之一,《荒原》自问世以来至今一直被公认是对20世纪初叶欧洲社会所作的最深刻、最广泛、最具有艺术感染力的诗体写照。诗以挽歌的风格描写了战争对物质文明和精神文明所造成的惨绝人寰的劫难,"荒原"这一主题意象不仅入木三分地再现战后社会与人的凄惨状况,而且还向麻木不仁、被社会假象和各种虚伪的学说所迷惑的读者敲响了寻求拯救与再生的警钟。全诗由五节构成,分别是《死者的葬礼》、《对弈》、《火戒》、《水边的死亡》与《雷霆的话语》,在内容上构成一个由死亡走向再生的过程,完整地体现了艾略特对"荒原"现状的认识以及对其未来出路的思考。此处节选的是诗中第一节的内容,也是诗中较为复杂并能够典型地体现艾略特的诗歌特征的部分。

有关《荒原》的主题思想,学术界几乎没有出现过异议,但该诗却素来以内容晦涩难懂闻名。主要原因在于艾略特颠覆了传统的叙事与抒情模式，内容不再局限于传统的文学题材和主题，而是将神话、神学、宗教、道德论理、科学、迷信等各个领域的内容全部纳入，从而使他的诗歌文本类似一个具有神秘特征的万花筒。此外，在他的作品中，主题内容不再主要依靠传统的思维逻辑来构建，而是代之以各种新颖的意象，通过单个意象和组合意象所传达的寓意、含蓄的启示、跨学科的关联、跨文化的联想，以及时空错位等途径，将貌似复杂、分散、甚至不相干的内容交织在一起，起到衬托主题的作用。例如，这一节第一行诗"四月是最残忍的月份"，似乎违背常理，令人困惑，因为春季的四月通常能够用明媚的阳光、鲜艳的花卉、郁郁葱葱的原野赋予人类一年之中最美好的时光，加之诗人在此刻意选择的词汇和句子结构，明显能够使得读者联想到英国诗人乔叟的名作《坎特伯雷故事集》的"序曲"中对四月春光的美好描写，更增强了概念与思维逻辑方面的矛盾与困惑。然而，当诗人将读者的视线聚焦到"死亡"，即战后荒凉、萧条的社会现状与心理状态，欧洲的"荒原"顿时浮现在读者的眼帘中，无须阐释和说明，四月具有讽刺意味的"最残忍"的本质就一目了然。同理，诗中反复使用的"丁香花"和"风信子"等意象也往往被艾略特赋予新的寓意，使这些原本用来表示青春、欲望、浪漫和再生的花朵，在与死亡、毁灭、道德、希望和拯救等思想概念串联的时候，能够产生新的魅力，激发读者的想象力与悟性。

思考题

1. In "The Burial of the Dead", whom do you find as the narrator/narrators? What narrative features can you find here that distinguish T. S. Eliot from his contemporary peers?

2. What biblical, mythological or literary references can you find in "The Burial of the Dead" that help T. S. Eliot encompass alluded meanings?

3. If you compare the poetry of Ezra Pound and that of T. S. Eliot, what similarities and differences can you find? Can you interpret them in view of the former's influence on the latter?

推荐作品

1. *The Love Song of J. Alfred Prufrock*
2. *Morning at the Window*
3. *Sweeney Among the Nightingales*

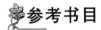 参考书目

1. Bush, Ronald. *T.S. Eliot: A Study in Character and Style*. London: Oxford University Press, 1984.
2. Miller, James E. *T. S. Eliot. The Making of an American Poet, 1888—1922*. University Park: The Pennsylvania State University Press, 2005.
3. Southam, B. C. *A Guide to the Selected Poems of T. S. Eliot*. New York: Harcourt Brace & Company, 1994.

第九单元

Robert Frost (1874—1963)
罗伯特·弗洛斯特

作者简介

罗伯特·弗洛斯特,出生于加利福尼亚州旧金山市,父母都受过良好教育,父亲毕业于哈佛大学,作过教师、记者,母亲是教师。他11岁时父亲去世,后随母亲移居马萨诸塞州劳伦斯镇(Lawrence),中学学习成绩优异,毕业后,进入达特茅斯学院(Dartmouth College),但仅仅学习了几个月便厌倦大学生活,离开学校,开始工作谋生,三年后娶妻生子。这期间他做过工人,教过书,当过记者,还曾有两年在哈佛大学学习文学和拉丁文,但并没有获得学位。1900年他和家人来到新罕布什尔州德利镇(Derry)附近乡间,经营祖父留给他的农庄,后兼作教师工作。弗洛斯特生活中的变迁并没有消磨掉他早在中学时期就开始的诗歌创作热情,他作为学生,曾在劳伦斯高中杂志上发表过自己的诗歌,20岁时在纽约《独立者》杂志(The Independent)上发表了诗歌《我的蝴蝶:哀歌》(My Butterfly: An Elegy, 1894)。但此后漫长的20年中,他的诗歌并没有得到认可,农庄经营并不成功,有限的收入往往入不敷出,写出的诗稿也大多被拒绝。1912年,他卖掉了农庄,举家移居到英国,寻求摆脱困顿的生活,集中精力于创作。在英国,他不久就先后出版了两本诗集:《一个男孩的意愿》(A Boy's Will, 1913 (英国版),1915(美国版))、《波士顿之北》(North of Boston, 1914(英国版),1915(美国版))。诗集立即得到了英美评论界的好评。他于1915年回到美国,此时已享誉美国诗坛。他在新罕布什尔州买下农庄。他的作品也陆续发表,其中4部诗集获得普利策奖:《新罕布什尔》(New Hampshire, 1923)、《诗集》(Collected Poems, 1930)、《又一片牧场》(A Further Range, 1936)以及《一株作证的树》(A Witness Tree, 1942)。其他作品包括:《山间》(Mountain Interval, 1916)、《诗选》(Selected Poems, 1923)、《西流的溪涧》(West-Running Brook, 1928)、《理智假面舞会》(A Masque of Reason, 1945)、《绣线菊》(Steeple Bush,

1947)、《慈悲假面舞会》(*A Masque of Mercy*, 1947)。在 1949 年出版了《诗歌全集》(*Complete Poems*)。

弗洛斯特的家乡新英格兰地区在他的诗歌里留下了浓郁的乡土色彩和背景,他因此被誉为"新英格兰诗人",他使用当地词汇和表达方式,语言朴实无华、清新、自然,口吻亲切。他坚持采用传统诗歌形式,精于无韵体诗和五音步抑扬格诗行;他巧妙运用韵律、词汇和句法产生他引以为豪的所谓"句子的声音"(sentence sounds),通过诗歌形式和主题内容的协调,来表现特定情绪和意蕴。他的诗歌的另一个特点是,诗人对最平常不过的事物、场景、事件的一点点情怀、感动,在读者玩味之余,不知不觉地从一时一地的情感被引向人生哲理的理解。正如弗罗斯特在 1939 年出版的《诗集》导言"论诗的形质"("The Figure a Poem Makes")中指出,诗歌创造的形象"始于愉悦,终于智慧"。他的诗歌背景是远离都市喧嚣的简单乡村生活和自然景色,在 19 世纪末美国开始的工业化、城市化进程中,弗罗斯特贴近自然的诗歌使人耳目一新,而简单、平凡的田园表象常常揭示个人面对外界搅扰时的道德价值或其中的教训;在纷扰的现代生活体验中,诗人内心世界远非自然那样平静有序,对于困扰的心灵来说,诗歌是"抵御迷茫的片刻镇定"(a momentary stay against confusion)。

弗洛斯特一生受到诸多荣誉和嘉奖,除 4 次获得普利策奖外,还被命名为 Phi Beta Kappa(希腊文:哲学是人生的指南)诗人,并获得了牛津、剑桥等著名大学的荣誉学位,他还是美国非正式的桂冠诗人。几乎没有其他诗人可以像他一样做到雅俗共赏,从而拥有最多的读者。在美国诗坛,作为"自然的诗人"(Francis Otto Matthiessen 语),弗洛斯特堪与诗坛巨匠、都市的诗人艾略特比肩而立。

The Tuft of Flowers

I went to turn the grass once after one
Who mowed it in the dew before the sun.

The dew was gone that made his blade so keen[①]
Before I came to view the levelled scene.

---

① keen:磨快了的。

I looked for him behind an isle of trees;
I listened for his whetstone in the breeze.

But he had gone his way, the grass all mown,
And I must be, as he had been—alone,

'As all must be,' I said within my heart,
'Whether they work together or apart.'

But as I said it, swift there passed me by
On noiseless wing a bewildered butterfly①,

Seeking with memories grown dim o'er② night
Some resting flower of yesterday's delight.

And once I marked③ his flight go round and round,
As where some flower lay withering on the ground.

And then he flew as far as eye could see,
And then on tremulous wing came back to me.

I thought of questions that have no reply,
And would have turned to toss the grass to dry;

But he turned first, and led my eye to look
At a tall tuft of flowers beside a brook,

A leaping tongue of bloom the scythe had spared
Beside a reedy brook the scythe had bared.

I left my place to know them by their name,
Finding them butterfly weed when I came.

---

① ...swift there pass me by on noiseless wing a bewildered butterfly...: swift there a bewildered butterfly passed me by on noiseless wing.
② o'er: over。
③ mark: 注意到。

The mower in the dew had loved them thus,
By leaving them to flourish, not for us,

Nor yet to draw one thought of ours to him,
But from sheer morning gladness at the brim.

The butterfly and I had lit upon①,
Nevertheless, a message from the dawn,

That made me hear the wakening birds around,
And hear his long scythe whispering to the ground,

And feel a spirit kindred to my own;
So that henceforth I worked no more alone;

But glad with him, I worked as with his aid,
And weary, sought at noon with him the shade;

And dreaming, as it were, held brotherly speech
With one whose thought I had not hoped to reach.

'Men work together,' I told him from the heart,
'Whether they work together or apart.'
(1906, 1913)

作品赏析

《花丛》是一首押韵两行诗。诗歌分为三部分。在第一部分,叙述者"我"来到地里翻晒刚刚被割草工割下的草,"我"此时形只影单,当"我"期盼同伴的目光寻找割草工时,他却已经离开;静寂中也自然聆听不到微风中割草工的磨刀声。此时此刻,叙述者的心境跃然纸上。同时,诗中创造的意境与"我"孤单的心境紧密呼应;象征黎明生机的晨露已经"踪迹全无";地上的花草也已"平整"地割倒;树木也成了孤立的"岛屿"。"我"意识到他与割草工一样必定都是孤单的,并且无论他们在一起还是各自一人,内心都必然孤单。诗的第二部分开始于一只飞舞的蝴蝶,寻觅昨日在此地逗留、嬉戏时的花朵,然而却遍寻不得。这也呼应了叙述者期盼同伴而不得的孤单心境。诗歌的第三部分标志着叙述者心境的转折。这时,蝴蝶将"我"的目光带到了一簇花丛,这显然是割草工有意留下的一簇花,但他

---

① light upon: 偶然发现。

美国诗歌选读

并不是为了引人注意,而只是因为"纯粹的清晨的喜悦"。蝴蝶与"我"从中读到的讯息是晨曦中的鸟鸣啾啾和长柄镰刀割草时的悦耳之音。此时无声胜有声。这是精神上的相通与共鸣,从此"我"无论和同伴在一起还是各自分离,都已不再"孤单"。

思考题

1. What did the speaker mean when he said "As all must be, whether they work together or apart"?
2. Why did the mower spare the tuft of flowers?
3. What was the message from the dawn that the speaker lit upon?
4. Why would the speaker want to hold brotherly speech with one whose thought he had not hoped to reach?

Mending Wall

Something there is that doesn't love a wall①,
That sends② the frozen-ground-swell under it,
And spills③ the upper boulders in the sun;
And makes gaps even two④ can pass abreast.
The work of hunters is another thing:
I have come after them and made repair
Where they have left not one stone on a stone,
But they would have the rabbit out of hiding,
To please the yelping dogs. The gaps I mean,
No one has seen them made or heard them made,
But at spring mending-time we find them there.
I let my neighbor know beyond the hill;

---

① Something there is that doesn't love a wall, ...: There is something that doesn't love a wall,...
② send: 导致,使得。
③ spill: 使落下。
④ two: 这里指两个人。

And on a day we meet to walk the line①
And set the wall between us once again.
We keep the wall between us as we go.
To each the boulders that have fallen to each②.
And some are loaves and some so nearly balls
We have to use a spell③ to make them balance:
"Stay where you are until our backs are turned!"
We wear our fingers rough with handling them.
Oh, just another kind of out-door game,
One on a side④. It comes to little more⑤:
There where it is we do not need the wall⑥:
He is all pine⑦ and I am apple orchard .
My apple trees will never get across
And eat the cones under his pines, I tell him.
He only says, 'Good fences make good neighbors.'
Spring is the mischief in me, and I wonder
If I could put a notion in his head:
'*Why* do they make good neighbors? Isn't it
Where there are cows? But here there are no cows.
Before I built a wall I'd ask to know
What I was walling in or walling out,
And to whom I was like⑧ to give offence.
Something there is that doesn't love a wall,
That wants it down. 'I could say' Elves' to him,
But it's not elves exactly, and I'd rather
He said it for himself. I see him there
Bringing a stone grasped firmly by the top
In each hand, like an old-stone savage armed⑨.

---

① walk the line：步行着查看、度量。
② To each the boulders that have fallen to each：各自负责滑落到各自一边的石头。
③ spell：咒语。
④ One on a side：各自在自己一边。
⑤ It comes to little more...：除此之外，并没有什么用。
⑥ There where it is...：It is there where...
⑦ He is all pine...：他那边都是松树……
⑧ like：likely.
⑨ ...an old-stone savage armed：武装起来的旧石器时代野蛮人。

He moves in darkness as it seems to me,
Not of woods only and the shade of trees.
He will not go behind his father's saying①,
And he likes having thought of it so well
He says again: 'Good fences make good neighbors.'
(1914)

　　春天来临,人们开始修补邻居之间损坏的石墙。诗中涉及两个邻居,叙述者"我"与邻居"他"对墙的看法显然不同。"他"相信好邻居需要篱笆隔开,这是"父辈"的经验之谈,至于这是为什么,他并不深究。而"我"的看法则对此有所反思。人们建造、修补保护各自利益的屏障,但是总有一些自然或非自然的因素却并不"喜欢"这样的人为屏障,并不时将其破坏。"我"一方面在修墙的季节主动告知邻居,一起完成修补工作;另一方面认为界墙对于保护他们之间的财产来说并没有什么意义,而邻居修补界墙的形象在"我"的眼中,像是仍然停留在黑暗中的"野蛮人"。按弗罗斯特的说法,这首诗承续另一首诗《花丛》(The Tuft of Flowers)关于个人与他人之间的隔离和相通的主题。个人自由和财产权利的保护和界定是美国个人主义传统的前提,也造成形式上个人与他人行为中的利益区隔,而在这样的文化背景中,个人独立自主被认为天经地义;同时,对个人财产的保护,爱默生(Ralph Waldo Emerson)的观点颇具代表性:符合自然规律的"更高法则年复一年写出一个又一个尊重财产的法令"。尽管弗罗斯特抱持着爱默生式个人主义观,相信独立于社群的个体自主性,但《补墙》对人们之间界限的自然规律性重新思考,因为自然似乎并不"喜欢"、甚至年复一年地破坏这样的界限。即便是维护这个界墙也需要邻居之间的默契和合作。的确,人们在相处中随时隔了一道界墙,尽管人们习惯于如何在各自一边行事,这从"我"和"他"的行为中表现了出来,但诗人似乎在不经意间表达了对墙的复杂、甚至矛盾的心态,从而令我们思考"界墙"寓意。

思考题

1. What is it that does not love a wall?
2. Why do good fences make good neighbors?
3. Why does it seem to the speaker that his neighbor moves in darkness?

---

① ...go behind his father's saying:深究他父亲的说法。

Stopping by Woods on a Snowy Evening

Whose woods these are I think I know.
His house is in the village though;
He will not see me stopping here
To watch his woods fill up with snow.

My little horse must think it queer
To stop without a farmhouse near
Between the woods and frozen lake
The darkest evening of the year①.

He gives his harness bells a shake
To ask if there is some mistake.
The only other sound's the sweep
Of easy wind② and downy flake③.

The woods are lovely, dark, and deep.
But I have promises to keep,
And miles to go before I sleep,
And miles to go before I sleep.

　　这是一首抒情诗。在雪夜跋涉旅途中,叙述者"我"乘坐马拉车来到渺无人迹的湖畔树林边,驻足凝望。林畔微风拂雪,夜色中的静寂树林令人流连不前。"我"似乎被一种近乎催人"安眠"的神秘力量所吸引。树林不仅仅"可爱",而是"幽暗"、"深邃",引人入胜。唯一能使"我"回到现实的是马儿触响的铃声和"我"意识到自己在现实世界中做出的"承诺"。如果不是这些承诺和责任要求完成尚未完成的旅途,"我"将难以摆脱自然的神秘美感吸引,探寻"幽暗"、"深邃"的未知。弗罗斯特曾说,他可以为这首诗加上40页的注脚,但他又没有明确说明他所要表达的思想。这为评论家的解读留下不小空间。一些评论家(如

---

① ...the darkest evening of the year: 冬至。
② easy wind: 微风。
③ downy flake: 绒毛般的雪花。

美国诗歌选读

John Ciardi)将雪夜林中的魅力解读为瞬间的"死亡欲望"(death wish)。的确,"寒冬"、"幽暗"、"冰雪"、"安眠"等意象的文化象征意义常与死亡相联系。弗罗斯特本人曾在讲演中对此说法嗤之以鼻。按照他自己的说法,"这只是说要赶快从那里逃走。"无论如何,"我"面临着旅途中一时一地自身价值和旅途目的的终极价值之间的冲突,或者说,内心欲求的"安眠"和职责担当之间的抉择。在更为宽泛的人生意义上,"我"不得不面对的冲突和抉择不也正是人生旅途时时不得不面对的困惑吗?

全诗分为4节,每节4行,韵脚为 aaba, bbcb, ccdc, dddd,前三节的韵律安排与第四节有所不同,韵脚变化产生的效果与诗中情绪的发展形成呼应。

思考题

1. What may snow symbolize?
2. Why must the speaker's horse think it queer to stop without a farmhouse near?
3. What may the dark, deep woods symbolize?
4. What may "sleep" symbolize?
5. Why is the speaker attracted to the dark, deep woods?

作品

The Death Of The Hired Man

Mary sat musing on the lamp-flame at the table
Waiting for Warren. When she heard his step,
She ran on tip-toe down the darkened passage
To meet him in the doorway with the news
And put him on his guard. 'Silas is back.'
She pushed him outward with her through the door
And shut it after her. 'Be kind,' she said.
She took the market things from Warren's arms
And set them on the porch, then drew him down
To sit beside her on the wooden steps.

"When was I ever anything but kind to him?
But I'll not have the fellow back," he said.

"I told him so last haying, didn't I?"
"If he left then", I said, "that ended it".
What good is he? Who else will harbor him
At his age for the little he can do?
What help he is there's no depending on①.
Off he goes always when I need him most.
"He thinks he ought to earn a little pay,
Enough at least to buy tobacco with,
So he won't have to beg and be beholden②".
"All right," I say, "I can't afford to pay
Any fixed wages, though I wish I could."
"Someone else can." "Then someone else will have to."③
I shouldn't mind his bettering himself
If that was what it was. You can be certain,
When he begins like that, there's someone at him④
Trying to coax him off with pocket-money,—
In haying time, when any help is scarce.
In winter he comes back to us. I'm done⑤.'

'Sh! not so loud: he'll hear you,' Mary said.

'I want him to: he'll have to soon or late.'

'He's worn out. He's asleep beside the stove.
When I came up from Rowe's I found him here,
Huddled against the barn-door fast asleep,
A miserable sight, and frightening, too—
You needn't smile-I didn't recognize him—
I wasn't looking for him⑥—and he's changed.
Wait till you see.'
     'Where did you say he'd been?'

---

① What help he is there's no depending on：There's no depending on what help he is。

② Beholden：受到恩惠，感到欠下人情。

③ Then someone else will have to：Then someone else will have to hire and pay you。

④ there's someone at him：有别人想要雇佣他。

⑤ done：结束了，完事了。

⑥ looking for him：期望看见他。

'He didn't say. I dragged him to the house,
And gave him tea and tried to make him smoke.
I tried to make him talk about his travels.
Nothing would do: he just kept nodding off.'

'What did he say? Did he say anything?'

'But little.'

                                                                                      'Anything? Mary, confess
He said he'd come to ditch the meadow for me.'

'Warren!'

                                                                         'But did he? I just want to know.'

'Of course he did. What would you have him say?
Surely you wouldn't grudge the poor old man
Some humble way to save his self-respect.
He added, if you really care to know,
He meant to clear the upper pasture, too.
That sounds like something you have heard before?
Warren, I wish you could have heard the way
He jumbled① everything. I stopped to look
Two or three times—he made me feel so queer—
To see if he was talking in his sleep.
He ran on② Harold Wilson—you remember—
The boy you had in haying four years since.
He's finished school, and teaching in his college.
Silas declares you'll have to get him back.
He says they two will make a team for work:
Between them they will lay③ this farm as smooth!
The way he mixed that in with other things.

---

① jumble: 把事情混乱地绞在一起。
② run on: 不停地说。
③ lay: 使,使成为……状态。

He thinks young Wilson a likely[①] lad, though daft[②]
On education—you know how they fought
All through July under the blazing sun,
Silas up on the cart to build the load,
Harold along beside to pitch it on.'

'Yes, I took care to keep well out of earshot.'

'Well, those days trouble Silas like a dream.
You wouldn't think they would. How some things linger!
Harold's young college boy's assurance piqued him.
After so many years he still keeps finding
Good arguments he sees he might have used.
I sympathize. I know just how it feels
To think of the right thing to say too late.
Harold's associated in his mind with Latin.
He asked me what I thought of Harold's saying
He studied Latin like the violin
Because he liked it—that an argument!
He said he couldn't make the boy believe
He could find water with a hazel prong—
Which showed how much good school had ever done him.
He wanted to go over that. But most of all
He thinks if he could have another chance
To teach him how to build a load of hay—'
'I know, that's Silas' one accomplishment.
He bundles every forkful in its place,
And tags and numbers it for future reference,
So he can find and easily dislodge it
In the unloading. Silas does that well.
He takes it out in bunches like big birds' nests.
You never see him standing on the hay
He's trying to lift, straining to lift himself.'

---

① likely：有希望的，有前途的。
② daft：傻的，愚钝的。

'He thinks if he could teach him that, he'd be
Some good perhaps to someone in the world.
He hates to see a boy the fool of books.
Poor Silas, so concerned for other folk,
And nothing to look backward to with pride,
And nothing to look forward to with hope,
So now and never any different.'

Part of a moon was falling down the west,
Dragging the whole sky with it to the hills.
Its light poured softly in her lap. She saw it
And spread her apron to it. She put out her hand
Among the harp-like morning-glory① strings,
Taut with the dew from garden bed to eaves,
As if she played unheard some tenderness
That wrought on him beside her in the night.
'Warren,' she said, 'he has come home to die:
You needn't be afraid he'll leave you this time.'

'Home,' he mocked gently.

          'Yes, what else but home?
It all depends on what you mean by home.
Of course he's nothing to us, any more
Than was the hound that came a stranger to us
Out of the woods, worn out upon the trail.'

'Home is the place where, when you have to go there,
They have to take you in.'

          'I should have called it
Something you somehow haven't to deserve.'②

Warren leaned out and took a step or two,
Picked up a little stick, and brought it back
And broke it in his hand and tossed it by.

---

① morning glory: 牵牛花。
② haven't to deserve: don't have to deserve.

'Silas has better claim on us you think
Than on his brother? Thirteen little miles
As the road winds would bring him to his door.
Silas has walked that far no doubt to-day.
Why doesn't he go there? His brother's rich,
A somebody—director in the bank.'

'He never told us that.'

          'We know it though.'

'I think his brother ought to help, of course.
I'll see to that if there is need. He ought of right
To take him in, and might be willing to—
He may be better than appearances①.
But have some pity on Silas. Do you think
If he had any pride in claiming kin
Or anything he looked for from his brother,
He'd keep so still② about him all this time?'

'I wonder what's between them.'

          'I can tell you.

Silas is what he is—we wouldn't mind him—
But just the kind that kinsfolk can't abide.
He never did a thing so very bad.
He don't③ know why he isn't quite as good
As anyone. Worthless though he is,
He won't be made ashamed to please his brother.'
'I can't think Si ever hurt anyone.'

'No, but he hurt my heart the way he lay
And rolled his old head on that sharp-edged chair-back.
He wouldn't let me put him on the lounge.
You must go in and see what you can do.

---

① appearances: 给别人留下的外表印象。
② still: 安静,不谈及。
③ don't: doesn't.

I made the bed up for him there to-night.
You'll be surprised at him—how much he's broken.
His working days are done; I'm sure of it.'

'I'd not be in a hurry to say that.'

'I haven't been. Go, look, see for yourself.
But, Warren, please remember how it is:
He's come to help you ditch the meadow.
He has a plan. You mustn't laugh at him.
He may not speak of it, and then he may.
I'll sit and see if that small sailing cloud
Will hit or miss the moon.'

         It hit the moon.
Then there were three there, making a dim row,
The moon, the little silver cloud, and she.

Warren returned-too soon, it seemed to her,
Slipped to her side, caught up her hand and waited.

'Warren,' she questioned.

       'Dead,' was all he answered.

  这是一首对话体田园诗,背景是新英格兰的乡村生活。场景是农舍外的门廊处。诗中的三个主要人物的关系和不同的行为处世观念引出了戏剧性的冲突、发展和高潮。农场主沃伦(Warren)为人精明、视商业社会的基本准则为真理,尽管这样的真理在现实中有时冷酷无情,但却是社会公正的基石。他的妻子玛丽(Mary)心地善良,善于理解他人,富有同情心。农场前雇工希莱斯(Silas)曾在农场最需要他的时候离开了农场,而当他贫病潦倒时再次回到农场,夫妻之间对是否应该接纳他意见不一。丈夫从抽象的责任、权利、公平、公正的原则角度评判此事,认为没有义务收留希莱斯;而妻子则以宽厚仁慈之心着眼于希莱斯此时此刻的不幸处境。通过两人的对话交流,从丈夫和妻子不同的性别视角,展示了不同人物的性格、他们之间的关系以及不同观念的冲突。希莱斯来到农场寻求他的最终归宿,从夫妻俩的对话中可以看出,希莱斯为人好胜、自尊,即便在如此困境中也不愿求助于自己有钱的银行家兄弟。是否收留他自然引出了两人对"家"的不同定义。沃伦的定义:家意味着在需要回家时,家人必须接受你。这显然是一个法律意义上的定义,家人对家庭成员的义务是不可回避的。依据这个定义,希莱斯的兄弟,而不是他的前雇主,才是他的家。更何况他们之间的雇佣关系由于希莱斯的原因而已经结束了,而即便通过雇佣关系建立起来任何个人关系也不构成法律上的家庭关系。但是玛丽对家的定义代表了一个完全不同的思维角度:家恰恰是可以忽略责权关系的地方。这两种定义似乎完全没有交集的地方。玛丽观察事物和思考角度也与沃伦截然不同,似乎难以相互协调,也形成了两种思维方式的鲜明对比。然而,随着观念冲突的展开,丈夫的态度开始改变,而沃伦握住了玛丽的手标志着戏剧高潮的结束。

试分析夫妻开始交流时的一些细节,他们之间的视角差异和冲突十分明显。

丈夫在谈论希莱斯时说:

When was I ever anything but kind to him?
But I will not have the fellow back,' he said.
'I told him so last haying, didn't I?
If he left then, I said, that ended it.
What good is he? Who else will harbor him
At his age for the little he can do?
What help he is there is no depending on.
Off he goes always when I need him most.

而妻子谈论希莱斯时说:

'He is worn out. He is asleep beside the stove,
When I came up from Rowe's I found him there,
Huddled against barn-door fast asleep,
A miserable sight, and frightening, too—
You needn't smile—I didn't recognize him—
I wasn't looking for him—and he's changed.
Wait till you see.'

丈夫对事实的描述就事论事,而他的结论也是对希莱斯的行为人们普遍会认同的看法;反观妻子对事件的描述,其间充满了并非每个人对同一事件都会同样感受到的个人情感因素。尽管她描述事件的事实信息量并不大,但她使用的语言充分表现了女性对细节的关注和在细节观察基础之上产生的怜悯之心,如"worn out," "huddled," "miserable sight," "frightening," "changed," 等。又如下面一段对话:

'Anything? Mary, confess
He said he'd come to ditch the meadow for me.
'Warren!'

'But did he? I just want to know.'
'Of course he did. What would you have him say?
...'

在以上的交流中,丈夫要求妻子讲出事实,而丈夫对事实的猜想恰恰也是正确的。妻子表面上不愿意谈及事实,但她是希望丈夫看到事实现象以外的真实情况。夫妻交谈内容不多,但内涵丰富,令人回味。

再看看从未出场的希莱斯,他的性格特质和内心世界通过夫妻交谈也逐步展开:寻找归宿时的打工借口,对哈罗德·威尔逊和他们之间的争论耿耿于怀,在富有的兄弟和前雇主之间做出的抉择,以及面对死亡的尊严。无需多余着笔,一个栩栩如生的角色同样在诗歌的戏剧高潮中丰满呈现出来。

思考题

1. Was Warren kind to Silas? If he was, as he said, how did his kindness differ from Mary's?
2. Why didn't Warren want Silas back? Was he justified in refusing to have Silas back?
3. What did Silas say he had come back for? Had he really come back to work for Warren?
4. Why did the days working with Harold Wilson trouble Silas so much?
5. Was Silas good at anything? How did he feel about himself?
6. How did Warren and Mary define the notion of home?
7. What underlying attitudes towards home did their different definitions reveal?
8. Why didn't Silas seek help from his rich brother?
9. Why didn't Silas let Mary put him on the lounge?

推荐作品

1. *After Apple Picking*
2. *Birches*
3. *Departmental*
4. *Home Burial*
5. *The Figure a Poem Makes*
6. *Fire and Ice*
7. *Nothing Gold Can Stay*

8. *The Road Not Taken*
9. *The Wood-Pile*

参考书目

1. Faggen, Robert. *The Oxford Companion to Robert Frost*. Cambridge: Cambridge University Press, 2001.
2. Marcus, Mordecai. *The Poems of Robert Frost: An Explication*. Boston, Mass.: G.K. Hall, 1991.
3. Thomson, Lawrance R., and R. H. Winnick. *Robert Frost: A Biography*. New York: Holt, Rinehart and Winston, 1982.
4. Wilcox, Earl J., ed. *The Man and the Poet*. Conway, AR: UCA Press, 1989.

第十单元

Wallace Stevens (1879—1955)
华莱士·史蒂文斯

作者简介

华莱士·史蒂文斯(Wallace Stevens, 1879—1955)，20世纪最主要的美国诗人之一。出生于宾夕法尼亚州的雷丁市，父亲是律师。1903年从纽约大学法学院毕业，次年取得律师资格，开始从事律师职业。1909年完婚。1916年进入保险业界，后迁居康涅狄格州，任哈特福德意外事故理赔保险公司的副总裁。

史蒂文斯对诗歌的兴趣始于哈佛大学，最初在校刊《哈佛之声》(Harvard Advocate)上刊登过习作，1914年开始在《诗刊》(Poetry)等杂志上发表较为成熟的作品，直到1923年才出版了第一部诗集《簧风琴》(Harmonium)。这部诗集包含史蒂文斯的许多著名诗作，首版却反响平平，史蒂文斯因此气馁，20年代几乎中断了诗歌创作，将事业重心转向了商务。该诗集到1931年再版时获得了公众认可，仅有八首新作添加。随后，史蒂文斯接连推出了三部诗集，从而奠定了他作为最具原创力的美国现代派代表诗人之一的地位。1946年，他入选美国艺术文学院(The American Academy of Arts and Letters)；1955年同时获得普利策诗歌奖和国家图书奖。

史蒂文斯平日往返于办公室与家之间，除了定期造访纽约市并且间或在国内各地旅游以外从未出过国，以艺术品收藏和美食为业余爱好，似乎过着平静庸常的生活，其诗人身份在法律和商务圈内鲜为人知。上下班途中与夜晚才是他放飞想象、诗情勃发的空间。借助于鲜明的感官视觉意象和词语的乐感听觉效果，他尝试着在缪斯的王国中实现想象与现实之间的时空转换。与威廉斯(William Carlos Williams, 1883—1963)等强调实物意象的其他现代派诗人相比，史蒂文斯在诗歌创作中并不刻意回避哲学思辨和抽象思维，其作品肃穆却不乏妙趣，厚重而不失率真，语言的乐趣与力量在挥洒自如的才情中得以淋漓尽致地体现。

史蒂文斯的主要作品还有:《秩序观念》(*Ideas of Order*,1935),《带蓝色吉它的男人》(*The Man with the Blue Guitar*, 1937),《一个世界的片段》(*Parts of a World*,1942),《秋天的晨曦》(*The Auroras of Autumn*, 1950),诗歌文论集《必要的天使》(*The Necessary Angel*, 1951)、《诗全集》(*Collected Poems*, 1954)等。史蒂文斯的创作始终带有"元诗歌"(metapoetry)的性质,晚年作品尤其注重诗歌写作的理论探索,70岁以后的诗歌则有渐趋晦涩的倾向。

Anecdote of the Jar

I placed a jar in Tennessee,
And round it was, upon a hill.①
It made the slovenly wilderness
Surround that hill.②

The wilderness rose up to it,
And sprawled around, no longer wild.
The jar was round upon the ground
And tall and of a port in air.③

It took dominion everywhere.
The jar was gray and bare.
It did not give of bird or bush,④
Like nothing else in Tennessee.

《坛子轶事》是史蒂文斯一首广为流传的代表诗作。诗中的说话人把一个坛子置于荒野中的小山上,荒野顿时成为陪衬,环绕着它,显出一种秩序来。于是坛子高高在上,气度非凡,颇似统治者,而荒野则如子民般臣服恭顺。然而,坛子虽统辖一切,却由于不具备繁殖能力而灰

---

① And round it was, upon a hill: 此句倒装,正常语序为"And it was round..."。
② It made the slovenly wilderness/Surround that hill: 该句使用 make sth. do 结构; surround, v. 围绕,包围。意思是:它使得散乱的荒野/都以此小山为中心。
③ of a port in air: port, 举止,姿态; air, 风度,气派。意为:气度非凡。
④ give of: 相当于 produce, generate, 派生, 滋生。

暗光秃,缺乏生命力。诗中各节都可见坛子与荒野的对比,比如第一节中round对slovenly。在诗歌技巧上,诗人运用了象征主义和超现实主义的表现手法。诗中的"I"代表任何诗人或艺术家。坛子象征艺术,而田纳西州的荒野则象征着自然。这两种相去甚远、看似不协调的事物并置,产生了一种超现实的效果。

从主题上看,本诗讨论的是艺术(art)与自然(nature)之间的关系。一方面,自然原是一片荒芜,却在艺术的影响之下呈现出一种秩序感。另一方面,自然本身有繁殖的能力,而艺术品却不具备这种能力。坛子的意象很容易使人联想到英国浪漫主义诗人济慈的《希腊古瓮颂》(Ode on a Grecian Urn)。济慈笔下的古瓮是自然与艺术的完美结合,艺术将永恒赋予转瞬即逝的自然;而史蒂文斯笔下的坛子则与自然完全隔绝对立起来,艺术在自然面前拥有绝对却无生命的权威。浪漫主义与现代主义艺术观之间的差异可从中窥见一斑。

《坛子轶事》这首诗很好地体现了诗人对艺术的独道见解,特别是"最高虚构"(supreme fiction)的诗歌创作理念。史蒂文斯认为,诗歌反映现实,而"此现实"却非"彼现实",因为艺术想像力将现实升华到一个更高境界。具体说来,史蒂文斯将诗歌历程解析为三种境界。第一种境界是把意识对象缩减为他所称的"第一观念"(the First Idea)以避免错觉和虚幻。第二种境界是对第一种境界的反省,发现它其实不适合人类居住其中,因为人类生活在"第一观念"之中就会缺乏自由意志,与动物生活在它们的自然中没有区别。第三种境界是诗人对"第一观念"进行再想象,重构现实和自我,从而进入"最高虚构"。这种"最高虚构"的结果是一种新现实,一个全新的诗性自我。总之,在史蒂文斯看来,诗歌及其他艺术类型有必要在现实生活中创造一种有意义的秩序和模式,即便是人为强加的也完全可以接受。

思考题

1. What does the jar symbolize in contrast to the wilderness?
2. What kind of relationship between art and nature is illustrated by this poem?
3. How does this poem reveal the poet's artistic vision? How does this modernist notion of art differ from that of Romanticism?

Thirteen Ways of Looking at a Blackbird①

1
Among twenty snowy mountains,

---

① blackbird: 乌鸫;黑鹂鸟。一种青黑色的山雀类小型鸣禽。

The only moving thing
Was the eye of the blackbird.

2

I was of three minds,
Like a tree
In which there are three blackbirds.

3

The blackbird whirled in the autumn winds.
It was a small part of the pantomime.

4

A man and a woman
Are one.
A man and a woman and a blackbird
Are one.

5

I do not know which to prefer,
The beauty of inflections①
Or the beauty of innuendoes,②
The blackbird whistling
Or just after.

6

Icicles filled the long window
With barbaric glass.
The shadow of the blackbird
Crossed it, to and fro.
The mood
Traced in the shadow
An indecipherable cause.③

---

① inflection: *n.* 变调，音调变化。
② innuendo: *n.* 暗讽。
③ An indecipherable cause: 一个无法破解之谜，这里可理解为"情绪 / 在暗影里找到了 / 无法破解的原因"，诗人将情绪的捉摸不定比做乌鸫穿梭在冰柱下的暗影。

美国诗歌选读

7

O thin men of Haddam,①
Why do you imagine golden birds?
Do you not see how the blackbird
Walks around the feet
Of the women about you?

8

I know noble accents
And lucid, inescapable rhythms;②
But I know, too,
That the blackbird is involved
In what I know.

9

When the blackbird flew out of sight,
It marked the edge
Of one of many circles.

10

At the sight of blackbirds
Flying in a green light,
Even the bawds of euphony③
Would cry out sharply.

11

He rode over Connecticut
In a glass coach.
Once, a fear pierced him,
In that he mistook
The shadow of his equipage④
For blackbirds.

---

① Haddam: 地名,哈达姆,位于美国康涅狄格州,曾经出现过"淘金热"。
② lucid, inescapable rhythms: 明晰的、不可避免的节奏。
③ the bawds of euphony: bawd 意为"鸨母,妓院老板"。所谓"谐音的老鸨"在这里指的是十分讲究和谐音韵的人。
④ equipage: n. 装备,这里指此人所乘的玻璃车辇,构成"杯弓蛇影"的意想。

12

The river is moving.
The blackbird must be flying.

13

It was evening all afternoon.①
It was snowing
And it was going to snow.
The blackbird sat
In the cedar-limbs.

  在这首诗中,诗人写了观察乌鸫的十三种方式,以感性的方式揭示了真相的多样性,其中包含了丰富的审美感受和哲理启示。十三首小诗虽描写对象相同,但内涵和风格迥异。
  该诗的第一种观察方式体现了大与小、动与静、黑与白的对比。乌鸫的眼睛所带来的动感不仅为画面增添了生机,而且令观察的主体和客体之间产生了一种交互性——在人观察乌鸫时候,它的一双眼睛也在观察人。第二种观察方式从观察乌鸫的外在视角转移到了人的内心世界,将人的思想比做了树上栖息的乌鸫,未知的心灵隐秘在诗人的灵感中得以外化,展现着生机活力,彰显出"有我"之境的妙趣。第三小节构成了一个完整的比喻。在秋风中盘旋的乌鸫像是一出哑剧中的一个不起眼的角色。观察者把乌鸫纳入了一个宏观体系。第四种观察方式则强调了男性与女性的和谐一体,以及人与自然的和谐一体,颇似阴阳合一、天人合一的哲学思想。第五小节将观察的角度移向乌鸫鸣叫的声音,表达了诗人对诗道的思考。两个关键词"inflections"和"innuendoes"有作"词形变化"与"词义暗示"之解,也有作"音调变化"与"词义暗讽"之解,在诗歌的表达方式方面,还是从音调上理解更好。音韵美与暗示美,孰重孰轻?鸣叫后的乌鸫给人留下了"余音绕梁"的联想。第六小节是一种借助于中介的观察方式。透过玻璃一样的冰柱,乌鸫只能显现出依稀的影子。中介给观察对象造成了一种陌生感。人捉摸不定的情绪在模糊的乌鸫影子中更显扑朔迷离,观察和情绪自然地交融在这个意象之中。第七小节最接近象征主义的诗歌,金鸟和乌鸫的象征意义不言而喻,体现了物质与精神、世俗与自然等价值观的取舍。第八小节似乎带有明显的后现代风格,诗人忽然从幕后跳到前台,说明自己的写作对象和写作目的了,这是借用后现代小说常用的"元叙述"表现手法。在第九小节中,观察者目光紧紧追随着乌鸫,直至乌鸫逐渐飞出视野。随着目力穷尽,视野却陡然开阔。远眺的动态变化体现在众多不断扩大的圆圈之中。第十小节里,乌鸫在绿光中飞舞,尽显色彩、活力之动态美。老鸨是一种善长行走而拙于飞翔的鸟儿,虽以悦耳的声音为骄傲的资本,却在乌鸫的轻舞飞扬面前难免因自惭形秽而失声痛哭起来。两种鸟儿放在一起观察,是一种衬托的写法。第十一小

---

① It was evening all afternoon:整个下午都是晚上,暗示下雪前的天色昏暗。

美国诗歌选读

节并不是真正的实物观察,乌鸦只在幻觉中闪现,成为想像中的恐惧之源,恰似"杯弓蛇影",承载了主观意识在观察客体上的投射。第十二小节与上句的河水流动和下句的乌鸦飞翔构成了一个动感视觉意象,看似简单,却不乏深意。河流形成了一个参照系,乌鸦在其中静止,观察者依靠河流的状态来推断乌鸦其实在动。简单的意象中蕴涵了动与静相对性的深刻哲理。第十三小节与开头照应,结尾将观察视角切换回雪景之中,雪花不断飘落,乌鸦栖息枝头,静态中产生出一种曲终人散却意犹未尽的意境。至此,观察者似乎已与环境完全融为一体。

从整体上看,这首诗似乎缺乏一个贯穿全文的主题和一个完整的结构,全诗体现了一种发散式的思维结构,诗人放开想像,由一个具体的事物产生自由联想。可以说,这十三种观察方式的每一种都是一次想像力的探险。同时,如同另一首代表作《雪人》所体现的,诗人的观察"我中有物,物中有我",视角客观冷峻,有效地除去了感情色彩的杂质。

思考题

1. What do you think of the symbolic implication of the blackbird image?
2. How does the observer in the poem embody the poet's own poetic vision?
3. Another one of Stevens's poems "The Snow Man" contains the lines "the listener, who listens in the snow, /And, nothing himself, beholds/Nothing that is not there and the nothing that is." Could you please illustrate Stevens's perspective with reference to "Thirteen Ways of Looking at a Blackbird"?

The Idea of Order at Key West①

She sang beyond the genius of the sea.
The water never formed to mind or voice,
Like a body wholly body, fluttering
Its empty sleeves; and yet its mimic motion②

---

① Key West:佛罗里达州的基韦斯特,位于美国最南端,大西洋和墨西哥湾交汇处的一个小岛,被称作"日落之家"。该镇南北宽一英里左右,东西大约五英里,隔海与古巴相望。值得注意的是,1934年,诗人创作其时正值美国经济大萧条期(Great Depression),社会动荡,失业现象普遍,在基韦斯特并无秩序可言。

② its mimic motion:模仿的运动。该小节强调了歌者与大海之间形成的反差,以及心灵与外在现实之间的关联。大海没有人的思想,"有如全然肉体的肉体",它发出的声音是空洞的,能做的也只是一种机械运动而已。这是人比"非人的"自然高明之处。

Made constant cry, caused constantly a cry,
That was not ours although we understood,
Inhuman, of the veritable ocean.

The sea was not a mask. No more was she.
The song and water were not medleyed sound①
Even if what she sang was what she heard,
Since what she sang was uttered word by word.
It may be that in all her phrases stirred
The grinding water and the gasping wind;②
But it was she and not the sea we heard.

For she was the maker of the song she sang.
The ever-hooded, tragic-gestured sea③
Was merely a place by which she walked to sing.
Whose spirit is this? we said, because we knew
It was the spirit that we sought and knew
That we should ask this often as she sang.

If it was only the dark voice of the sea
That rose, or even colored by many waves;
If it was only the outer voice of sky
And cloud, of the sunken coral water-walled,④
However clear, it would have been deep air,
The heaving speech of air⑤, a summer sound
Repeated in a summer without end
And sound alone. But it was more than that,
More even than her voice, and ours, among
The meaningless plungings of water and the wind,⑥
Theatrical distances⑦, bronze shadows heaped

---

① medleyed sound：混响。
② in her phrases stirred/The grinding water and the gasping wind：歌者歌唱的是大海，歌声中仿佛海水涌动、风声呼啸，与大海发出的声音融为一体。接下来的诗句指出：在两种声音的混响之中，我们听到的首先是歌声。
③ The ever-hooded, tragic-gestured sea：永恒笼罩、手势悲凉的大海。拟人化描写。
④ the sunken coral water-walled：被海水环绕的珊瑚暗礁。
⑤ The heaving speech of air：空气的激荡言辞，比喻空气流动所发出的呼啸声。
⑥ The meaningless plungings of water and the wind：水与风无意义的起伏跌宕。
⑦ Theatrical distances：夸张的距离，指的是大海的辽阔、海天之间的空旷等。

美国诗歌选读

On high horizons①, mountainous atmospheres
Of sky and sea.②

It was her voice that made
The sky acutest at its vanishing.③
She measured to the hour its solitude.④
She was the single artificer⑤ of the world
In which she sang. And when she sang, the sea,
Whatever self it had, became the self
That was her song, for she was the maker. Then we,
As we beheld her striding there alone,
Knew that there never was a world for her
Except the one she sang and, singing, made.

Ramon Fernandez⑥, tell me, if you know,
Why, when the singing ended and we turned
Toward the town, tell why the glassy lights,
The lights in the fishing boats at anchor there,
As the night descended, tilting in the air,⑦
Mastered the night and portioned out the sea,⑧
Fixing emblazoned zones and fiery poles,
Arranging, deepening, enchanting night.

Oh! Blessed rage for order⑨, pale Ramon,
The maker's rage to order words of the sea,

---

① bronze shadows heaped/On high horizons：高高的海平线上堆积的青铜色阴影。
② mountainous atmospheres/Of sky and sea：海天之间如山的大气云层。
③ It was her voice that made/The sky acutest at its vanishing：黄昏消逝前，女子的歌声让天空变得锐利无比，此处意为天空在暮色中显现出鲜明的轮廓，与海水界限分明。
④ She measured to the hour its solitude：她一小时一小时地测量着它的孤寂。天色渐暗，天空的轮廓逐渐变得模糊起来，直至完全消失在暮色中，与大海完全隔绝。
⑤ artificer：n. 工匠，巧匠，艺术家。歌者扮演了造物者的角色，用歌声构建了自己的世界，也是唯一的世界。
⑥ Ramon Fernandez：雷蒙·费尔南德。根据上下文推测，与诗人一起漫步海边的男子，诗人当时倾诉和发问的对象。也是最后一小节中的"苍白的雷蒙"所指，此处暗示朋友在生命的追问和神性的顿悟面前的情感反应。
⑦ tilting in the air：这个分词短语的主语应为海边停泊的渔船的玻璃般的灯火，在空气中倾斜，指的是灯火射出的光柱划破夜色。
⑧ portioned out the sea：把海面划割成若干部分。
⑨ Blessed rage for order：秩序的神圣激情，造物主对秩序的狂热追求。

Words of the fragrant portals①, dimly-starred,
And of ourselves and of our origins,
In ghostlier demarcations②, keener sounds.

作品赏析

《基韦斯特的秩序观》这首诗创作于1934年，是史蒂文斯出色的早期代表作之一，也是他最为晦涩难懂的诗作之一，有着很大的阐释空间。

诗歌的叙事情节很简单：诗人与友人漫步于基韦斯特的海滨，偶然听到一名女子面向大海在歌唱。歌声与大海发出的声音交汇，引发了诗人对人生与美的深刻思考，特别是现实与想像之间的关联。歌声消散后，诗人在返回小镇的途中产生顿悟(epiphany)。

从主题上看，早期评论家，比如弗兰克·克默德(Frank kermode)，往往把该诗解读为史蒂文斯对艺术创造过程的描述、对想像力改变现实的力量之赞美，认为它传承了华兹华斯(William Wordsworth)、济慈(John Keats)等人所代表的浪漫主义诗歌遗风。然而，新近的评论家则主张：这首诗强调的与其说是歌声(即艺术)本身，不如说是歌声对听者造成的影响，其中包含着诗人的诗歌创作理念，代表了诗人在想像与现实、心灵与肉体、智力与情感等二元对立之间找寻平衡点的努力。如同史蒂文斯的许多诗作，此诗描述的是叙述者的心理活动，探究的是思维过程、感知结构以及想像力。

在1935年(即此诗问世大约一年以后)的一封信中，史蒂文斯是这样评论诗人的角色的："我们没有开始从这个世界获得它最终会通过诗人来传递的信息。如果诗歌带来秩序感，而且每一首合格的诗作都会带来秩序感，如果秩序意味着和平，即便那种特定的和平是一种幻像，那么如今上上下下每个人都承认不再有价值的诸多其他事物不也同样是幻像吗？生命的更新难道不是一件举足轻重的事情吗？"正是诗人的"陌生化"视角给司空见惯的庸常生活带来永恒的新鲜感和启示。

思考题

1. Please make an analysis of the images of the woman singer and the sea, and explain their relationship from the poet's perspective.

2. Enchanted by the singer, the listener/speaker begins to muse on the beauty of her song and its relationship to his own life, particularly his ideas on reality and imagination. He experiences a kind of epiphany—a moment of insight. What kind of epiphany does he experience?

3. According to critics, the poem dramatizes important conflicts for Stevens. What are they? Please illustrate your points with details and examples.

---

① portal: *n.* 大门，入口。the fragrant portals: 芬芳的入口，大概指的是天堂之门。
② ghostlier demarcations: 更为朦胧的划界，更多属于幽灵的界阈。

The Course of a Particular

Today the leaves cry, hanging on branches swept by wind,
Yet the nothingness of winter becomes a little less.①
It is still full of icy shades and shapen snow②.

The leaves cry... One holds off and merely hears the cry.
It is a busy cry, concerning someone else.
And though one says that one is part of everything.③

There is a conflict, there is a resistance involved;
And being part is an exertion that declines:④
One feels the life of that which gives life as it is.

The leaves cry. It is not a cry of divine attention,⑤
Nor the smoke-drift of puffed-out⑥ heroes, nor human cry.
It is the cry of leaves that do not transcend themselves,

In the absence of fantasia, without meaning more
Than they are in the final finding of the ear, in the thing
Itself, until, at last, the cry concerns no one at all.

《一个特例的过程》是史蒂文斯的晚期诗作，发表于1950年。哈罗德·布卢姆(Harold Bloom)在《华莱士·史蒂文斯评传》中说，这首诗是史蒂文斯最巧妙的作品，"整首诗通过与'树叶叫喊'这种现象性的真理相比较否定了价值不大的叫喊，当读者一步步认识到这一点时会大吃一惊"(p.354)。

---

① the nothingness of winter becomes a little less：树叶在风中的叫喊声给冬天的苍白无聊增添了一点内容，冬天的虚无从而减少了些许。
② shapen snow：积雪。
③ one is part of everything：一个人、一件事物是万物的一个部分，即万物合一。
④ an exertion that declines：拒绝的努力，与前句的"resistance"呼应。
⑤ divine attention：神灵的关注。
⑥ puffed-out：膨胀的，自我吹嘘的。

该诗集中体现了诗人晚期的哲学思辨倾向。

首先，诗中包含了史蒂文斯晚期常用的一个融合(integration)概念，所见所闻所知所感等融合为一个和谐的整体，从客观事物到主观感知最终都通过某种仪式性的沉思或冥想(meditation)而达到一种合一状态。与此同时，在史蒂文斯看来，融合包含着一种拒绝，感知主体要与现实保持一定距离，正如《雪人》中所描述，"他在雪中倾听，/完全不是他自己，看见／一切，以及一切存在中的空无"。

其次，"事物本身"也是史蒂文斯诗歌创作理念中一个相当重要的概念，承载了诗人对想象与现实、心灵与肉体、自然与文明、秩序与混乱、在场与缺席等诸多问题的深刻思考，其中不无矛盾和暧昧。可参照史蒂文斯的诗作《不是关于事物的理念而是事物本身》(*Not Ideas about the Thing But the Thing Itself*)加以理解。

另外，对于听者来说，树叶"没有超越自身"，故而其喊叫声终究毫无意义而言。以读者接受的视角看来，"树叶叫喊"给诗人／艺术家带来的启示在于：在诗人的创作中，只有想象力才能使外部现实产生意义；而困顿于"事物本身"只能造成空洞的表征，亦即意义的缺席。

思考题

1. What does the leaves' cry signify, both in relation to the winter context and the listener?
2. How does the line "One feels the life of that which gives life as it is" carry Stevens's idea of "integration"?
3. How do you understand Stevens's concept of "the thing itself" with reference to multiple poetic contexts?

推荐作品

1. *Harmonium*(1923)(诗集)
2. *The Collected Poems of Wallace Stevens*(1954)(诗全集)
3. *Letters of Wallace Stevens*(1966)(ed. by Holly Stevens)(书信集)

参考书目

1. Axelrod, S.G., ed. *Critical Essays on Wallace Stevens*. Boston: G.K. Hall, 1988.
2. Bloom, Harold, ed. *Wallace Stevens: Modern Critical Views*. New York: Chelsea, 1986.
3. Cook, Eleanor. *A Reader's Guide to Wallace Stevens*. Princeton: Princeton University Press, 2007.
4. Serio, John N., ed. *The Cambridge Companion to Wallace Stevens*. New York: Cambridge University Press, 2007.

第十一单元

William Carlos Williams (1883—1963)
威廉·卡洛斯·威廉斯

作者简介

威廉·卡洛斯·威廉斯,生于新泽西州,父亲经商、母亲绘画,家境殷实。于宾夕法尼亚大学学医期间结识著名诗人庞德,并建立起终生友谊。他一生行医为业,同时笔耕不止,创作了大量的诗歌、散文和剧本。1909年,威廉斯出版第一部诗集——《诗集》(Poems)。1913年在伦敦出版诗集《性情》(The Tempers),显示出其捕捉美国生活韵律和语言特色的能力。20世纪20年代,威廉斯创作了一批散文和小说,除诗歌散文集《春天及其他》(Spring and All, 1923)和《冬日降临》(The Descent of Winter, 1927)外,还有《美国杰出小说》(The Great American Novel, 1923),《与美国情投意合》(In the American Grain, 1925),《帕格尼之旅》(A Voyage to Pagany, 1928)和《一月》(January: A Novelette, 1932)。其中,《与美国情投意合》成就最高。此外,威廉斯还写过《白骡》(White Mule, 1937)等反映德国移民生活的三部曲。1944年发表的诗集《楔子》(The Wedge)反映出身兼诗人和医生双重身份的威廉斯在第二次世界大战期间的痛苦。经过近二十年的努力,长诗《帕特森》(Paterson)的第一卷于1946年问世。从某种意义上讲,《帕特森》是对艾略特关于20世纪机械文化下传统价值的失落的回应,其对美国人共同的文化历史元素的追寻抗击了美国社会的琐碎和零乱。诗中的帕特森集医生和诗人于一体,在一个叫做帕特森的工业小镇里过着常人生活,尽管不喜欢镇上人的行为方式,却认为他们有权选择自己的行为。通过帕特森的日常生活体验、原汁原味的语言以及诗歌的节奏,威廉斯向读者展示了普通人生活的诗意。此后到1958年,《帕特森》共出五卷,并于1962年写出第六卷的一部分,完整地表现了美国多民族的语言特色和行为习惯,美国的活力和暴力,以及美国人寻求共同历史文化认同感的努力。1962年,威廉斯的最后一部诗集《布鲁盖尔的绘画

美国诗歌选读

及其他》(*Pictures from Brueghel and Other Poems*)出版,该诗集次年于诗人谢世后获得普利策诗歌奖。威廉斯在其近半个世纪的诗歌创作生涯中不断创新,通过精选场景,巧妙构造诗歌结构,翻新句法、词汇和标点等手法,创造出了大量简洁质朴、清新鲜明的意象,让读者自己去发现"真"中的美,自己去玩味医院里红色手推车和绿色玻璃的意义,而无需借助象征手法,正如他在《帕特森》第一卷中所说:"思想存于事物"("no ideas but in things.")。

The Young Housewife

At ten A.M. the young housewife
moves about in negligee① behind
the wooden walls of her husband's house.
I pass solitary in my car.

Then again she comes to the curb②
to call the ice-man, fish-man, and stands
shy, uncorseted③, tucking in
stray④ ends of hair, and I compare her
to a fallen leaf.

The noiseless wheels of my car
rush with a crackling sound over
dried leaves as I bow and pass smiling.

《少妇》一诗发表于1916年,选入《1909—1917年诗集》(*Poems 1909—1917*),是威廉斯的早期作品。在美国20世纪诗人中,休斯、弗洛斯特和威廉斯三人以创作大量的妇女画像著称。此类诗也在威廉斯最著名的诗歌作品之列。威廉斯对妇女的态度丰富多变,总体上趋于积极肯定,但也不乏男权意识。该诗表面上用简洁的文字白描出开车过路的诗人(医生)

---

① negligee:来自法语 négligé,妇女长睡衣;穿戴不整。
② curb:路边。也是公共交通与私有财产的分界线。
③ uncorseted:没穿紧身胸衣的。
④ stray:零落的。

同一名乡间少妇礼貌的一次不期而遇。但是,因诗人的无际的幻觉,该诗含意丰富,妙趣横生。诗里障碍和牢笼意象明显:"木头围墙"、"她丈夫的房子"、"路边"、"汽车"等。然而,手握汽车方向盘的诗人的视力(更准确地说是想象)却穿过"木头围墙",看到围墙后面穿睡裙的少妇。或许,他把自己想象成脚跨战马的骑士,正冲破障碍砸碎牢笼,营救被关押的贵夫人。但是,诗行的排列组合和选词造句又让人觉得诗人是一个不怀好意地窥视少妇的好色之徒,尤其是第2行和第7行的结尾,很容易造成错觉。当然,这也是诗人的幽默所在。尽管少妇"塞起"的是"零落"(stray)的几缕头发,但因为"stray"一词同时有"出轨"的意思,诗人似乎在不怀好意地希望少妇呼唤的不是"ice-man","fish-man",而是他本人的服务,他甚至把少妇比喻为"一片落叶",并想象着用车轮碾碎"落叶"。不过,诗人最终没有冲破社会行为规范和道德准则的约束,而是从幻觉中清醒,走出白日梦,彬彬有礼地向少妇颔首微笑而过,使幻觉中的男权意识显得荒诞可笑。

思考题

1. Are there any parallels between the speaker and the young housewife?
2. What are we to make of the implicit connection between the woman as a leaf and the leaves crushed by the car's wheels?
3. How does the speaker's fantasy structure the details, progress, and interrelation of elements in the poem?

The Red Wheelbarrow

so much depends
upon

a red wheel
barrow

glazed with rain
water

beside the white
chickens

美国诗歌选读

《红色手推车》选自1923年出版的《春天及其他》，是威廉斯最著名的诗篇，为他赢得"红色手推车诗人"的称号。该诗通过形式突出客观意象。全诗仅一个完整的句子。首行奠定诗的基调，随后的每一行都依赖（"depends upon"）第一行，中心词"红色手推车"（a red wheel barrow）自然地成为诗的中心意象。"红色"使整个意象鲜活明亮，雨水冲刷后更是焕然一新、熠熠生辉。"手推车"和"雨水"两词分别被分割开来，排列在两行，不仅延长了只有单音节词的第3行和第5行，而且也使第4行的"车"（barrow）和第6行的"水"（water）两个词更加醒目、清晰。而"glazed"和"rain"的两个词的中间韵使手推车听起来圆润饱满。最后两行中的"白色"同前面的"红色"相互衬托，使画面更加生动，而"鸡群"又使本来静止的画面具有动感。"手推车"本是最简单的机械工具，司空见惯，而诗歌这种艺术形式却通过结构美、色彩美和音乐美赋予其全新的意义。

 思考题

1. What in the poem catches the eye?
2. How do the three prepositions help to create a kind of contingent spatial rhyme?
3. What do you think "depends" upon the first line of the poem?

Nantucket

Flowers through the window
lavender① and yellow

changed by white curtains—
Smell of cleanliness—

Sunshine of late afternoon—
On the glass tray

a glass pitcher②, the tumbler③

---

① lavender：淡紫色的。
② pitcher：（有嘴和柄的）大水罐。
③ tumbler：平底酒杯。

turned down, by which

a key is lying—And the
immaculate① white bed

《南塔科特岛》选自《1929—1935 年诗集》(*Poems 1929—1935*)。题目为马萨诸塞州的一个真实地名，同时也是《白鲸》中伊什梅尔出海捕鲸的出发地。可是，诗的正文却呈现出同这一文化传统毫不相干的另一面。在岛上的某个房间，叙述人由外及内观察房间，获得五种意象，分别由五个句子片段、三种颜色、八个物体、两种感觉描绘出。整首诗像一组水彩画，颜色逐渐变淡，由淡紫色和黄色到白色，再到洁白无瑕。白色同"干净"、"无瑕"两种感觉相互交织，和花朵、托盘、水罐、酒杯、钥匙等其他静物，以及诗歌工整的结构和节奏一起，组成一幅洁白无瑕、宁静祥和、怡然自得的图画。

思考题

1. How does Williams break up the expected syntax and semantic patterns?
2. It is said that Williams's use of words tends to strip the detail of any interpretative ambiguity. What kind of room is the speaker in?
3. What can you tell from the change of colors in the poem?

Silence

Under a low sky—
this quiet morning
of red and
yellow leaves—

a bird disturbs
no more than one twig
of the green leaved
peach tree

---
① immaculate：纯洁无瑕的。

美国诗歌选读

 **作品赏析**

《寂静》选自发表于第二次世界大战期间的诗集《楔子》。诗人在诗集前言里指出,诗人创作是把"他认为身边相互关联的词组合到一起,不加会影响词汇确切意义的扭曲,强烈地表现其感知和热情,以便言语揭示出新发现"。作品的艺术性并不在于诗人说了些什么,而在于他创造出什么,感知之强烈,诗就会按照其内在规律验证其真实。《寂静》呈现的是诗人用色彩和构图创造出的凌晨万籁俱寂的画面。天空低垂,满目红叶黄林。静悄悄中,一只小鸟摇动了长着绿叶的桃树枝。寥寥数笔,画意入诗。画面以暖色为背景,红黄相间,然而着意涂抹的则是冷色调的绿色,对比强烈。小树枝被小鸟抖动了,小鸟则若隐若现,不仅使寂静中有了生机,也更显出树林的静谧。诗中有画,静中有动,亦虚亦实,使人如临其境,如睹其景,留下了悠悠不尽之意。或许还有几分不解:红叶黄林显然在写秋天,刘梦得《秋词》云:"山明水净夜来霜,数树深红出浅黄",那么为什么单单这颗桃树绿叶犹存呢?难道诗人用对比鲜明的颜色不仅仅是要给人强烈的视觉冲击,而是要借用绿色的象征意义?是啊,万物有盛衰,颜色随之变,在"战争是当今世界第一也是唯一的大事"(《楔子》前言)的背景下,难道诗人不能发现一点点希望么?

思考题

1. How do you understand the syntax of the first stanza: "Under the low sky of red and yellow leaves" or "this quiet morning of red and yellow leaves"?
2. What is foregrounded in the second stanza: the bird or the twig?
3. How do you interpret the different colors in the poem?

 作品

Landscape with the Fall of Icarus

According to Brueghel[①]
when Icarus fell
it was spring

a farmer was ploughing
his field

Brueghel: "Landscape with the Fall of Icarus"

---

① Pieter Bruegel:16世纪佛兰芒画家,创作了大量反映乡村生活和风景的绘画作品,注重细节刻画。威廉斯的这首诗乃根据布鲁盖尔的同名绘画而作。

the whole pageantry①

of the year was
awake tingling
near

the edge of the sea
concerned
with itself

sweating in the sun
that melted
the wings' wax

unsignificantly
off the coast
there was

a splash quite unnoticed
this was
Icarus drowning

《伊卡洛斯坠海的风景》选自《布鲁盖尔的绘画及其他》。该诗根据 16 世纪佛兰芒画家布鲁盖尔的同名绘画而作,借助希腊神话人物——伊卡洛斯的悲剧表达诗人对死亡和不被承认的惋惜之情。希腊神话里,建筑师和雕刻家代达罗斯(Daidalos)被囚禁后用蜡制成双翼装在自己和儿子伊卡罗斯身上飞走,代达罗斯曾警告儿子不要飞近太阳,但是,伊卡洛斯得意忘形,飞近太阳,蜡翼遇热融化,伊卡洛斯坠海身亡。诗人借助布鲁盖尔之口,声言伊卡洛斯的悲剧发生在万物复苏的春天,加重了悲剧的震撼力。伊卡洛斯和农夫一样辛勤劳作、播种着希望,他努力高飞,不断达到新境界。不幸的是,他没有收获成功就坠落大海。更可悲的是,这悲壮的一幕竟然如石沉大海,无人知觉,无人敬仰!对一位不断追求艺术新高度和社会认可的诗人来说,这惨烈的风景可歌可泣!诗歌语言直白,不用标点,仿佛让人看到伊卡洛斯垂直坠落的情景。而最后一个词用的是带双元音的现在分词,表示"淹死"在进行中,迫使读者不仅看到这悲惨的一幕,而且还要感受死亡的痛苦。

---

① pageantry: 壮观;季节更迭。

思考题

1. Is there any difference between Williams's peom and Brueghel's painting?
2. What is the perspective of the poem?
3. Is Icarus's upward flight in any way significant in the poem?

推荐作品
1. *First Praise*
2. *Portrait of a Lady*
3. *Spring and All*
4. *To Elsie*
5. *Paterson*

参考书目

1. Ahearn, Barry. *William Carlos Williams and Alterity: The Early Poetry.* Cambridge: Cambridge University Press, 1994.
2. Lowney, John. *The American Avant-Garde Tradition: William Carlos Williams, Postmodern Poetry, and the Politics of Cultural Memory.* Lewisburg: Bucknell University Press, 1997.
3. Schmidt, Peter. *William Carlos Williams, the Arts, and Literary Tradition.* Baton Rouge: Louisana State University Press, 1988.
4. Whitaker, Thomas R. *Williams Carlos Williams.* Rev. ed. Twayne's United States Authors Ser. 139. Boston: Twayne, 1989.

第十二单元

Langston Hughes (1902—1967)
兰斯顿·休斯

作者简介

兰斯顿·休斯,生于密苏里州,随外祖母在堪萨斯州生活到十三岁。外祖母的两任丈夫均为激进的废奴主义者。外祖母去世后随母亲到伊利诺伊州同住。在俄亥俄州上高中期间在校办刊物上发表诗作。1921年秋,他进入哥伦比亚大学学习,一年后辍学。其间,他对哈莱姆地区产生浓厚兴趣,迅速成为哈莱姆文学艺术圈的活跃分子,并最终成为哈莱姆文艺复兴的代言人和记录者。其自传《大海》(The Big Sea, 1940)至今仍是研究那个时期的第一手资料。1923年,他作为水手随货船访问了三十余个非洲港口。1925年,他原发表在《危机》(Crisis)杂志上的《疲惫的布鲁斯》("The Weary Blues")一诗获得《机会》(Opportunity)杂志举办的文学竞赛诗歌类一等奖。1926年,休斯的第一本诗集以《疲惫的布鲁斯》为名出版,发表《黑人艺术家与种族之大山》一文,主张黑人艺术家增加民族自豪感,保持艺术独立性,奠定了他在哈莱姆文艺复兴运动中的主导地位。同年,他获得白人富婆梅森(Charlotte Osgood Mason)的资助,进入宾夕法尼亚州的林肯大学学习。1927年,休斯发表第二部诗集《好衣服拿给犹太人》(Fine Clothes to the Jew),但未获成功。在梅森的说服下,休斯创作了长篇小说《并非无笑》(Not Without Laughter, 1930)。1930年两人发生争执,资助关系终止,对休斯打击很大。之后,休斯在思想上转向左翼,开始在《新大众》(New Masses)杂志发表诗作,于1932年访问苏联,1933年访问上海。1934年发表的短篇小说集《白人的方式》(The Ways of White Folks)充满了对种族关系的悲观失望情绪。随后几年,休斯转向戏剧创作。1942年,休斯开始为美国黑人办的报纸《芝加哥卫士》(Chicago Defender)撰写专栏。1943年,幽默的贫民人物辛普尔(Jesse B. Semple 或 Simple)出现在这个专栏里,休斯借此讨论严肃的种族问题。因为辛普尔幽默可爱,专栏大获成功,故事连载了

美国诗歌选读

20年。1947年,休斯用为百老汇音乐剧写歌词挣的钱实现了他在哈莱姆购房的梦想。1951年,他发表了著名的诗集《延迟的梦之蒙太奇》(*Montage of a Dream Deferred*),借鉴当时新出现的快节奏爵士乐的不和谐音表现北方城市黑人生活不断蔓延的绝望感,开辟出诗歌创作的新领地。其后,他又发表了二十余部作品,其中包括1956年发表的根据他在苏联的经历创作的第二部自传《我漫游,我思考》(*I Wonder as I Wander*)和1962年发表的植根于黑人文化和音乐的长诗《问你妈妈》(*Ask Your Mama*)。休斯将美国黑人音乐明快的节奏运用到诗歌中,努力表现黑人,尤其是下层黑人的活力,被誉为"哈莱姆桂冠诗人"、"黑人民族桂冠诗人"。

The Weary Blues①

Droning a drowsy syncopated② tune,
Rocking back and forth to a mellow croon,
    I heard a Negro play.③
Down on Lenox Avenue④ the other night
By the pale dull pallor of an old gas light
    He did a lazy sway...
    He did a lazy sway...
To the tune o' those Weary Blues.
With his ebony hands on each ivory key⑤

---

① blues:布鲁斯(又译蓝调)音乐,原为美国南方黑人民间的一种即兴演唱形式,常表现悲伤的主题(美国人认为蓝色为忧郁、悲哀的颜色),速度舒缓,节拍常为四二拍、四四拍,旋律多含切分节奏,常于大调音阶上降半音,而且带有滑音、颤音,使歌唱听起来哀声怨语,悲恸凄楚。布鲁斯演唱风格自由,生活气息浓厚,假声、呻吟、哭泣、嘟囔、呼喊都可以用来渲染表达情绪,烘托气氛。布鲁斯的发展经历了乡村布鲁斯、古典布鲁斯和城市布鲁斯三个阶段。乡村布鲁斯采用上升或下降的自然滑音,一般三句构成一段,没有固定的段数,可以即兴演唱很多段,有时采用班卓琴和吉他进行伴奏。古典布鲁斯,常有作曲者参与,不完全靠歌手即兴演唱,曲式更加规整,经常有爵士乐队伴奏。城市布鲁斯主要反映城市生活的感受,结构固定,四四拍,12小节分成三句,每4小节为一句,第一、二句重复。伴奏可能是乐队,或者是钢琴,伴奏和声更加规范。
② syncopated:被切分的;syncopation:切分音。
③ 诗的前三行为一个句子,从表面上看,出现了语法上的"无依着"现象,即前两行分词短语的逻辑主语和第三行句子主语不一致。这里,诗人通过这一结构表现布鲁斯音乐使歌手(分词短语的逻辑主语)和听众(句子主语)合二为一的效果,暗示布鲁斯音乐表达的不仅仅是个人情感,而是黑人的民族情感。
④ Lenox Avenue:纽约市哈莱姆区的一条主要街道。
⑤ With his ebony hands on each ivory key:注意该行中黑(ebony hands)白(ivory key)之间的关系,以及黑人乐手用白人乐器创造出自己的艺术形式的寓意。歌手低沉的歌声表现了"黑人的灵魂"(a black man's soul),布鲁斯帮助黑人界定身份。乌黑的手敲击在乳白色的琴键上,使产生于西方文化的钢琴倾诉着黑人的悲伤,白人的音乐形式被黑人文化改变。

He made that poor piano moan with melody.
　　　　O Blues!
Swaying to and fro on his rickety stool
He played that sad raggy① tune like a musical fool.
　　　　Sweet Blues!
Coming from a black man's soul.
　　　　O Blues!
In a deep song voice with a melancholy tone
I heard that Negro sing, that old piano moan—
　　　　"Ain't got nobody in all this world,
　　　　Ain't got nobody but ma self.
　　　　I's gwine to quit ma frownin'
　　　　And put ma troubles on the shelf."②
Thump, thump, thump, went his foot on the floor.
He played a few chords then he sang some more—
　　　　"I got the Weary Blues
　　　　And I can't be satisfied.
　　　　Got the Weary Blues
　　　　And can't be satisfied—
　　　　I ain't happy no mo'
　　　　And I wish that I had died."
And far into the night he crooned that tune.
The stars went out and so did the moon.
The singer stopped playing and went to bed
While the Weary Blues echoed through his head.
He slept like a rock or a man that's dead.

《疲惫的布鲁斯》发表于1923年。休斯在自传《大海》里说这首诗包含着他幼年在堪萨斯州最早听到的布鲁斯歌曲。诗歌用第一人称描述了一天夜晚在哈莱姆街道上听布鲁斯歌手演唱的情景，通过选词、重复句子、引用布鲁斯歌词表达悲哀之情和布鲁斯歌曲舒缓的节奏，从而使读者感受到布鲁斯歌手的情绪。无名歌手扭动身躯，手弹钢琴，脚拍地板，用"懒洋洋的切分调"低沉哀婉地唱出自己的希望、孤独与失望。手脚上的活力同低沉的音调

---

① raggy：相当于ragged，一般指衣衫褴褛的。这里指乐声狂躁刺耳。
② 没有受过正规教育的美国黑人使用的英语，有不符合语法规范的地方，如用双重否定表示否定"Ain't got nobody",ain't为助动词的否定式形式;ma: my; "I's gwine to": I'm going to; frownin': 省音现象在美国黑人英语中比较常见。

美国诗歌选读

形成反差,揭示歌手内心的冲突。诗歌引用了两段布鲁斯歌词,第一段为 8 小节,表现的歌手是决心忘却烦恼,面对生活的愿望。但是,相对第二段 12 小节,8 小节显得短小,暗示实现这种愿望的渺茫,从而深化了歌手的孤独。第二段通过两句重复进一步强化歌手的疲惫、失落和绝望。忧伤的布鲁斯似乎成了歌手拥有的一切,既是他表达"黑人的灵魂"的途径,也是他展示自己生命活力的舞台。他用布鲁斯宣泄生活在白人主宰的社会里的孤独,让白人的钢琴发出黑人的呐喊。他通宵达旦地演唱,直到精疲力竭,内心的感受得到完全的释放,然后安然入睡。布鲁斯因此界定了他的身份,显然也打动了作为诗歌叙述人的听众,使他用另一种艺术形式表现出歌手孤独、疲惫的感情,以及歌手通过布鲁斯音乐拒绝接受现状,力图展示活力,维护尊严的复杂心理。布鲁斯因此成为联系歌手和听众(诗人)的纽带。

 思考题

1. What figure of speech is used in the first line, and what effect does it have?
2. How does the poet create a "rocking" or "swaying" effect?
3. How does the poem express pride in African-American forms of expression?

Let America be America again

Let America be America again.
Let it be the dream it used to be.
Let it be the pioneer on the plain
Seeking a home where he himself is free.

(America never was America to me.)

Let America be the dream the dreamers dreamed—
Let it be that great strong land of love
Where never kings connive nor tyrants scheme①
That any man be crushed by one above.

---

① connive:共谋。scheme:搞阴谋。

(It never was America to me.)

O, let my land be a land where Liberty
Is crowned with no false patriotic wreath①,
But opportunity is real, and life is free,
Equality is in the air we breathe.

(There's never been equality for me,
Nor freedom in this "homeland of the free.")

Say, who are you that mumbles② in the dark?
And who are you that draws your veil across the stars?

I am the poor white, fooled and pushed apart,
I am the Negro bearing slavery's scars.
I am the red man driven from the land,
I am the immigrant clutching the hope I seek—
And finding only the same old stupid plan
Of dog eat dog, of mighty crush the weak.

I am the young man, full of strength and hope,
Tangled in that ancient endless chain
Of profit, power, gain, of grab the land!
Of grab the gold! Of grab the ways of satisfying need!
Of work the men! Of take the pay!
Of owning everything for one's own greed!
I am the farmer, bondsman to the soil.
I am the worker sold to the machine.
I am the Negro, servant to you all.
I am the people, humble, hungry, mean—
Hungry yet today despite the dream.
Beaten yet today—O, Pioneers!
I am the man who never got ahead,
The poorest worker bartered through the years.

---

① wreath：花环。
② mumble：嘟哝。

美国诗歌选读

Yet I'm the one who dreamt our basic dream
In that Old World while still a serf of kings,
Who dreamt a dream so strong, so brave, so true,
That even yet its mighty daring sings
In every brick and stone, in every furrow turned
That's made America the land it has become.
O, I'm the man who sailed those early seas
In search of what I meant to be my home—
For I'm the one who left dark Ireland's shore,
And Poland's plain, and England's grassy lea①,

And torn from Black Africa's strand I came
To build a "homeland of the free."

The free?

Who said the free? Not me?
Surely not me? The millions on relief today?
The millions shot down when we strike?
The millions who have nothing for our pay?
For all the dreams we've dreamed
And all the songs we've sung
And all the hopes we've held
And all the flags we've hung,
The millions who have nothing for our pay—
Except the dream that's almost dead today.

O, let America be America again—
The land that never has been yet—
And yet must be—the land where every man is free.
The land that's mine—the poor man's, Indian's, Negro's, ME—
Who made America,
Whose sweat and blood, whose faith and pain,
Whose hand at the foundry, whose plow in the rain,
Must bring back our mighty dream again.

---

① lea: ley, 草地，牧地。

Sure, call me any ugly name you choose—
The steel of freedom does not stain.
From those who live like leeches on the people's lives,
We must take back our land again,
America!

O, yes,
I say it plain,
America never was America to me,
And yet I swear this oath—
America will be!

Out of the rack and ruin① of our gangster death,
The rape and rot of graft②, and stealth, and lies,
We, the people, must redeem
The land, the mines, the plants, the rivers.
The mountains and the endless plain—
All, all the stretch of these great green states—
And make America again!

《让美国再次成为美国》发表于1938年，针对当时美国经济萧条，社会矛盾突出，美国标榜的自由、平等被肆意践踏等现象，诗人呼吁美国兑现美国梦。事实上，休斯一直为黑人实现以自由、平等为主要内容的美国梦而摇旗呐喊。他首先认为自己是美国人（"I, too, am America"），也有权要求得到美国承诺过的那些"不可剥夺的权力"，在《自由之犁》（*Freedom's Plow*）里，他十分肯定地宣称"美国是个梦"，强调这个"共同培育"出的梦属于"所有建设者"。在他看来，美国延缓了"黑肤色兄弟"的美国梦，并警告说延迟的梦（dream deferred）会爆炸。本诗通过现实中丑陋阴暗的美国与理想中平等自由的美国的对比，不仅抨击了种种背离美国梦的卑鄙行径，而且满怀信心地期待着真正的自由和博爱的到来。因此，诗歌超越了愤怒，在绝望中表现出希望：虽然美国梦受到破坏，却仍然存在并终将实现。更为重要的是，休斯并非仅仅为本民族实现美国梦而呼吁，而是把穷苦白人、印第安人、移民等所有相信并追求美国梦的工农大众都包括在内，强调自由、民主、博爱属于所有人，建设一个没有虚伪、压迫、饥饿和歧视的美国是所有美国人的梦想。诗歌运用了大量的排比，感情浓烈，气势磅礴。

---

① rack and ruin：破坏。
② graft：贪污。

美国诗歌选读

思考题

1. Why does the speaker believe America is his land? Find out his justification in the poem.
2. In this poem of 1938, Hughes says America never was, has never been, but will be America, and in another poem published in 1951, he asks "What happens to a dream deferred?" and suggests that it may "explode". Can you see any change in his belief in the American Dream?
3. The American society has changed a great deal since Hughes wrote the poem. Do you think the poem is still of contemporary value?

Madam and the Phone Bill

You say I O.K.ed
LONG DISTANCE?
O.K.ed it when?
My goodness, Central,
That was *then*!

I'm mad and disgusted
With that Negro now.
I don't pay no REVERSED
CHARGES① nohow.

You say, I will pay it—
Else you'll take out my phone?
You better let
My phone alone.

I didn't ask him

---

① reversed charges: 由受话方支付的电话费。

To telephone me.
Roscoe knows darn① well
LONG DISTANCE
Ain't free.

If I ever catch him,
Lawd, have pity!
Calling me up
From Kansas City

Just to say he loves me!
I knowed that was so.
Why didn't he tell me some'n
I don't know?

For instance, what can
Them other girls do
That Alberta K. Johnson
Can't do—*and more, too?*

What's that, Central?
You say you don't care
Nothing about my
Private affair?

Well, even less about your
PHONE BILL does I care!

Un-humm-m!... Yes!
You say I gave my O.K.?
Well, that O.K. you may keep—

But I *sure* ain't gonna pay!

---

① darn：damn 的委婉语。

美国 诗歌选读

《女士与电话单》通过一位黑人女子同话务员的对话刻画了一个质朴可爱、坚强倔强、性格鲜明的黑人女子形象，同时也揭示出下层黑人生活的艰辛。诗歌表层表现的是黑人女子拒付恋人（或丈夫）打的由受话方付费的长途电话费，并因此同话务员产生冲突。在这个层面上，一位淳朴但称不上宽厚，高傲甚至带几分蛮横的黑人女子形象跃然纸上。然而，诗歌深层暗含的则是种族和性别冲突。黑人男子 Roscoe 无钱支付打给恋人或妻子的长途电话费的事实，揭示了在种族主义压迫下的下层黑人男子经济上的无能。不仅如此，他还不顾后果地把付费的负担转嫁给自己的心上人，让女人为他付账，其传统意义上的（男）人（man）身份丧失殆尽。黑人女子生活则更加艰辛，她们不但要承受种族压迫，而且还要承受男人外出谋生给她们留下的孤独，承担男人随时转嫁的经济的、精神的和身体的剥削。本诗最健康的地方是，没有把女子当作双重压迫的无助牺牲品来描写。相反，诗中的女子更像是一位同官僚机构和男权世界抗争的女勇士，勇敢地在一个男人缺席的孤独世界里捍卫着自己的权利、尊严和财产（"You better let/My phone alone"），毫不隐讳地宣布不为他们买单（"I sure ain't gonna pay!"），她拒付的不仅仅是电话费，"pay" 可以理解为多种意义上的付出，包括拒绝资助支持男人剥削女人的官僚机构。她态度明朗，声音洪亮，毋庸置疑，显示出 "女士"（"madam"）的尊严与权威。在其震慑之下，"中心"（"Central"）交换台的话务员最终茫然失语。诗歌于诙谐幽默中揭示严肃的问题。

思考题

1. How is Alberta K. Johnson different from other female characters in American literature?

2. It has been argued that Roscoe maintains romantic relationships with "other girls". Do you find the argument justified?

3. This poem is written in the form of a black woman's voice on the phone. Is the form important to the theme?

推荐作品

1. *The Negro Speaks of Rivers*
2. *Dreams*
3. *Dream Variations*
4. *I, Too*
5. *As I Grew Older*
6. *Lynching Song*
7. *Freedom's Plow*
8. *What happens to a dream deferred?*

参考书目

1. Emanuel, James A. *Langston Hughes.* New York: Twayne Publishers, 1997.
2. Miller, R. Baxter. *The Art and Language of Langston Hughes.* Lexington: UP of Kentucky, 1989.
3. Tracy, Steven C. *Langston Hughes and the Blues.* Urbana: U of Illinois P, 1988.

第十三单元

E. E. Cummings (1894—1962)
E. E. 肯明斯

作者简介

E. E. 肯明斯生于马萨诸塞州剑桥市,其父曾任哈佛大学教授。肯明斯自幼喜爱绘画和文学,就读哈佛大学期间推崇现代艺术,开始现代主义诗歌创作。第一次世界大战期间,他在法国救护车队当志愿者,曾被错误地关押几个月,后来他用超现实主义手法把这段经历写进《巨大的房间》(*The Enormous Room*, 1922)一书,痛斥独裁主义。战后他在巴黎学习绘画,同时从事诗歌创作。他的第一部诗集《郁金香与烟囱》(*Tulips and Chimneys*, 1923)包括爱情诗、讽刺诗和自然诗,受格特鲁德·斯泰因、艾米·洛威尔等先锋派的影响,在句法、词性、形式等方面别出心裁,形成自己的特色。以后陆续发表《诗四十一首》(*XLI Poems*, 1925)、《万岁》(*ViVa*, 1931)、《不谢》(*No Thanks*, 1935)、《诗九十五首》(*95 Poems*, 1958)等十余部诗集,都以形式实验和反对极端科学主义为特征。其诗作形式常参差不齐,词语任意分裂,标点符号违反常规,一般不用大写(包括 i 和 e. e. cummings),其目的是用文字游戏构建的视觉效果抗争科技产品对人们视觉造成的冲击。但是,形式的怪异掩盖不住肯明斯敏锐的艺术洞察力和卓越的抒情诗才。他的爱情诗绸缪凄婉,韵味十足;他的自然诗朴实纯真,如春风拂面。同时,他善于讥讽现实生活中的阴暗面,常以漫画式的笔调嘲讽和鞭挞现代资本主义社会中充满尔虞我诈的竞争和人与人之间冷漠的关系。总之,肯明斯以极为广泛的题材,把浪漫的生活态度和前锋派的表现形式融为一体。

Thy fingers make early flowers of

Thy fingers make early flowers of
all things.
thy hair mostly the hours love:
a smoothness which
sings, saying
(though love be a day)
do not fear, we will go amaying①.

thy whitest feet crisply are straying.
Always
thy moist eyes are at kisses playing,
whose strangeness much
says; singing
(though love be a day)
for which girl art thou flowers bringing?

To be thy lips is a sweet thing
and small.
Death, Thee i call rich beyond wishing
if this thou catch,
else missing.
(though love be a day
and life be nothing, it shall not stop kissing).

《你的妙手让万物生花》是诗集《郁金香与烟囱》里的一首诗（后来，Gwyneth Walker 为这首诗谱曲，可查 www.gwynethwalker.com）。肯明斯强调自然的感觉和感情，厌恶冷冰冰的规则。这首歌词里，爱情冲破规则的樊篱达到永恒。无论生命或者爱情多么短暂（"though love be a day and life be nothing"），恋爱中的美丽长存。在叙述人眼里，他的恋人完美无缺，她

---

① amaying: 应该是 amazing。为了同下阙 straying, playing 押韵作了变动。

美国诗歌选读

的手指、头发、双脚、双眼和双唇，一切都恰到好处，而且还会永远如此（"Always"一词是全诗中少数几个大写的单词之一。）不仅如此，恋人还温柔地打消了他对生命短暂的顾虑，主动引导他全心投入接吻，使叙述人终于领悟到，只要能饱尝恋人的双唇，即使死了也极其富有。歌词反复赞美恋人身体的不同部位，各段落连贯而流畅，每段第三行用扬扬格，第二、四、五行用普通韵律，结构整齐，节奏明快。

思考题

1. What does "it" in the last line refer to, love, life, or Death, or something else?
2. What is the tone of the poem?
3. Is there any fusion between the physical reality and emotional existence in the poem?

Your little voice Over the wires came leaping

your little voice
                  Over the wires came leaping
and i felt suddenly
dizzy
    With the jostling① and shouting of merry flowers
wee② skipping high-heeled flames
courtesied③ before my eyes
              or twinkling over to my side
Looked up
with impertinently④ exquisite faces
floating hands were laid upon me
I was whirled and tossed into delicious dancing
up
  Up

---

① jostle：推撞。
② wee：极小的，很少的。
③ courtesy：n. 礼貌，殷勤。这里用作动词，同其他动词一起构成对声音拟人，似乎说话的人从声音中走出。
④ impertinently：傲慢地。

     with the pale important
        stars and the Humorous
           moon
    dear girl
    How i was crazy how i cried when i heard
        over time
  and tide① and death
  leaping
  Sweetly
    your voice

  《你的声音随着电波跳跃而至》是一首爱情诗,乍看起来描绘的是叙述人接到恋人电话时的幸福体验,那声音如山花烂漫,似火焰跳跃,银铃般清脆,令他头晕目眩,飘飘欲仙。连用的两个"up"(而且第二个以大写字母开头)表示叙述人的幸福登峰造极、黯星淡月。然而,电话里的声音标志主体的不在场,有一种缺失感。全诗使用过去时,幸福到"疯癫"("crazy")的极致后,突然在一行几乎令人喘不过气的诗行里加入"哭泣"("cried"),随即又指出所描绘的声音是"历经岁月和死亡"而来,反差之大让人感觉好像从巅峰跌落到深渊。显然,他是对已经失去的声音和爱情做甜蜜而痛苦的回忆。诗歌因此蕴涵凄迷起来,那令人心醉令人发狂的声音哪里去了?"死亡"的是肉体还是感情?声音背后的故事幽渺莫测。虽然甘甜的声音已经随那段岁月一去不复返,但是每当它出现在幻觉或梦境时,还是让叙述人百感交集,既为记忆里那热烈的声音和鲜活的面孔激动不已,也为现实中人去声消而痛哭流涕。爱之深,失去爱才痛之切。诗歌在现实的电话线与温馨浪漫的假象中开头,于无形的岁月、冷冰冰的死亡和凄婉哀楚的幻觉中结束,余味无穷。

思考题

1. How is "voice" made alive in the poem?
2. What role does the capitalization of words play in the poem?
3. The poem begins with "voice" coming over "wires" and ends with voice coming over "time and tide and death". Is it the same voice the speaker is talking about?

---

① time and tide:岁月。

美国 诗歌 选读

My sweet old etcetera

my sweet old etcetera
aunt lucy during the recent

war could and what
is more did tell you just
what everybody was fighting

for,
my sister

isabel created hundreds
(and
hundreds) of socks not to
mention shirts fleaproof earwarmers

etcetera wristers etcetera, my

mother hoped that

i would die etcetera
bravely of course my father used
to become hoarse talking about how it was
a privilege and if only he
could meanwhile my

self etcetera lay quietly
in the deep mud et

cetera
(dreaming,
et

cetera, of
Your smile
eyes knees and of your Etcetera)

《我亲爱的老什么什么》是一首反战诗。叙述人的家人（代表传统社会观念）认为战死沙场是一种殊荣，用勇气、忠诚等观念动员叙述人上前线，动之以情，晓之以理，父亲不惜声嘶力竭，姐姐为其缝衣备袜。然而，身处前线的叙述人卧倒在深泥潭里，感到被遗弃、被愚弄，只能靠幻想某个姑娘的音容笑貌和身体部位忘却战场的残酷，理想主义和现实之间形成鲜明的对比。诗中"什么什么"（"etcetera"）以不同的形式出现八次，其语法性质逐渐改变。第一次出现起强调形容词"sweet old"作用；第二、三次连续出现强调姐姐为战士考虑之细致，准备物品之齐全；再次出现时修饰动词（"I would die etcetera / bravely"）；第七次出现时被分割为两部分，一方面可以表示叙述人因绝望而气弱，奄奄一息，同时也把诗的最后两行里叙述人看重的东西同前文那些虚无的价值和残酷的现实隔开，进一步强化了括号内内容有别于其他部分；最后一次出现时竟然变成以大写字母开头的名词，代替的显然是一个不雅的词，其突出位置和形式是叙述人对传统观念和战争本身的抗议。诗歌对比强烈，讽刺调侃有度。

思考题

1. What is the irony in the family members' actions?
2. Why does the speaker's sister prepare "fleaproof earwarmers" and "wristers" for him?
3. Words like "Aunt Lucy", "Isabel" and "I", which are normally capitalized, are not capitalized, while "Your smile" and "your Etcetera" are. What do you think the poet is trying to convey with the arrangement?

Anyone lived in a pretty how town

anyone lived in a pretty how town
(with up so floating many bells down)
spring summer autumn winter
he sang his didn't he danced his did.

美国诗歌选读

Women and men (both little and small)
cared for anyone not at all
they sowed their isn't they reaped their same
sun moon stars rain

children guessed (but only a few
and down they forgot as up they grew
autumn winter spring summer)
that noone① loved him more by more

when by now and tree by leaf
she laughed his joy she cried his grief
bird by snow and stir by still
anyone's any was all to her

someones married their everyones
laughed their cryings and did their dance
(sleep wake hope and then) they
said their nevers they slept their dream

stars rain sun moon
(and only the snow can begin to explain
how children are apt to forget to remember
with up so floating many bells down)

one day anyone died i guess
(and noone stooped to kiss his face)
busy folk buried them side by side
little by little and was by was

all by all and deep by deep
and more by more they dream their sleep
noone and anyone earth by april
wish by spirit and if by yes.

---

① noone：把 no one 写在一起。

Women and men (both dong and ding①)
summer autumn winter spring
reaped their sowing and went their came
sun moon stars rain

《住在漂亮那么样镇的任何人》在语言使用方面堪称肯明斯的代表作。诗歌打破词类和句法的常规用法，使用迭句和句型重复，对比小人物"anyone, noone"和大人物"someones, everyones"不同的人生，讽刺了代表现代资本主义社会的"the pretty how town"大人物的空虚与冷漠。诗第一、四、七、八阕描述小人物的生活方式。虽然受大人物的蔑视，他们富有爱心，彼此理解相互欣赏（"she laughed his joy she cried his grief"），活得朴实自然，充实快乐（"he sang his didn't he danced his did"），死得安然（"little by little and was by was"），虽死犹生（"and more by more they dream their sleep"）。与之对照，第二、五、九阕则描绘了大人物的另一种生活方式。他们生活单调呆板（"reaped their same"，"went their came"，机械地 "dong and ding"）却盛气凌人（"cared for anyone not at all"），好高骛远却好逸恶劳（"they/said their nevers they slept their dream"），过着行尸走肉般的生活（"said their nevers they slept their dream"）。夹在中间的第三、六两阕描述的是介于小人物和大人物之间的孩子，少数孩子以其童真读懂小人物的爱心，但是随着年龄的增长，他们也被大人物的价值观同化，忘却了小人物的善良（"down they forgot as up they grew."）。诗歌口气戏谑，节奏简单，照应小人物的生活。

思考题

1. The poet breaks conventions in the use of words, particularly in their parts of speech. Do you find these words confusing in their meaning?

2. The order of the four seasons and the natural phenomena of the "sun moon stars rain" are inverted in different ways with the discription of different people. What do you think the poet tries to convey in the arrangement?

3. The past tense is used in most stanzas of the poem. Why do you think the poet switches to the present tense when describing the afterlife of "noone and anyone"?

---

① dong and ding: 铃声的象声词。

美国诗歌选读

推荐作品

1. *Buffalo Bill's*
2. *O sweet spontaneous*
3. *space being (don't forget to remember) Curved*
4. *since feeling is first*

参考书目

1. Dendinger, Lloyd N., ed. *E. E. Cummings: The Critical Reception*. New York: Burt Franklin, 1981.
2. Kidder, Rushworth M. *E. E. Cummings: An Introduction to the Poetry*. New York: Columbia University Press, 1979.
3. Marks, Barry A. *E.E. Cummings*. Twayne's United States Authors Series No. 46. Boston: Twayne, 1997.

第十四单元

Elizabeth Bishop (1911—1979)
伊丽莎白·毕晓普

作者简介

著名女诗人,近年来名声鹊起,越来越多的人研读她的诗。她的童年充满苦难:她8个月大时父亲因病去世,5岁时母亲因精神问题永久住院。毕晓普起初与外公、外婆住在新斯科舍的格瑞特村。在祖父母家住过一段,后由于身体原因,搬到姨妈家居住。在瓦莎女子学院读书时,毕晓普见到玛瑞安·穆尔。这次会面是她人生的转折点。在穆尔的鼓励下,毕晓普放弃医学,成了一名诗人。1934年她从瓦莎女子学院毕业后,毕晓普经常旅行,曾在很多地方居住,这包括纽约市、佛罗里达的基韦斯特、华盛顿、西雅图、旧金山、波士顿以及欧洲。1951年一个旅游奖学金让她踏上了巴西。她非常喜欢巴西,在那里居住了16年。对她来说,旅行和写作是解脱痛苦的最好方式。在旅行过程中,毕晓普与许多人保持通信联系。后来这些信件结集出版,称作《一种艺术》(One Art: The Selected Letters of Elizabeth Bishop, 1994)。除了写作,毕晓普在哈佛大学教了七年的写作课,并且担任国会图书馆的诗歌顾问。

毕晓普的诗从一开始就以旅居国外和各地旅行为核心。这从她的诗集的名字即可看出,先后发表诗集《北方与南方》(North and South, 1946)、《寒冷的春天》(A Cold Spring, 1955)、《旅行的问题》(Questions of Travel, 1965)、《诗歌全集》(The Complete Poems, 1969)、《地理之三》(Geography III, 1976)。自1945年起,她几乎年年获奖,例如1956年获普利策奖,1970年获国家图书奖,1977年获全国图书批评家奖。她的小说《在村庄里》(In the Village)获《党派评论》(Partisan Review)小说奖。她还是唯一获得了纽斯达特国际文学奖(the Nenustadt International Prize for Literature)的美国作家。

毕晓普创作诗歌非常严谨,常常将所写的诗钉在墙上,思考措辞。因此虽然她的创作生涯长达五十多年,但她总共才写了一百多首诗。她曾对她的

美国 诗歌选读

学生说:"用字典,这比评论家好得多。"她的诗一旦写成,就不再修改,与她的好友洛厄尔对诗的不断修正形成鲜明对比。毕晓普的诗多描写自然风景和动物,以类似植物学家、地理学家和人类学家的好奇,对熟悉的事物进行细致入微的客观描述,将其陌生化,变得有些不真实,从而取得意味深长的寓言般效果。

The Fish

I caught a tremendous fish
and held him beside the boat
half out of water, with my hook
fast in a corner of his mouth.
He didn't fight.
He hadn't fought at all.
He hung a grunting weight,
battered and venerable①
and homely. Here and there
his brown skin hung in strips
like ancient wallpaper,
and its pattern of darker brown
was like wallpaper:
shapes like full-blown roses
stained and lost through age.
He was speckled with barnacles,
fine rosettes of lime,
and infested
with tiny white sea-lice,
and underneath two or three
rags of green weed hung down.
While his gills were breathing in
the terrible oxygen

---

① venerable:由于上了岁数,值得尊敬。

—the frightening gills,
fresh and crisp with blood,
that can cut so badly—
I thought of the coarse white flesh
packed in like feathers,
the big bones and the little bones,
the dramatic reds and blacks
of his shiny entrails①,
and the pink swim-bladder②
like a big peony.
I looked into his eyes
which were far larger than mine
but shallower, and yellowed,
the irises backed and packed
with tarnished tinfoil
seen through the lenses
of old scratched isinglass③.
They shifted a little, but not
to return my stare.
—It was more like the tipping
of an object toward the light.
I admired his sullen face,
the mechanism of his jaw,
and then I saw
that from his lower lip
—if you could call it a lip—
grim, wet, and weaponlike,
hung five old pieces of fish-line,
or four and a wire leader
with the swivel still attached,
with all their five big hooks
grown firmly in his mouth.
A green line, frayed at the end
where he broke it, two heavier lines,

---

① entrails：内部器官。
② bladder：鱼漂。
③ isinglass：在普通玻璃出现之前用于镶窗户。

and a fine black thread
still crimped from the strain and snap
when it broke and he got away.
Like medals with their ribbons
frayed and wavering,
a five-haired beard of wisdom
trailing from his aching jaw.
I stared and stared
and victory filled up
the little rented boat,
from the pool of bilge①
where oil had spread a rainbow
around the rusted engine
to the bailer rusted orange,
the sun-cracked thwarts②,
the oarlocks on their strings,
the gunnels③—until everything
was rainbow, rainbow, rainbow!
And I let the fish go.

毕晓普热爱大自然和动物。她详细地描写她见到的景物和户外经历。在一封给穆尔的信中,毕晓普讲述了写《鱼》这首诗的缘由:"前天我意外地钓到一条鹦嘴鱼。它们是可爱的鱼——它们是彩虹色的,每个鳞片都有银边,一张公牛似的嘴巴像绿松石;眼睛很大,带有野性,眼球也是青绿色的——他们的样子很滑稽。"

《鱼》这首诗揭示了诗人关于生存问题的观点:人生就和鱼的一生一样,充满坎坷、险阻,但是我们应该和鱼一样不屈不挠,与命运抗争。诗中的鱼仿佛是挂满勋章的英勇形象。毕晓普曾提到鱼"如果不像罗伯特·弗罗斯特,可能像欧内斯特·海明威!我留下了最后一行,因此它不是这俩人"。鱼的勋章即是它嘴上的五个鱼钩。它们表现了鱼的坚毅、勇敢,与死亡的抗争。这些鱼钩见证了历史,即这条鱼的一生。如今鱼已经上了岁数,离死不远了。它坦然地面对死亡,不再有挣扎。有评论家认为鱼"集徽章似的外表、浓缩的多数和历史于一身。但它仍旧是一个矛盾体,回到它从未完全离开过的变迁中。"

诗人用海明威式的简洁语言描述鱼。诗句的主语和谓语没有修饰词。叙述人的视角不是全能的,而是有局限的、单向的:I caught, I thought, I looked, I stared and I stared。但是

---

① bilge:船底部的死水。
② thwarts:小船上的座。
③ gunnels:船舷。

即使是这种简洁的虚张声势也有一种神秘氛围。诗人用了一连串出人意料的明喻。这些明喻暗示了一个家庭繁荣衰败的完整循环,由此我们对自然中的相似模式有了一定的认识(Full-blown roses, rosettes, and the confusion as to whether it is the wallpaper shapes or the full-blown roses that are "stained and lost through age.")。我们感受到了历史的沧桑,时间的无情。诗中对鱼眼睛的描写也使人深切地感受到了这种沧桑感 (I looked into his eyes/ which were far larger than mine/ but shallower, and yellowed,/ the irises backed and packed/ with tarnished tinfoil/ seen through the lenses/ of old scratched isinglass.)。对毕晓普来说,出水的鱼是静态的自然。它的美丽和脆弱属于时间。诗人"stared and stared",即使鱼没有回视她。她的想象将"pool of bilge/ where oil had spread a rainbow"转变为欣喜若狂的彩虹。

在这首诗中,毕晓普陌生化的手法得到充分展现。诗人细致入微地描写鱼的皮肤、眼睛、下颚、伤口甚至它身上的海草和寄生物、渔线,使一条普通的鱼变得很陌生。在诗的结尾处是一个令人刻骨铭心的升华:诗人的描写渐渐扩大到小船、船上的积水、水上的油彩。这时她戛然而止"当一切都成为/彩虹,彩虹,彩虹!/我把鱼放走了。"当读到这里,真的感觉到物质世界的丰富和神圣在眼前升起、发出虹彩,迫使你把你那卑微的占有欲给"放走了"。

思考题

1. Notice the rhythm of the sentence structure. Is it conversational, or does it have a regular, metrical rhythm?
2. Picture the fish as the speaker describes it. What emotional effect does this description have on you?
3. Why doesn't the fish fight for his survival this time?
4. Whose victory fills up the boat?
5. What effects does the ending have on the readers?

Sestina[①]

September rain falls on the house.
In the failing light, the old grandmother

[①] sestina: 六节诗,一种由六节六行诗以及结尾的一节三行诗构成的诗体。每节六行诗的最后一个词会出现在下面一节,但次序不同。但此诗并不完全符合规律。

sits in the kitchen with the child
beside the Little Marvel Stove,
reading the jokes from the almanc①,
laughing and talking to hide her tears.

She thinks that her equinoctial② tears
and the rain that beats on the roof of the house
were both foretold by the almanac,
but only known to a grandmother.
The iron kettle sings on the stove.
She cuts some bread and says to the child,

It's time for tea now; but the child
is watching the teakettle's small hard tears
dance like mad on the hot black stove,
the way the rain must dance on the house.
Tidying up, the old grandmother
hangs up the clever almanac
on its string. Birdlike, the almanac
hovers half open above the child,
hovers above the old grandmother
and her teacups full of dark brown tears.
She shivers and says she thinks the house
feels chilly, and puts more wood in the stove.

It was to be, says the Marvel Stove.
I know what I know, says the almanac.
With crayons the child draws a rigid house
and a winding pathway. Then the child
puts in a man with buttons like tears
and shows it proudly to the grandmother.

But secretly, while the grandmother
busies herself about the stove,

---

① almanac: 历书, 年历, 天文历。
② equinoctial: 春分或秋分的。

the little moons fall down like tears
from between the pages of the almanac
into the flower bed the child
has carefully placed in the front of the house.

Time to plant tears, says the almanac.
The grandmother sings to the marvellous stove
and the child draws another inscrutable① house.

作品赏析

毕晓普的诗以不露声色而闻名,她对自白派诗人描写自身的痛苦经历很反感。但是,她的悲惨童年不可能不留下痕迹。特别是母亲的长期不在场对她的心理和情感产生了巨大的影响。毕晓普曾写了几首诗,讲述自己的祖母以及在新斯科舍的格瑞特村的生活。《六节诗》是其中的一首。这是一首自传体诗,是成年诗人对自己童年的回忆。诗人通过对无处不在的眼泪的轻描淡写,揭示了由于母女关系的缺失而导致的祖孙之间的代沟和亲密。这首诗起初命名为《早期悲伤》,后来毕晓普改用诗的形式来命名。诗的场景是祖母和孙女在厨房里。厨房里的物品也是大家熟悉的:历书,茶壶和炉子。她们想尽办法阻止"秋分的眼泪",但它还是无处不在:九月的雨,茶壶冒出的水气结成的水滴,茶杯里的茶水,孩子画的纽扣,洒下的月光。祖孙二人尽力掩饰自己的悲伤,相互安慰:祖母偷偷藏起眼泪,孩子不说什么,但在她的画中表露了一切。悲伤是无处不在的,如同各种形式的眼泪一样。

在这首诗中,毕晓普再次运用了陌生化手法:家庭应该是人们最熟悉的,但是毕晓普反其道而用之。在她的笔下,家是"神秘的"。她们家庭特有的忧伤被含蓄地表达了出来。

易于记忆的六行诗体有好几个作用。它强调名词,增强了诗的形象性。通过反复加强了意象,使其萦绕于心。这种形式还暗示着孩子的初级语言,不能分辨时态,因而突出了回忆。毕晓普还创造性地使用了这种诗体,允许节奏较大的变化以及名词序列的松散顺序,以此表示在场景范围内物品之间的联系。孩子无法表述隐藏的或过去的事,或将来的事,所以这些事从物品中神秘地表现出来。这是一个孩子不能表述的事实,但是她通过绘画表达了出来:代沟,母亲的缺失,以及更宽泛的失去感。

总之,这首诗像是一幅画,定格在成年诗人心中,充满了淡淡的忧伤,使读者产生共鸣。

---

① inscrutable:神秘莫测的。

美国诗歌选读

思考题

1. What is "only known to a grandmother"?
2. What are the meanings of the italicized words?
3. What is the meaning of the child's painting?
4. In what way is the form repeated and varied?

The Armadillo

for Robert Lowell

This is the time of year①
when almost every night
the frail, illegal fire balloons appear.
Climbing the mountain height,

rising toward a saint
still honored in these parts②,
the paper chambers flush and fill with light
that comes and goes, like hearts.

Once up against the sky it's hard
to tell them from the stars—
planets, that is —the tinted ones:
Venus going down, or Mars.

or the pale green one③. With a wind,
they flare and falter, wobble and toss;

---

① This is the time of year：圣约翰日。圣约翰是耶稣的早期门徒之一，据说曾被投进油锅，却奇迹般地生还，毫发未损。后来，圣约翰和伊利亚一样升入天堂。每年的5月6日人们纪念圣约翰，而12月27日为圣约翰宴会日。
② these parts：里约热内卢，巴西。
③ Uranus：天王星。

but if it's still they steer between
the kite sticks of the Southern Cross①,

receding, dwindling, solemnly
and steadily forsaking us,
or, in the downdraft from a peak,
suddenly turning dangerous.

Last night another big one fell.
It splattered like an egg of fire
against the cliff behind the house.
The flame ran down. We saw the pair

of owls who nest there flying up
and up, their whirling black-and-white
stained bright pink underneath, until
they shrieked up out of sight.

The ancient owls' nest must have burned.
Hastily, all alone,
a glistening armadillo left the scene,
rose-flecked, head down, tail down,

and then a baby rabbit jumped out,
short-eared, to our surprise.
So soft!—a handful of intangible ash
with fixed, ignited eyes.

Too pretty, dreamlike mimicry!
O falling fire and piercing cry
and panic, and a weak mailed fist
clenched ignorant against the sky!

---

① the Southern Cross：在南半球可见到的一个星座,星星排列成一个十字架的形状。

美国诗歌选读

作品赏析

在狂欢时刻,文化准则遭到颠覆,受压抑的欲望得到表现。但同时宗教信仰却得到加强。这是人们的精神追求和日常道德相冲突的时刻。毕晓普有好几首诗都以狂欢为场景,《犰狳》是其中一首。这首诗描述了在圣约翰日,里约热内卢的狂欢场景。在这一天放飞载有烟火的气球是一个传统节目。毕晓普曾向她的医生安妮·鲍曼讲述写这首诗的初衷。她写道:"这是圣约翰日……下着倾盆大雨。这很糟糕,因为在这一天要放烟火、点篝火等等。但是又很好,因为不会有那么多的森林大火和事故。载有烟火的气球被认为是非法的,但是每个人都放飞这种气球。它们太美了。……一个人对它们有两种不同的想法。"后来,同年8月,她在给友人的信中提到:"现在我们所有的风景,所有的山都烧黑了。幸存的树烧成淡黄或白色……看起来非常像一张照片的底片,丑陋,但在某种意义上很美。"诗人的矛盾心理溢于言表。

《犰狳》的第一节诗描写了载有烟火的气球的自杀式升天,代表的是在节日里被激发的人类超凡脱俗、探索宇宙的欲望:when almost every night/the frail, illegal fire balloons appear./Climbing the mountain height,/rising toward a saint/still honored in these parts。"易破裂的,非法的气球"被比喻成心脏,成为欲望和人类局限的象征。接下来,诗人集中表达了载着烟火的气球的后果与崇高的愿望大相径庭。观察者的视角是从上往下的。当气球落地时,崇高变得很怪诞:receding, dwindling, solemnly/and steadily forsaking us,/or, in the **downdraft from a peak,/suddenly turning dangerous**。诗人通过诗行的长短不齐和音步的不断变化表现了观察者情绪的波动。接着有四节诗诗人注视自然秩序的衰微,表现了动物世界、自然界的不堪一击,这是人类想要超凡脱俗的后果。在诗人的眼中,有重生的时刻:从天而降的火球被描写成一个破壳的蛋,落到家庭生活的中心———一所房子后面,惊扰了猫头鹰的巢和兔子的洞穴。结束的场景很壮观,也很恐怖。观察者注意到被点燃的兔子的耳朵和犰狳的玫瑰色斑点。在此处诗人描述的是世俗世界的苦难和对导致这种苦难的力量的没有希望的抗争。随着视角从载有烟火的气球移到地上受炙烤的动物,美学距离被粉碎,诗人极其愤怒。在诗的结尾处用斜体字强调并且用犰狳作为主题意象,突出了痛苦和残忍。诗人似乎是在揭示人们想要超凡脱俗是危险的梦,让人们清醒地回到可怕的、无意义地受苦的现实。为了崇高的事业,殉道者可以忍受肉体上的苦痛,但是我们凡夫俗子必须反抗我们所受的折磨。

思考题

1. What does the first line mean? Why does the poet choose a carnivalized moment?
2. What are the meanings of the italicized sentences?
3. What is the metrical form of the poem?
4. What is the theme of the poem?

推荐作品

1. Bishop, Elizabeth. *The Complete Poems, 1927—1979.* New York: Farrar, Straus, and Giroux, 1983.
2. ——*The Collected Prose.* New York: Farrar, Straus, and Giroux, 1984.

参考书目

1. Costello, Bonnie. *Elizabeth Bishop: Questions of Mastery.* Cambridge: Harvard UP, 1990.
2. Fountain, Gary & Brazeau, Peter, eds. *Remembering Elizabeth Bishop: An Oral Biography.* Amherst: U of Massachusetts P, 1994.
3. Harrison, Victorica. *Elizabeth Bishop's Poetics of Intimacy.* Cambridge: Cambridge UP, 1993.
4. Monteiro, *George. Conversations with Elizabeth Bishop.* Jackson: UP of Mississippi, 1996.

第十五单元

Randall Jarrell (1914—1965)
兰德尔·贾雷尔

作者简介

兰德尔·贾雷尔出生在田纳西州的纳什维尔,毕业于范德比尔特大学,获心理学学士(1936)和文学硕士(1939),执教于肯庸大学期间(1937—1939),与兰瑟姆、洛厄尔等结为朋友,一度受新批评派的影响,但后来在《批评时代》一文(The Age of Criticism)中对滥用术语的文学理论提出批评。第二次世界大战期间,担任航空塔操作员(1942—1946),该经历使他亲睹战争的残酷与士兵的困惑,诗集《为外国人流血》(Blood for a Stranger, 1942)、《小朋友,小朋友》(Little Friend, Little Friend, 1945)及《损失》(Losses, 1948)反映作者对战争和已逝童年的思考。曾任《国家》(一译为《民族》)(The Nation)编辑,撰写了有关惠特曼、弗洛斯特等诗人的评论文章。1947年以在北卡罗那大学女子学院的教学经历为基础撰写了早期校园小说《一所大学的写照》(Pictures from an Institution, 1954),讽刺了女子学院的生活。贾雷尔不仅是才华出众的诗人,而且是独具慧眼的评论家,《诗歌与时代》(Poetry and the Age, 1953)集中体现了作者的文学批评观:提倡在阅读文学作品的基础上撰写评论文章,反对脱离文学作品滥用理论术语。"批评存在的理由是它所批评的剧本、故事与诗歌。"他认为,判断评论家的标准在于他对文学作品是否有所感悟,"好的批评家最鲜明的特点是,他真正感受到艺术作品的品质及真实的特质——不是总会感受到,但经常会。"去世后出版的《失落的世界》(The Lost World, 1965)借用戏剧独白、多元叙述视角等手法记录了作者对童年的回忆以及对成人社会的观察。其诗作受弗洛伊德的精神分析影响,既反映外部社会又流露内心世界。贾雷尔曾写道,"诗歌反映无意识活动及有意识活动,反映我们的生活及思想。"

A Lullaby

For wars his life and half a world away
The soldier sells his family and days.
He learns to fight for freedom and the State;
He sleeps with seven men within six feet.

He picks up matches and he cleans out plates;
Is lied to like a child, cursed like a beast.
They crop his head, his dog tags ring① like sheep
As his stiff limbs shift wearily to sleep.

Recalled in dreams or letters, else forgot,
His life is smothered like a grave, with dirt;
And his dull torment mottles like a fly's
The lying amber② of the histories.

这首战争诗的题名《摇篮曲》寓意深刻,一方面哀悼命丧战场的士兵,韵律较为严格的诗行使他们暂时得到片刻安宁,另一方面又为世人敲响警钟,使他们从孩提时代就清楚地意识到战争的残酷及士兵的可悲。然而,战争的残酷不仅表现在对士兵生命的摧毁,而且体现在对他们精神上的摧残。发起战争背后的理由冠冕堂皇,这使人的生命更显得毫无价值。诗中,主动和被动语态的交替使用,逐步强化士兵任人宰割的事实。一系列的明喻以及头韵突出了士兵所遭受的非人待遇。青春岁月就这样葬送在疆场上,被历史的垃圾堆掩埋。该诗充满了对统治者的尖锐批判,饱含对受害者的深切同情。

---

① dog tags:(俚)士兵挂在颈部的身份识别牌;ring:给牲口套鼻圈,这里比喻士兵像套着鼻圈的绵羊。
② amber:琥珀色,比喻时间的流逝

美国诗歌选读

1. Why does the poet use "sells" to describe the soldier's fate?
2. What does the word "they" in the second stanza refer to?
3. What do the animal images imply about the soldier's life?

Next Day

Moving from Cheer to Joy, from Joy to All[①],
I take a box
And add it to my wild rice, my Cornish game hens[②].
The slacked or shorted, basketed[③], identical
Food-gathering flocks[④]
Are selves I overlook. Wisdom, said William James[⑤],

Is learning what to overlook[⑥]. And I am wise
If that is wisdom.
Yet somehow, as I buy All from these shelves
And the boy takes it to my station wagon,
What I've become
Troubles me even if I shut my eyes.

When I was young and miserable and pretty
And poor, I'd wish
What all girls wish: to have a husband,
A house and children. Now that I'm old, my wish
Is womanish:

---

① Cheer, Joy, All：分别是肥皂的商品名。
② Cornish game hens：一种肉鸡。
③ slacked, shorted, basketed：购物者忘记买的东西、需要买的东西、装入购物篮里的东西。
④ food-gathering flocks：指购买大批物品的顾客。
⑤ William James：威廉·詹姆斯，美国哲学家(1842—1910)。
⑥ 出自威廉·詹姆斯的《心理学原理》(Principles of Psychology)。

That the boy putting groceries in my car

See me. It bewilders me he doesn't see me.
For so many years
I was good enough to eat: the world looked at me
And its mouth watered. How often they have undressed me,
The eyes of strangers!
And, holding their flesh within my flesh, their vile

Imaginings within my imagining,
I too have taken
The chance of life. Now the boy pats my dog
And we start home. Now I am good.
The last mistaken,
Ecstatic, accidental bliss, the blind

Happiness that, bursting, leaves upon the palm
Some soap and water—
It was so long ago, back in some Gay
Twenties, Nineties①, I don't know... Today I miss
My lovely daughter
Away at school, my sons away at school,

My husband away at work—I wish for them.
The dog, the maid,
And I go through the sure unvarying days
At home in them. As I look at my life,
I am afraid
Only that it will change, as I am changing:

I am afraid, this morning, of my face.
It looks at me
From the rear-view mirror, with the eyes I hate,
The smile I hate. Its plain, lined look

---

① Gay Twenties, Nineties: 20世纪20年代, 19世纪90年代, 指代"我"过去的快乐时光。

美国诗歌选读

Of gray discovery
Repeats to me: "You're old." That's all, I'm old.

And yet I'm afraid, as I was at the funeral
I went to yesterday.
My friend's cold made-up face, granite among its flowers,
Her undressed, operated-on, dressed body
Were my face and body.
As I think of her I hear her telling me

How young I seem; I *am* exceptional;
I think of all I have.
But really no one is exceptional,
No one has anything, I'm anybody,
I stand beside my grave
Confused with my life, that is commonplace and solitary.

这首诗采用第一人称，反映上世纪60年代女性对自我身份的困惑，透露出作者对迷失自我的女性的同情，清楚地再现诗人探究人的心理这一特点。诗中，"我"面临中年危机，开始质疑自我的身份：在母亲和妻子的角色之外，自己在社会中究竟占什么地位？女性受传统观念的束缚，依赖漂亮的长相寻找异性建立家庭，从此养尊处优，但缺乏经济和精神上的独立。然而，年老色衰后，女性不再具有被男性"凝视"的资格，也同时失去其存在的理由。这里，不难看出男权思想对女性的危害。

除第二节和第九节外，其余八节的最后一行均与下一节的第一行连续，使句义完整，如此排列不仅清晰地展现"我"的思考过程，而且也构成一定悬念，驱使读者继续阅读，发现"我"的思想。此外，还采用意识流的手法，揭示了容颜上的改变如何导致人生发生转变这一事实。通过重复一些富有象征含义的词汇，更加强了"我"的孤独感和无望。

思考题

1. Do you think "I" have the wisdom that William James had once defined? Why or why not?
2. What does "I stand beside my grave" (last stanza) imply?
3. How does the title "Next Day" relate to "my" memories about the past and "my" wish at present?

第十五单元

1. *Eighth Air Force*
2. *The Woman at the Washington Zoo*
3. *Losses*

参考书目

1. Bryant, J. A. *Understanding Randall Jarrell.* Columbia: University of South Carolina Press, 1986.
2. Burt, Stephen. *Randall Jarrell and His Age.* New York: Columbia University Press, 2002.
3. Pritchard, William H. *Randall Jarrell: a literary life.* New York: Farrar, Straus and Giroux, 1990.

第十六单元

Robert Lowell (1917—1977)
罗伯特·洛威尔

作者简介

罗伯特·洛威尔是美国自白派诗人的代表人物之一,被公认为美国二战后最重要的诗人。洛威尔出身新英格兰名门,家族包括著名诗人詹姆斯·拉塞尔·洛威尔和艾米·洛威尔。他从小立志成为一名诗人。他按照家人的安排,先后就读于上流社会的圣公会寄宿学校和哈佛大学。但他在哈佛大学学习两年后,出于对新英格兰文化传统的不满,转到肯庸学院,投到兰塞姆门下。1944 年,发表诗集《不同的国度》(Land of Unlikeness)。这段时期,由于深受艾伦·塔特和兰塞姆新批评派的影响,洛威尔的诗倾向于欧洲文学传统,格律工整,形式严谨,频繁使用象征、暗喻。诗的主题围绕波士顿、天主教和战争,反映了诗人内心的骚动不安以及他的宗教思想。1946 年发表诗集《威利勋爵的城堡》(Lord Weary's Castle)。他仍然沿袭文学传统,讲究格律,内涵丰富,反复使用象征、比喻等修辞手法,但比以前的诗成熟、自然。诗的主题涉及诗人的家庭出身、他的先祖,尤其是当时社会中道德的沦丧和精神上的颓废。诗集出版后广受好评,于 1947 年获普利策奖。

1951 年,发表诗集《卡瓦纳家庭的磨房》(Mills of the Kavanaughs)。其后几年,洛威尔在诗歌创作上经历了痛苦的转型,他借鉴 W.C.威廉斯的创作风格,加上自己的探索,一改往昔晦涩、引经据典的传统诗歌创作风格,写出了著名的自白诗文集《人生研究》(Life Studies, 1959),获国家图书奖。这是一个自传体诗集。其中诗一反艾略特新批评派的"非个性"诗风,采用了自由体,以第一人称叙述家庭生活中的压力,特别是父母和孩子间的关系,夫妻之间的关系。诗人试图重塑自己的童年和青年时期,从自己的人生经历反映社会、历史的变革。

洛威尔还著有《致联邦死难烈士》(For the Union Dead, 1964),《笔记本》

(*Notebook*, 1970),《海豚》(*The Dolphin*, 1973),《日复一日》(*Day by Day*, 1977), 以及根据梅尔维尔和霍桑的小说改编的戏剧集《古老的光荣》(*Old Glory*, 1964)。洛威尔的诗歌创作代表了现代诗歌的两大潮流:一是坚持传统,引经据典,借助修辞手段,尽可能不表露情感;二是揭开了自白诗运动的序幕,以惊人的方式描述自己的体验。从自白派开始,学院派和非学院派诗歌的界限逐渐模糊。

The Quaker Graveyard in Nantucket

(*for Warren Winslow, Dead at Sea*)
Let man have dominion over the fishes of the sea and the fowls of the air and the beasts and the whole earth, and every creeping creature that moveth upon the earth.

I

A brackish reach of shoal off Madaket①—
The sea was still breaking violently and night
Had steamed into our North Atlantic Fleet,
When the drowned sailor clutched the drag-net. Light
Flashed from his matted head and marble feet,
He grappled at the net
With the coiled, hurdling muscles of his thighs:
The corpse was bloodless, a botch of reds and whites,
Its open, staring eyes
Were lustreless dead-lights②
Or cabin-windows on a stranded hulk
Heavy with sand. We weight the body, close
Its eyes and heave it seaward whence it came,
Where the heel-headed dogfish barks its nose
On Ahab's③ void and forehead; and the name

---

① 诗人的表兄弟,二战时死于美国军舰的沉没。
② 引自《旧约·创世记》1:26,"使他们管理海里的鱼,空中的鸟,地上的牲畜,和全地,并地上所爬的一切昆虫。"
③ 楠塔基特岛上的小镇和港口。

Is blocked in yellow chalk.
Sailors, who pitch this portent at the sea
Where dreadnaughts shall confess
Its hell-bent deity,
When you are powerless
To sand-bag this Atlantic bulwark, faced
By the earth-shaker①, green, unwearied, chaste
In his steel scales: ask for no Orphean lute
To pluck life back②. The guns of the steeled fleet
Recoil and then repeat
The hoarse salute.

II

Whenever winds are moving and their breath
Heaves at the roped-in bulwarks of this pier,
The terns and sea-gulls tremble at your death
In these home waters. Sailor, can you hear
The Pequod's sea wings, beating landward, fall
Headlong and break on our Atlantic wall
Off 'Sconset③, where the yawing S-boats④ splash
The bellbuoy, with ballooning spinnakers,
As the entangled, screeching mainsheet clears
The blocks: off Madaket, where lubbers lash
The heavy surf and throw their long lead squids
For blue-fish? Sea-gulls blink their heavy lids
Seaward. The wind's wings beat upon the stones,
Cousin, and scream for you and the claws rush
At the sea's throat and wring it in the slush
Of this old Quaker graveyard where the bones
Cry out in the long night for the hurt beast
Bobbing by Ahab's whaleboats in the East.

---

① 在暴风雨时可以把水挡在外面的船舷窗上的窗板。该意象来自梭罗的《科德角》第一章"海难"的第 4—11 行。
② 梅尔维尔小说《白鲸》中的捕鲸船装廓德号的船长。他追捕白鲸,但最后白鲸颠覆他的船只使他葬身海中。
③ 波塞冬,希腊神话中的海神。
④ 在希腊神话中,俄耳甫斯(Orpheus)试图利用他的音乐的力量把他的妻子欧律狄刻(Eurydice)带离冥界。

III

All you recovered from Poseidon died
With you, my cousin, and the harrowed brine
Is fruitless on the blue beard of the god,
Stretching beyond us to the castles in Spain,
Nantucket's westward haven. To Cape Cod
Guns, cradled on the tide,
Blast the eelgrass about a waterclock
Of bilge and backwash, roil the salt and sand
Lashing earth's scaffold, rock
Our warships in the hand
Of the great God, where time's contrition blues
Whatever it was these Quaker sialors lost
In the mad scramble of their lives. They died
When time was open-eyed,
Wooden and childish; only bones abide
There, in the nowhere, where their boats were tossed
Sky-high, where mariners had fabled news
Of IS①, the whited monster. What it cost
Them is their secret. In the sperm-whale's slick
I see the Quakers drown and hear their cry:
"If God himself had not been on our side,
If God himself had not been on our side,
when the Atlantic rose against us, why,
Then it had swallowed us up quick."

IV

This is the end of the whaleroad② and the whale
Who spewed Nantucket bones on the thrashed swell
And stirred the troubled waters to whirlpools
To send the Pequod packing off to hell:
This is the end of them, three-quarters fools,
Snatching at straws to sail
Seaward and seaward on the turntail whale,

---

① 楠塔基特岛上的小镇。
② 赛艇的一种。

美国诗歌选读

Spouting out blood and water as it rolls,
Sick as a dog to these Atlantic shoals:
*Clamavimus*①, O depths. Let the sea-gulls wail

For water, for the deep where the high tide
Mutters to its hurt self, mutters and ebbs.
Waves wallow in their wash, go out and out,
Leave only the death-rattle of the crabs,
The beach increasing, its enormous snout
Sucking the ocean's side.
This is the end of running on the waves;
We are poured out like water. Who will dance
The mast-lashed master of Leviathans②
Up from this field of Quakers in their unstoned graves?

V

When the whale's viscera go and the roll
Of its corruption overruns this world
Beyond tree-swept Nantucket and Woods Hole
And Martha's Vineyard③, Sailor, will your sword
Whistle and fall and sink into the fat?
In the great ash-pit of Jehoshapat④
The bones cry for the blood of the white whale,
The fat flukes arch and whack about its ears,
The death-lance churns into the sanctuary, tears
The gun-blue swingle⑤, heaving like a flail,
And hacks the coiling life out: it works and drags
And rips the sperm-whale's midriff into rags,
Gobbets of blubber spill to wind and weather,
Sailor, and gulls go round the stoven timbers
Where the morning stars sing out together
And thunder shakes the white surf and dismembers

---

① 很可能引自《新约·启示录》17:18: "你所看见的兽,先前有,如今没有(Behold the beast and was and is not and yet is.)"
② 海。
③ 拉丁文, "We have called." 引自《旧约·诗篇》130:1, "耶和华阿,我从深处向你求告。"
④ 旧约中的海怪。
⑤ 马萨诸塞州大西洋沿岸的小镇,在 Martha's Vineyard 的对面。

The red flag hammered in the mast-head①. Hide,
Our steel, Jonas Messias②, in Thy side.

VI OUR LADY OF WALSINGHAM③

There once the penitents took off their shoes
And then walked barefoot the remaining mile;
And the small trees, a stream and hedgerows file
Slowly along the munching English lane,
Like cows to the old shrine, until you lose
Track of your dragging pain.
The stream flows down under the druid tree④,
Shiloah's⑤ whirlpools gurgle and make glad
The castle of God. Sailor, you were glad
And whistled Sion⑥ by that stream. But see:

Our Lady, too small for her canopy,
Sits near the altar. There's no comeliness
At all or charm in that expressionless
Face with its heavy eyelids. As before,
This face, for centuries a memory,
*Non est species, neque decor*⑦,
Expressionless, expresses God: it goes
Past castled Sion. She knows what God knows,
Not Calvary's Cross nor crib at Bethlehem
Now, and the world shall come to Walsingham.

VII

The empty winds are creaking and the oak
Splatters and splatters on the cenotaph⑧,

---

① 楠塔基特附近的岛屿。
② "决定谷",上帝评判世界的场所(《旧约·约珥书》3:1—16)。"评判日。据一些预言家所说,世界在火中消亡"(洛厄尔的注释)。
③ 木质的像刀一样的工具。
④ 指《白鲸》结尾下沉的裴廓德号桅杆上钉着的旗子。
⑤ 在基督教文学中经常比较约拿(Jonah)和耶稣基督。约拿的经历被认为是耶稣复活的预言。
⑥ 献给童贞女马利亚的圣地,在英格兰诺福克郡的 Walsingham Priory.
⑦ 古代异教徒凯尔特人祭司奉为圣树的像树。
⑧ 古巴勒斯坦小镇。

The boughs are trembling and a gaff
Bobs on the untimely stroke
Of the greased wash exploding on a shoal-bell
In the old mouth of the Atlantic. It's well;
Atlantic, you are fouled with the blue sailors,
Sea-monsters, upward angel, downward fish:
Unmarried and corroding, spare of flesh
Mart once of supercilious, wing'd clippers,
Atlantic, where your bell-trap guts its spoil
You could cut the brackish winds with a knife
Here in Nantucket, and cast up the time
When the Lord God formed man from the sea's slime
And breathed into his face the breath of life,
And blue-lung'd combers lumbered to the kill.
The Lord survives the rainbow of His will.

《楠塔基特岛上贵格会教徒墓地》是诗集《威利勋爵的城堡》中的名篇。是他早期诗歌风格的典型代表。他引经据典，不仅引用《圣经》和希腊神话，而且还引用美国文学的经典著作，甚至诗集的题目也来自苏格兰的古民谣《拉姆金》。民谣中威利勋爵拒绝付给瓦工拉姆金工钱。拉姆金闯入城堡进行了恶意的报复。威利勋爵的城堡是一座"忘恩负义，不履行义务，犯罪与惩罚"的宅第，象征着现代世界。在这本诗集中，正如评论家伦德尔·嘉雷尔所说，洛威尔攻击"一切封闭的，向内的，小集团的事物，一切盲目的或受束缚的事物：旧的规则，帝国主义，军国主义，资本主义，沙文主义，政权，父亲，正统的波士顿人，……富人"。它关注的焦点是诗人所熟悉的新英格兰。

《楠塔基特岛上贵格会教徒墓地》是一首挽歌，表面上是悼念洛威尔的表兄华伦·文思洛。华伦在二战中由于美国海军军舰的沉没而淹死。实际上，洛威尔(此诗)探讨了一些困扰他的问题：(有关)生与死，拯救的可能性，在自然和上帝面前人类最终的(是否)无能为力(等问题)。

该诗的头12行几乎直接引自梭罗对一位沉船死难者的描写(《科德角》)。在此洛威尔引入了人类进化的主题，把它当作上帝计划的一部分。上帝创造人始于海，因而人死于海很正常。也就是说，人的进化过程是可逆的：创造暗含毁灭。因此，溺水的水手和裴廊德号的船长艾哈伯一样，葬身于海洋是他们的宿命。海洋是波塞东主宰的世界，即使是承认海洋威力的仪式也不能使波塞东息怒，无法挽救溺水的水手或者他的伙伴的生

---

① 成为希伯来人政府和生活中心的耶路撒冷的小山。后用来描述以色列人，教堂和圣城。
② 拉丁语，"他无佳形美容。"(《旧约·以赛亚书》)53:2)
③ 为纪念葬在别处的人所建的墓碑。

命。因此,该诗的开篇是向死亡的威力致敬。诗人是忧郁的,无助的。

在下几节诗中,这一主题得到深化,同时诗人加入了对社会和政治的批评。华伦·文思洛的死亡地点和情形使人自然地联想到贵格会教徒和他们对财富的寻求。对诗人来说,贵格会教徒是不人道的、残酷的象征。是他们引起了人们精神上的异化,也是他们的贪婪导致了现代战争。对上帝所创生物鲸鱼的剥削和毁灭暗示了现代战争中人对同胞的不人道。在这种意义下,诗中对《创始记》的引言赋予了讽刺意味。"畏神"的贵格会教徒用这段文字警告他们的贪婪。他们不但忘记了因为对抗波塞东而受到的惩罚,他们也背离了基督教教义,因此也被剥夺了被上帝宽恕的可能性,由此也丧失了自身被拯救的可能性。

总之,诗人在诗中表明现代人的贪婪、对权力的膜拜以及对同胞的屠戮只能导致灾难。

这首诗还典型地代表了洛威尔早期诗歌的风格,具有鲜明的现代派诗歌的特色。全诗引经据典,包括《圣经》、希腊神话、美国文学的经典著作和宗教等方面。另一方面,诗人不仅采用十分复杂的韵脚,而且还采用头韵、谐音或只押元音的韵脚以及句行的长短不一等技巧。

思考题

1. There are symbols in the poem. Could you name some of them and tell what they stand for?
2. What do (is implied in the) allusions to Herman Melville's *Moby Dick* imply? What do you think is the reason that Lowell used the allusions to Melville's *Moby Dick*?
3. What is Lowell's vision of the time in the poem?
4. Why does the poet describe a tranquil pastoral scene in Staza VI?
5. What is the metrical form of the poem?

美国诗歌选读

Skunk Hour①

(for Elizabeth Bishop)
Nautilus Island's② hermit
heiress still lives through winter in her Spartan cottage,
her sheep still graze above the sea.
Her son's a bishop. Her farmer
is first selectman③ in our village;
she's in her dotage.

Thirsting for
the hierarchic privacy
of Queen Victoria's century,
she buys up all
the eyesores facing her shore,
and lets them fall.

The season's ill—
we've lost our summer millionaire,④
who seemed to leap from an L.L. Bean⑤
catalogue. His nine-knot yawl⑥
was auctioned off to lobstermen.
A red fox⑦ stain covers Blue Hill.⑧

And now our fairy⑨
decorator brightens his shop for fall;

---

① 洛威尔宣称该诗受了毕晓普的诗《犰狳》的启发写成。
② Nautilus Island：缅因州一岛名，洛威尔曾在附近一小镇居住过。诗中提到的 Blue Hill 也在这一带。
③ 由选举产生的掌管小镇事务的官员。
④ summer millionaire：指此人是个短暂的暴发户。
⑤ 位于缅因州佛里波特市的邮购衣服和体育用品的商店。
⑥ 双桅帆船。
⑦ red fox：指颜色。大自然都受到玷污。
⑧ 缅因州 Bangor 附近的海滨小镇。
⑨ fairy：(俚语)同性恋者，此节末尾说他也想结婚了，说明世界之混乱。

his fishnet's filled with orange cork,
orange, his cobbler's bench and awl;
there is no money in his work,
he'd rather marry.

One dark night,
my Tudor Ford climbed the hill's skull;
I watched for love-cars. Lights turned down,
they lay together, hull to hull,
where the graveyard shelves on the town....
My mind's not right.

A car radio bleats,
"Love, O careless Love...."① I hear
my ill-spirit sob in each blood cell,
as if my hand were at its throat....
I myself am hell,②
nobody's here—

only skunks, that search
in the moonlight for a bite to eat.
They march on their soles up Main Street:
white stripes, moonstruck eyes' red fire
under the chalk-dry and spar spire
of the Trinitarian Church.

I stand on top
of our back steps and breathe the rich air—
a mother skunk with her column of kittens swills the garbage pail.
She jabs her wedge-head in a cup
of sour cream, drops her ostrich tail,
and will not scare.

---

① 民歌"粗心的爱"的歌词。
② 约翰·弥尔顿的《失乐园》(第四册,第 75 行)撒旦的话语"which way I fly is hell; myself am Hell."的改写。

美国诗歌选读

作品赏析

这首诗选自诗集《人生研究》。该诗集分四部分：一、《阿尔卑斯山外》；二、散文《里维尔街91号》；三、《致迈道克斯·福特》、《致乔治·桑特亚纳》、《致戴尔莫·施瓦茨》、《讲给哈特·克兰的话》；四、十五首诗。《臭鼬出没的时刻》是这十五首诗中的一首。

洛威尔曾写文章讲述他所创作的《臭鼬出没的时刻》。他提到"头四节诗描绘的是没落的缅因海边小镇的一幅节奏缓慢，多少亲切的景象。风景中满是无生育能力的人，但对悲伤的前景我的语调尽可能忍耐、幽默和随意。诗中……是随意的、不确定的自然和衰亡。然后在第六、七节诗中所有的都复活了。这是一个黑夜……。我的夜晚不优美，是世俗的、清教的和不可知的。在我的心中……到达了最黑暗的时刻，一个人只能用自杀来解脱。这时在最后两节诗中模模糊糊地出现了一队臭鼬……它们既是堂吉诃德式的，也是粗暴荒谬的……"

该诗的诗行短小，语言是对话式的，就好象诗人在直接、客观地向读者述说。我们似乎在聆听一个苦恼的人深夜独自在家的思绪。前四节诗里，诗人描绘了一幅衰弱无力的景象，是一个自私的、没有爱的、病态的环境。在第一、二节诗中描写了一个女继承人，她依旧拥有羊群，她依旧可以染指教堂和政府，但是一句"in her dotage"表明她的王国是虚幻的。她奢侈、有些古怪、自私、无生气。在第三节诗中描写了一个自杀的百万富翁。他的死打击了度假胜地的经济。第四节诗中描写了一个同性恋装潢师，是小镇新经济的代表。他在抱怨赚不到钱。他的生活毫无意义，也没有目标。这几节诗中，死亡的意象在层层叠加。这些繁复的形象实际上表明了诗中的"我"自身的问题所在。他确实也知道他的思想有问题。黑漆漆的夜里，他在途经地狱。他对生活、对人类、对自己失去了信心，死亡的想法萦绕于心。对他来说死是解脱的最好办法。正在这时，"我"看到了一只臭鼬母亲带着小臭鼬们在堂而皇之地觅食。它们肆无忌惮，大啃大嚼，充满了乐趣。"我"受到了震动，惊叹于它们旺盛的生命力和繁殖力。"我"意识到这些动物身上有值得学习的地方，使"我"恢复了生活下去的勇气。

思考题

1. In the poem, there are a lot of words which imply death. Can you pick them out?
2. There are some words related to Christianity. What do these words imply?
3. What are the meanings of the words "red", "Blue" and "orange" in the poem?
4. Why does the poet mention cars, car radio and the song?

For the Union Dead

*"Relinquunt Omnia Servare Rem Publicam."*①
The old South Boston Aquarium stands
in a Sahara of snow now. Its broken windows are boarded.
The bronze weathervane cod has lost half its scales.
The airy tanks are dry.

Once my nose crawled like a snail on the glass;
my hand tingled
to burst the bubbles
drifting from the noses of the cowed, compliant fish.

My hand draws back. I often sigh still
for the dark downward and vegetating kingdom
of the fish and reptile. One morning last March,
I pressed against the new barbed and galvanized

fence on the Boston Common. Behind their cage,
yellow dinosaur steamshovels were grunting
as they cropped up tons of mush and grass
to gouge their underworld garage.

Parking spaces luxuriate live civic
sandpiles in the heart of Boston.
A girdle of orange, Puritan-pumpkin colored girders
braces the tingling Statehouse,

shaking over the excavations, as it faces Colonel Shaw②
and his bell-cheeked Negro infantry

---

① 拉丁语："他放弃了一切,为共和国服务。"
② 罗伯特·肖上尉(1837—1863),美国内战中马赛诸塞州第54黑人团的的指挥官。

on St. Gaudens' shaking Civil War relief,①
propped by a plank splint against the garage's
earthquake.

Two months after marching through Boston,
half the regiment was dead;
at the dedication,
William James② could almost hear the bronze Negroes
breathe.

Their monument sticks like a fishbone
in the city's throat.
Its Colonel is as lean
as a compass-needle.

He has an angry wrenlike vigilance,
a greyhound's gentle tautness;
he seems to wince at pleasure,
and suffocate for privacy.

He is out of bounds now. He rejoices in man's lovely,
peculiar power to choose life and die—
when he leads his black soldiers to death,
he cannot bend his back,
On a thousand small town New England greens,
the old white churches hold their air
of sparse, sincere rebellion; frayed flags
quilt the graveyards of the Grand Army of the Republic.③

The stone statues of the abstract Union Soldier
grow slimmer and younger each year—

---

① 美国雕塑家奥古斯督·圣·Gaudens(1848—1907)所建的纪念碑,在波士顿州政府对面的波士顿广场上。请查人名译名字典,找出中文,或直接用英语。
② 美国哲学家(1842—1910),小说家亨利·詹姆斯的哥哥。在他的"纪念碑奠基典礼上的致辞"(1897年5月)中,威廉·詹姆斯说,"被社会摈弃的黑人徒步走来,他们真诚地对待自然,人们几乎可以听到他们行进时的呼吸(There on foot go the dark outcasts, so true to nature that one can almost hear them breathing as they march.)。"
③ 前联邦军队成员组成的内战老兵组织。

wasp-waisted, they doze over muskets
and muse through their sideburns....

Shaw's father wanted no monument
except the ditch,
where his son's body was thrown
and lost with his "niggers."①

The ditch is nearer.
There are no statutes for the last② war here;
on Boylston Street③, a commercial photograph
shows Hiroshima boiling

over a Mosler Safe, the "Rock of Ages"
that survived the balst. Space in nearer.
When I crouch on my television set,
the drained faces of Negro school-children rise like balloons.

Colonel Shaw
is riding on his bubble.
he waits
for the blessed break.

The Aquarium is gone. Everywhere,
giant finned cars nose forward like fish;
a savage servility
slides by on grease.

作品赏析

这首诗纪念了美国内战中牺牲的将士，慨叹现代社会人心不古，不再怀有崇高理想，而是自私自利、唯利是图。

诗中有几个意象。其一是水族馆。它的由过去的兴盛到如今的废弃表现了过去和现在之间的巨大鸿沟。诗人记得过去"我的鼻子曾经

---

① 南部联盟对肖上尉的军队的称呼。在 1863 年 7 月 18 日进攻南卡罗来纳的南部邦联的 Wagner 的战役中，肖上尉和他的大部分士兵牺牲，被葬在一起。现在在英语里，'nigger' 有贬义，不能用来指黑人。
② 第二次世界大战，1939—1945。
③ 波士顿的一条街道。

美国 诗歌 选读

像蜗牛般在玻璃上爬，/我的手跃跃欲试／想捅破那些被吓唬得／服贴的鱼鼻子上冒出的气泡。",而如今"古老的波士顿水族馆站在／一片白雪的沙漠中,破窗钉着木板,／青铜的鳕鱼形风标掉了大半鳞片,／贮水池已经干涸。"水族馆是自然界的象征。自然界遭受了严重的破坏。其二是肆无忌惮的挖土机。为了修停车场,挖土机的作业动摇了州政府和烈士纪念浮雕,可谓轰轰烈烈。其三是联邦烈士纪念浮雕。该浮雕是为了纪念在南北战争中牺牲的烈士而立的。他们为了南北统一、废除奴隶制献出了一切,甚至生命,但是当今的人们已将他们渐渐遗忘。在他的"纪念碑奠基典礼上的致辞"中,威廉·詹姆斯说,"他们行军时人们几乎可以听到他们的呼吸"。可见当时的人们对烈士的景仰和怀念。而如今浮雕在摇摇欲坠,一天比一天消瘦,表明年久失修,少有人来凭吊。现代人已将他们渐渐遗忘,不再有烈士们的为崇高事业可牺牲生命的理想主义。将士们换来的是怎样的一个现实呢？奴隶制虽然废除,但是种族歧视依然存在,黑人和白人的地位仍然不平等,黑人仍在为自己的权益作斗争。黑人学生为了取消种族隔离在学校举行游行示威的新闻照片就是很好的例证。其四是莫斯勒公司的保险箱的广告牌。广告牌上是广岛核爆炸的一片火海下安然无恙的保险箱。如今的人们都在关注自己的区区小利,想着如何守住自己的财富。他们一心想买结实耐用的保险箱,而对无数在战争中无辜死去的人们不闻不问。现代人的冷漠、无情、贪婪可见一斑。诗人在慨叹现代人的道德败坏,对物质享受的追求泯灭了人们的良知。其五是汽车。代表现代工业文明成就的汽车在招摇过市。由于工业文明,环境遭到污染、破坏。

该诗结构严谨、富含意象、内涵丰富。

 思考题

1. In the third stanza, what does the poet have in mind when he says "my hand draws back" imply?
2. Why does the poet mention steamshovels?
3. What does the poet's intend to convey to the reader with his des (c)ription of Colonel Shaw imply?
4. What is the metrical form of this poem?

推荐作品

1. Lowell, Robert. *Land of Unlikeness*. Cummington: Commington Press, 1944.
2. ——. *Lord Weary's Castle: The Mills of the Kavanaughs*. Harvest: Harcourt Publishers Ltd, 1983.
3. ——. *Life Studies & For the Union Dead*. NY: Farrar, Straus, and Giroux, 1967.
4. ——. *Notebook: Poems*. NY: Farrar, Straus, and Giroux, 1995.
5. ——. *Day by Day*. NY: Farrar, Straus, and Giroux, 1977.

参考书目

1. Hamilton, Ian. *Robert Lowell: A Biography.* New York: Random House, 1982.
2. Ostroff, Anthony. *The Contemporary Poet as Artist and Critic: Eight Symposia.* New York: Little, Brown, Boston, 1964.
3. Parkinson, Thomas, ed. *Robert Lowel: A Collection of Critical Essays.* Englewood Cliffs: Prentice-Hal Inc., 1968.
4. Perloff, Marjorie G. *The Poetic Art of Robert Lowell.* Ithaca & London: Cornell UP, 1973.
5. Rosenthal, M.L. *The Modern Poets: A Critical Introduction.* London: Oxford UP, 1960.
6. P. Mariani. *Lost Puritan: A Life of Robert Lowell.* New York: W.W. Norton, 1996.
7. 常耀信:《精编美国文学教程》,南开大学出版社,2005年。
8. 彭予:《美国自白诗探索》,社会科学文献出版社,2004年。
9. 王卓:《后现代主义视野中的美国当代诗歌》,山东文艺出版社,2005年。
10. 张子清:《二十世纪美国诗歌史》,吉林教育出版社,1995年。

第十七单元

Gwendolyn Brooks (1917—2000)
格温朵琳·布鲁克斯

作者简介

格温朵琳·布鲁克斯生于美国堪萨斯州，在芝加哥长大。自小受父母熏陶，16岁开始在《芝加哥捍卫者》(*Chicago Defender*)发表作品。黑人诗人詹姆斯·韦尔登·约翰逊和兰斯顿·休斯不仅向她介绍 T. S. 艾略特等诗人的作品，而且鼓励她创作，休斯还成为她的导师和朋友。布鲁克斯1936年大学毕业后在大学任教。1967年菲斯克大学的第二届黑人作家会议(the Fisk University Second Black Writers' Conference)对布鲁克斯有很大影响，之后，布鲁克斯积极投身黑人民权运动和黑人艺术运动(the Black Arts movement)，并成为宣扬"黑人美学"("the Black aesthetics")的主要人之一。她的诗歌也更富有强烈的政治性。1968年她当选为伊利诺州的桂冠诗人，并成为美国全国艺术与文学院(National Institute of Arts and Letters)的成员以及美国国会图书馆的诗歌顾问。布鲁克斯曾与由黑人青年组成的黑石突击队(the Blackstone Rangers)共同举办诗歌研讨会，用黑人口头语言进行创作。

布鲁克斯著作等身，1945年的《布朗兹维尔一条街》(*A Street in Bronzeville*)生动再现黑人的悲惨生活以及黑人在第二次世界大战服军役期间所受到的种族歧视。叙事诗集《安妮·艾伦》(*Annie Allen*, 1949)谱写了黑人女性的成长过程，以其现实主义主题及反传统的文学形式赢得普利策奖(1950)，成为第一位获此殊荣的黑人女诗人。小说《莫德·玛莎》(*Maud Martha*, 1953)采用口头叙事的方法讲述了黑人女性寻找身份的过程。《吃豆的人》(*The Bean Eaters*, 1960)中的《我们真酷》(*We Real Cool*)最为经典。《在麦加》(*In the Mecca*, 1968)通过戏仿十四行诗的写作形式，揭露黑人遭受非人待遇这一事实。《骚动》(*Riot*, 1969)以及《家庭相片》(*Family Pictures*, 1970)采用黑人语言，强调黑人意识，并由黑人出版社出版，突出了作者作为黑人的鲜明立场。自传《第一部分报导》和《第二部分报导》(*Report from Part One*, 1972; *Report from Part Two*, 2003)记录了她的生活经历以及创作历程。《在蒙哥马利以及其他诗歌》(*In Montgomery: And Other Poems*, 2003)收集有1971年出版的诗歌,歌颂了阿拉巴马的民权运动者。布鲁克斯的诗歌饱含丰富的黑人文化,涉及普通黑人的生活点滴,写作形式多样化,包括歌谣、自由诗、灵歌等,极大丰富了美国黑人诗歌创作的内容与形式。她秉信文化的多样性:"我认为所有人都应互相了解,因为我们身上承载了许多各式各样的文化。不去了解这些文化就是怀疑、回避或者毁坏该文化。"

We Real Cool

      The Pool Players.
      Seven at the Golden Shovel.

We real cool. We
Left school. We

Lurk① late. We
Strike straight. We

Sing sin. We
Thin gin②. We

Jazz③ June. We
Die soon.

  从诗歌前面两行文字看,不难判断该诗出自七位青少年的口吻。诗中的不规范语言表明这些孩子是黑人,他们敢于挑战白人中产阶级主张接受教育的价值观,从某种意义上说,这是对种族歧视的反叛。然而,正如诗人所说:这首诗反映出这些孩子自我身份的不确定

---

① lurk:潜伏。
② thin:将酒稀释;gin:杜松子酒。
③ jazz:作动词用,演奏爵士乐。

性，他们在背离传统观念时的心理较为盲目："'Kilroy is here. We are.'"一方面，孩子们的叛逆行为使他们获得片刻自由，这种反叛精神令人肃然起敬。另一方面，他们又明知自己的反叛徒劳无益，这使读者对他们的境况深表同情。该诗的创作时期为20世纪60年代，正值黑人民权运动。诗人从独特的视角反映黑人青少年的反叛与迷茫，表达出她的矛盾心理。

整齐的押韵以及不断重复的"我们"，连同一系列的头韵，使读者强烈感受到"我们"的力量。而且，这种有力的反抗有其连续性和节奏感，具体表现在每节中同一行及下一行的头韵用词。例如，第一节与第二节的"left, lurk, late"；第二节与第三节出现的"strike, straight, sing, sin"；第三节与第四节出现的"gin, jazz, June"；全诗四节通过上述相应的头韵首尾相连，突出强调了黑人孩子齐心协力共同反抗的事实。与前面几节有所不同的是，第四节的最后一行没有出现"we"，"我们"的消失生动形象地再现七位黑人少年的金色岁月悄然流逝这一事实。

思考题

1. Are "we" really cool?
2. How do you understand "We jazz June"?
3. Brooks once said that "we" should be read softly. Read the poem this way and discuss your findings.

Kitchenette building

We are things of dry hours and the involuntary plan,
Grayed in①, and gray. "Dream" makes a giddy② sound, not strong
Like "rent," "feeding a wife," "satisfying a man."

But could a dream send up through onion fumes
Its white and violet, fight with fried potatoes
And yesterday's garbage ripening in the hall,
Flutter, or sing an aria③ down these rooms

---

① Grayed in: gray 作动词用，囚禁在灰色的楼房。
② giddy: 令人头晕的。
③ aria: 咏叹调。

Even if we were willing to let it in,
Had time to warm it, keep it very clean,
Anticipate a message, let it begin①?

We wonder. But not well! not for a minute!
Since Number Five② is out of the bathroom now,
We think of lukewarm water, hope to get in it.

  这首诗具有浓郁的黑人生活气息,集中反映了黑人对梦想的质疑以及对生活的洞察。"我们"无法描绘美好幸福的图景,因为梦想与现实之间的距离相差甚远。诗人采用拟人手法,逼真地描述出黑人对梦想的理解。梦想的一切品质与"我们"拥挤不堪的居所格格不入,其中不乏反讽意味。这些反差表现在色彩、声音、气味的意象上面,暗淡无光的日子囚禁着"我们",绚丽多彩的梦想只能加剧现实中的痛感;房租、生存等现实问题不可回避,要歌唱梦想,恐怕也需要足够的空间和洁净的场所;在油烟滚滚、垃圾满地的地方,梦想似乎不好光顾。通过调动这些感官意象,诗人试图解释"我们"拒绝梦想的原因。第一节表明"我们"的非人生活现状,第二节的反问句延伸至第三节,并使用排比句,进一步凸显出黑人捉襟见肘的现实生活,使梦想的存在显得缺乏底气。第四节简明扼要地点出梦想的多余与现实的紧迫。黑人的梦想应立足于现实,并且黑人只有依靠自己的力量,争取改善非人的现实生活,才能实现自己的梦想。该诗未采用传统的押韵方法,然而黑人的生活原本就缺乏韵律,印证了诗人的现实主义创作手法。

思考题

1. How do you understand "things of dry hours and the involuntary plan"?
2. What do "rent", "feeding a wife" and "satisfying a man" suggest about the blacks' life?
3. Can you relate this poem to Langston Hughes' "Dreams"?

---

① let it begin:让梦想开始(实现),接第二节。
② number 5:暗指黑人狭窄的居住空间,这么小的地方住了起码5个人。

美国诗歌选读

My dreams, my works, must wait till after hell

I hold my honey and I store my bread
In little jars and cabinets of my will①.
I label clearly, and each latch and lid
I bid, Be firm till I return from hell.
I am very hungry. I am incomplete.
And none can tell when I may dine again.
No man can give me any word but Wait,
The puny light②. I keep eyes pointed in;
Hoping that, when the devil days of my hurt
Drag out to their last dregs and I resume
On such legs as are left me, in such heart
As I can manage, remember to go home,
My taste will not have turned insensitive
To honey and bread old purity③ could love.

  这首诗基本采用了莎士比亚式十四行诗的格式，由三个韵脚类似的四行连句诗和一个双韵句构成，韵脚格式为ababcdcdefefgg。与传统的莎士比亚式十四行诗的主题不同，这首诗并没有抒发爱情，而是用质朴的语言表达黑人对基本温饱生活的渴望。通过戏仿传统的诗歌模式，该诗深刻揭示了诗人对黑人贫困现状的关注以及对美国社会的种族歧视与阶级压迫的批判。黑人所遭遇的黑暗现实与地狱相差无几，温饱问题直接威胁到黑人的生存。

  诗中采用了第一人称、头韵、排比、夸张等手法，生动勾勒出黑人生不如死的事实，使读者对以"我"为代表的黑人表示同情。

---

① my will：（在）我的想象中。
② puny light：比喻希望渺茫。
③ old purity：比喻在世的"我"。

1. What does "Be firm till I return from hell" suggest about the credibility of the wish?
2. What does "Wait" imply about the speaker's attitude?
3. How do you interpret the last two lines?

1. *I Am a Black*
2. *The Bean Eaters*
3. *The Coora Flower*

参考书目

1. Gayles, Gloria Jean Wade, ed. *Conversations with Gwendolyn Brooks*. Jackson: UP of Mississippi, 2003.
2. Kent, George E. *A Life of Gwendolyn Brooks*. Lexington, Kentucky.: UP of Kentucky, 1989.
3. Mootry, Maria K. et al, eds. *A Life Distilled: Gwendolyn Brooks, Her Poetry and Fiction*. Urbana: U of Illinois P, 1987.
4. Wright, Stephen Caldwell. *On Gwendolyn Brooks: Reliant Contemplation*. Ann Arbor: U of Michigan P, 1996.

第十八单元

Allen Ginsberg (1926—1997)
艾伦·金斯堡

作者简介

艾伦·金斯堡，美国当代诗人。出生于新泽西州一中学教师家庭。父亲也是诗人，母亲长期患精神病，在金斯堡心灵中投下过阴影。1948年毕业于哥伦比亚大学，选修过大文学批评家特里林(Lionel Trilling)的课程，结识了后来成为"垮掉一代"重要人物的凯鲁亚克(Jack Kerouac)等人，在校期间曾因写过淫秽诗句一度被校方赶出学校。此后干过电焊工、饭店刷盘者、杂志书评人等工作。1955年在旧金山一次诗歌朗诵会上朗诵了他的诗《嚎叫》，一举成名，成了"垮掉一代"文学运动的代表。

金斯堡既是诗人，也是活跃的社会活动者，积极投入人权、反战运动，鼓吹同性恋，并身体力行，通过吸毒体验幻觉，但后来又摒弃毒品，转向赞同佛教禅学。1974年金斯堡与几个年轻诗人共同创立凯鲁亚克写作项目，讲授诗歌创作，同时在布鲁克林学院授课，并且成为了该校的终身教授，一直到去世。

金斯堡早期曾写过严格的律诗。后师承威廉斯，寻求口语及具有明显呼吸节奏感的语句。同时，在形式上效仿惠特曼，并从英国十八世纪诗人布莱克(William Blake)那里获取神秘气氛，创造了他自己的独特风格。他的诗节奏鲜明，语调铿锵有力，诗情一泻千里，自由奔放。内容以描写当代美国人精神苦闷及压抑的心理为主，同时也对美国社会进行大胆的批判和直截了当的攻击。1974年获美国全国图书奖。诗集有《嚎叫及其他诗》、《现实三明治》等。

金斯堡的诗歌创作，尤其是其对口语传统的重视和运用，以及无拘无束、大胆直露的诗风在五六十年代的美国形成了一道独特的风景线，引起了美国诗坛的广泛关注，大诗人威廉斯为《嚎叫》写了序言，甚至把他与金斯堡的通信放到了他的长诗《派特森》中，而另一著名诗人罗威尔(Robert Lowell)则从金斯堡的诗歌得到启发，开始重视口语的运用。有些评论者认为金斯堡也许是唯一一位在全世界享有声誉的当代美国诗人。

Howl

For Carl Solomon

I saw the best minds of my generation destroyed by madness, starving hysterical naked,

dragging themselves through the negro streets at dawn looking for an angry fix,①

angelheaded hipsters burning for the ancient heavenly connection to the starry dynamo② in the machinery of night,

who poverty and tatters and hollow-eyed and high sat up③ smoking in the supernatural darkness of clod-water flats floating④ across the tops of cities contemplating jazz,

who bared their brains to Heaven under the El and saw Mohammedan⑤ angels staggering on tenement roofs illuminated,

who passed through universities with radiant cool eyes hallucinating Arkansas and Blake-light tragedy among the scholars of war,

who were expelled from the academies for crazy & publishing obscene odes on the windows of the skull,⑥

who cowered in unshaven rooms in underwear, burning their money in wastebaskets and listening to the Terror through the wall,

who got busted in their pubic beards⑦ returning through Laredo⑧ with a belt of marijuana for New York,

who ate fire in paint hotels or drank turpentine in Paradise Alley,⑨ death, or purgatoried their torsos⑩ night after night

---

① fix: 俚语, 意为吸毒者自我注射。
② angelheaded... dynamo: 渴望与星星般闪光的古代仙人接上联系的、有着天使般头脑的嬉皮士们。burning for, 渴望, dynamo, 口语, 精力充沛的人。
③ who…sat up: 他们衣衫褴褛、眼神空虚、神魂颠倒地坐于。high, 口语, 意为"喝醉的, 被毒品麻醉的"。
④ floating: 这里指吸毒后蒙蒙胧胧感到飘越过。
⑤ Mohammedan: 穆罕默德。
⑥ publishing... skull: 在窗户上写下流的诗。金斯堡在这里提及自己在哥伦比亚大学时的经历。
⑦ who... beards: 他们赤身裸体地被抓住。bust, 俚语, 逮捕, pubic, 阴部的。
⑧ Laredo: 拉雷多, 美国德克萨斯一城市。
⑨ drank... Alley: 在天堂小巷里饮松节油, Paradise Alley, 指纽约下东部一平民区。
⑩ purgatoried their torsos: 把他们的身体投入炼狱。purgatoried, 源自名词, purgatory, 此处做动词用, 意为投入炼狱。

with dreams, with drugs, with waking nightmares, alcohol and cock and endless balls,

incomparable blind streets of shuddering cloud and lightning in the mind leaping toward poles of Canada & Paterson,① illuminating all the motionless world of Time between,

Peyote solidities of halls,② backyard green tree cemetery dawns, wine drunkenness over the rooftops, storefront boroughs of teahead joyride③ neon blinking traffic light, sun and moon and tree vibrations in the roaring winter dusks of Brooklyn,④ ashcan rantings and kind king light of mind,

who chained themselves to subways for the endless ride from Battery⑤ to holy Bronx on benzedrine⑥ until the noise of wheels and children brought them down shuddering mouth-wracked and battered bleak of brain all drained of brilliance in the drear light of Zoo,

who sank all night in submarine light of Bickford's⑦ floated out and sat through the stale beer afternoon in desolate Fugazzi's,⑧ listening to the crack of doom on the hydrogen jukebox,

who talked continuously seventy hours from park to pad to bar to Bellevue⑨ to museum to the Brooklyn Bridge,

a lost battalion of platonic conversationalists⑩ jumping down the stoops off fire escapes off windowsills off Empire State⑪ out of the moon,

yacketayakking⑫ screaming vomiting whispering facts and memories and anecdotes and eyeball kicks and shocks of hospitals and jails and wars,

whole intellects disgorged in total recall for seven days and nights with brilliant eyes, meat for the Synagogue cast on the pavement,⑬

who vanished into nowhere Zen⑭ New Jersey leaving a trail of ambiguous

---

① Paterson：美国新泽西一地区，金斯堡出生地。
② Peynote solidities of halls：充满致幻剂的大厅。peynote，植物名称，可用此提取致幻剂。
③ teahead joride：大麻烟鬼驾车兜风。
④ Brooklyn：纽约一城区。
⑤ Battery：纽约市区一公园。Bronx：纽约一城区。
⑥ Benzedrine：安菲他明(中枢兴奋剂)。
⑦ who... Bickford's：他们整夜沉没在比克佛德的水下光芒中。Bickford：自助餐厅。
⑧ Fugazzi's：纽约格林威治村一酒吧，文人聚集地。
⑨ pad：俚语，公寓。Bellevue：纽约曼哈顿一精神病院。
⑩ a lost battalion of platonic conversationalists：一大队晕头转向的柏拉图式的健谈者。
⑪ Empire State：指 Empire State Building，纽约帝国大厦。
⑫ yacketayakking=yak，俚语，谈个没完没了。
⑬ meat for the Synagogue cast on the pavement：扔在人行道上的给犹太教徒的肉。
⑭ Zen：禅宗，50年代在"垮掉一代"中盛行。

picture postcards of Atlantic City Hall,

suffering Eastern sweats and Tangerian bone-grindings and migraines of China① under junk-withdrawal in Newark's bleak furnished room,②

who wandered around and around at midnight in the railroad yard wondering where to go, and went, leaving no broken hearts,

who lit cigarettes in boxcars boxcars boxcars racketing③ through snow toward lonesome farms in grandfather night,

who studied Plotinus Poe St. John of the Cross④ telepathy and bop kabbalah⑤ because the cosmos instinctively vibrated at their feet in Kansas,

who loned it through the streets of Idaho seeking visionary indian angels who were visionary indian angels,

who thought they were only mad when Baltimore gleamed in supernatural ecstasy,

who jumped in limousines with the Chinaman of Oklahoma on the impulse of winter midnight streetlight smalltown rain,

who lounged hungry and lonesome through Houston seeking jazz or sex or soup, and followed the brilliant Spaniard to converse about America and Eternity, a hopeless task, and so took ship to Africa,

who disappeared into the volcanoes of Mexico leaving behind nothing but the shadow of dungarees and the lava and ash of poetry scattered in fireplace Chicago,

who reappeared on the West Coast investigating the F.B.I. in beards and shorts with big pacifist eyes sexy in their dark skin passing out incomprehensible leaflets,

who burned cigarette holes in their arms protesting the narcotic tobacco haze of Capitalism,⑥

who distributed Supercommunist pamphlets in Union Square⑦ weeping and undressing while the sirens of Los Alamos⑧ wailed them down, and

---

① Eastern... China：东方人的焦虑,(摩洛哥)丹吉尔人的刺骨病,中国人的偏头痛病。sweats, 焦虑, migraine, 偏头痛。
② Newark：新泽西州一城市。
③ racketing：纵情欢闹。
④ Plotinus Poe St. John of the Cross：Plotinus (A.D. 205?—270) 罗马哲学家。Edgar Allan Poe (1809—1849) 美国诗人，John of the Cross (1542—1591) 西班牙诗人。
⑤ telepathy and bop kabbalah：心灵感应术和具有神秘特征的事物。
⑥ protesting the narcotic tobacco haze of Capitalism：抗议麻醉、毒人的资本主义烟雾。
⑦ Union Square：纽约联合广场。
⑧ Los Alamos：洛斯阿拉莫斯，美国新墨西哥州中北部城镇，著名的原子能研究中心。

wailed down Wall, and the Staten Island ferry① also wailed,

who broke down crying in white gymnasiums naked and trembling before the machinery of other skeletons,

who bit detectives in the neck and shrieked with delight in policecars for committing no crime but their own wild cooking pederasty② and intoxication,

who howled on their knees in the subway and were dragged off the roof waving genitals and manuscripts,

who let themselves be fucked in the ass by saintly motorcyclists, and screamed with joy,

who blew③ and were blown by those human seraphim, the sailors, caresses of Atlantic and Caribbean love,

who balled in the morning in the evenings in rose gardens and the grass of public parks and cemeteries scattering their semen freely to whomever come who may,

......

"垮掉一代"文学运动虽然时间不长,但仍在美国文学史上写下了重要一笔。二战以后,美国经济快速发展,进入"富裕社会"阶段,但社会气氛却很是压抑,以冷战和对抗共产主义为名义的麦卡锡主义于50年代初在美国正甚嚣尘上,一些美国青年对现实不满,其中一部分——他们日后被称为"垮掉一代",便以"脱俗"的方式来发泄不满。他们留长发、着异装、弃学业、蔑视传统,流迹于社会底层,吸毒纵欲,寻求刺激,形成了一个独特的圈子,向传统社会发动了攻击。金斯堡这首诗如实地反映了"垮掉青年"的苦闷、压抑的心理情绪。

《嚎叫》的出版发行在社会上引起了很大的震动。1956年旧金山警察以《嚎叫》含有淫秽内容的理由逮捕了一家销售该诗集的书店经营者,但次年法庭判定《嚎叫》合法,肯定了其有"拯救心灵"的价值。

《嚎叫》被誉为50年代的"荒原"。它以冲天的怨气表达了"我这一代精英"的痛苦、自暴自弃以及疯狂的行为。生活对他们来说是一个梦魇,为了逃避生活,也是为了表示抗议,他们吸毒、狂欢,在幻觉中让自己的神经得到麻痹。

金斯堡曾称他的诗是"垮掉派——嬉皮士——神秘宗——意象派"的综合体。所选的《嚎叫》中的这段诗就是一个典型的例子。诗人将沉溺于幻觉中的嬉皮士们疯狂、神秘的生活形态与具体的现实生活有机地结合起来,构成了一个个既超脱现实又触手可摸

---

① Wall and Staten Island ferry：(纽约)华尔街和斯塔腾岛渡口。
② cooking pederasty：能引起性欲的鸡奸。
③ blew：俚语,吸毒。

的"意象",再配上一气呵成的平行诗行及咒语似的节奏,给读者造成了既惊诧不已又痛快淋漓的感觉。按照"垮掉一代"的重要人物凯鲁亚克的说法,"垮掉"(beat)一词,原意含有"贫穷潦倒、过流浪汉生活"的意思,后来被发展成表示一种反抗姿态的新的道德态度。可以说,无论从细节描述还是从意义引申方面来说,《嚎叫》都体现了这层意思。

这首诗用了大量的口语、俚语且不避秽语,烘托了"垮掉派"、嬉皮士们的行为方式。当然,诗中也掺杂了许多不健康的内容,作为读者,这是应该意识到的。

America

America I've given you all and now I'm nothing.
America two dollars and twentyseven cents January 17, 1956.
I can't stand my own mind.
America when will we end the human war?
Go fuck yourself with your atom bomb.
I don't feel good don't bother me.
I won't write my poem till I'm in my right mind.
America when will you be angelic?
When will you take off your clothes?
When will you look at yourself through the grave?
When will you be worthy of your million Trotskyites?①
America why are your libraries full of tears?
America when will you send your eggs to India?②
I'm sick of your insane demands.
When can I go into the supermarket and buy what I need with my good looks?
America after all it is you and I who are perfect not the next world.
Your machinery is too much for me.
You made me want to be a saint.
There must be some other way to settle this argument.
Burroughs is in Tangiers③ I don't think he'll come back

---

① Trotskyites:指俄国早期共产党托洛茨基的跟随者,理想主义者。
② 印度当时正遭遇饥荒,而美国农业收成有很多剩余。
③ Burroughs is in Tangiers: William Burroughs,是金斯堡在哥伦比亚大学结识的朋友,"垮掉派"成员,著有小说《赤裸的午餐》(*Naked Lunch*),Tangiers,摩洛哥一城市。

it's sinister.
Are you being sinister or is this some form of practical joke?
I'm trying to come to the point.
I refuse to give up my obsession.
America stop pushing I know what I'm doing.
America the plum blossoms are falling.
I haven't read the newspapers for months, everyday somebody goes on trial for murder.
America I feel sentimental about the Wobblies.①
America I used to be a communist when I was a kid I'm not sorry.
I smoke marijuana② every chance I get.
I sit in my house for days on end and stare at the roses in the closet.
When I go to Chinatown I get drunk and never get laid.③
My mind is made up there's going to be trouble.
You should have seen me reading Marx.
My psychoanalyst thinks I'm perfectly right.
I won't say the Lord's Prayer.
I have mystical visions and cosmic vibrations.
America I still haven't told you what you did to Uncle Max④ after he came over from Russia.

I'm addressing you.
Are you going to let your emotional life be run by Time Magazine?
I'm obsessed by Time Magazine
I read it every week.
Its cover stares at me every time I slink past the corner candystore.
I read it in the basement of the Berkeley Public Library.
It's always telling me about responsibility. Businessmen are serious.
Movie producers are serious. Everybody's serious but me.
It occurs to me that I am America.
I am talking to myself again.

---

① Wobblies：指世界产业工人组织,1905 年在芝加哥建立的一个带有革命倾向的组织。
② marijuana：大麻。
③ get laid：得到满足。
④ Uncle Max：金斯堡妈妈妹妹的丈夫,从俄国移民到美国。

Asia is rising against me.

I haven't got a chinaman's chance.

I'd better consider my national resources.

My national resources consist of two joints① of marijuana millions of genitals an unpublishable private literature that goes 1400 miles an hour and twentyfive-thousand mental institutions.

I say nothing about my prisons nor the millions of underprivileged who live in my flowerpots under the light of five hundred suns.

I have abolished the whorehouses of France, Tangiers is the next to go.

My ambition is to be President despite the fact that I'm a Catholic.

America how can I write a holy litany② in your silly mood?

I will continue like Henry Ford my strophes are as individual as his automobiles more so they're all different sexes.

America I will sell you strophes $2500 apiece $500 down on your old strophe

America free Tom Mooney③

America save the Spanish Loyalists④

America Sacco & Vanzetti⑤ must not die

America I am the Scottsboro boys.⑥

America when I was seven momma took me to Communist Cell meetings they sold us garbanzos⑦ a handful per ticket a ticket costs a nickel and the speeches were free everybody was angelic and sentimental about the workers it was all so sincere you have no idea what a good thing the party was in 1935 Scott Nearing was a grand old man a real mensch Mother Bloor the Silk-strikers' Ewig-Weibliche made me cry I once saw the Yiddish orator Israel Amter plain.⑧ Everybody must have been a spy.

---

① two joints of：（俚语）两卷。

② litany：连祷。

③ Tom Mooney：美国加州工运鼓动者,1916 年被控告炸弹谋杀,判死刑,1939 年被赦免。

④ Spanish Loyalists：指西班牙内战期间反对独裁者佛朗哥者。

⑤ Sacco & Vanzetti：1927 年意大利移民 Nicola Sacco 和 Bartolomeo Vanzetti 被告杀人抢劫被执行死刑,此案在世界各地引起抗议,认为案件处理与他们激烈的政治观点有关。

⑥ The Scottsboro boys：指 1931 年在美国阿拉巴马州强奸两个白人女人后被判刑的九个黑人。一些自由派人士和激进人士认为判定根据不足,四年后减刑。

⑦ garbanzos：鹰嘴豆。

⑧ Scott Nearing, Ella Bloor, Israel Amter：30 年代著名的美国社会主义者和共产主义者,mensch,尊敬的。

America you don't really want to go to war.
America it's them bad Russians.
Them Russians them Russians and them Chinamen. And them Russians.
The Russia wants to eat us alive. The Russia's power mad. She wants to take our cars from out our garages.
Her wants to grab Chicago. Her needs a Red *Readers' Digest*. Her wants our auto plants in Siberia. Him big bureaucracy running our fillingstations.
That no good.   Ugh.   Him make Indians learn read.   Him need big black niggers. Hah. Her makes us all work sixteen hours a day. Help.
America this is quite serious.
America this is the impression I get from looking in the television set.
America is this correct?
I'd better get right down to the job.
It's true I don't want to join the Army or turn lathes in precision parts factories, I'm nearsighted and psychopathic anyway.
America I'm putting my queer shoulder to the wheel.①

—Berkeley, January 17, 1956

作为"垮掉一代"文学派别的发言人,金斯堡的一些诗歌不仅表现和描述了"垮掉一代"异样的、另类的和与传统社会格格不入的行为方式,以及心中的郁闷,更是把矛头直指美国本身,对美国政府的一些行为进行批评乃至抨击,言辞直接,情绪激烈,被一些评论者认为是"政治诗"。这首题为"美国"的诗歌与金斯堡的成名作《嚎叫》齐名,也是一首政治意味强烈的诗作。诗人对美国拥有原子弹、好战的姿态、对穷国袖手不管以及对激进人士的压抑等等表示了强烈的不满。诗人也毫不掩饰地表明了自己的政治态度。金斯堡的母亲在30年代曾带金斯堡参加过一些美国共产党人的活动。在五十年代冷战气氛异常严峻时期,在诗中如此直白地表明自己的政治观点,没有足够的勇气和正义感恐怕是难以做到的。有意思的是,诗人同时也讲述了自己"吸大麻"、"酗酒"等一些代表"垮掉一代"的行为方式,这种政治表白与情绪发泄间的穿插结合是这首诗的一个显著特征。另一个特点则是诗人采用的讽刺手法,在诗的第二节以及第三节的部分诗行,诗人的身份转换成了"美国",似乎是在为美国进行辩护,当然实际上是对美国的行为进行了嘲讽。这样的角度转换更增加了抨击的力度。

金斯堡曾回忆说上中学时老师讲授惠特曼让他印象至深,终身不忘。惠特曼式风格

---

① putting my shoulder to the wheel:把意见态度坚持到底。put one's shoulder to the wheel,全力以赴;queer,古怪的,不同的,(俚语)同性恋的。

的运用在这首诗里显而易见。口语句式、平行诗行,间插故事叙述以及语气词的使用等语言特征与整首诗直抒胸臆式的情绪表露的主调完美结合。

思考题

1. How does Ginsberg describe the madness which destroys the best minds of his generation?
2. What are the central images that may pin down the meaning of the excerpt of "Howl" presented here?
3. What does America symbolize in the poem "America"?
4. What makes this poem so political?

推荐作品

1. *A Supermarket in California*
2. *Sunflower Sutra*
3. *Kaddish*
4. *American Change*

参考书目

1. Jonah Raskin, *Allen Ginsberg's Howl and the Making of the Beat Generation*, Berkeley: U of California P, 2004.
2. Don Byrd, "Allen Ginsberg: Overview" in *Contemporary Poets*, 6th ed. Ed. Thomas Riggs, St. James Press, 1996.

第十九单元

John Ashbery (1927—)
约翰·阿什贝利

作者简介

约翰·阿什贝利，美国后现代诗歌的核心代表人物之一。1953年出版第一部诗集《图兰朵及其他诗歌》(*Turandot and Other Poems*)，1955—1957年作为研究法国文学的富布莱特学者留学法国蒙特贝利埃和巴黎。1958年起作为纽约《先锋论坛报》欧洲版的艺术评论再度驻巴黎，为《艺术新闻》和《艺术国际》报道欧洲的艺术展品和展览会。1965年回到纽约担任《艺术新闻》的执行编辑至1972年。1974年起，阿什贝利开始在布鲁克林学院任教。

阿什贝利与弗兰克·奥哈拉(Frank O'Hara)、肯尼思·柯克(Kenneth Koch)、詹姆斯·斯凯勒(James Schugler)并称"纽约派诗人"(New York Poets)。他们对20年代四五十年代纽约派抽象画家，如杰克逊·波拉克(Jackson Pollock)，有着共同爱好，并且致力于将该派绘画技巧运用到诗歌创作中。事实上，该派是以地域为基础的松散组合，其成员风格各有不同；总体来说，他们刻意回避现实主义，强调艺术的生产特性，因而被归于超现实主义流派，通常以诗作中的大众意象、超现实主义思维方式和积极向上的幽默感著称。

阿什贝利的诗歌被评论家称作"诗歌的诗歌"，主题多是关于诗歌本身的；关注的焦点不是经验本身，而是经验渗透意识的方式，旨在揭示甚至颠覆意义建构的人为性。一度深受美国现代派诗人华莱士·史蒂文斯(Wallace Stevens, 1879—1955)的诗风影响，阿什贝利的诗作充满了哲性思考，言辞犀利。尽管作品经常取材于浪漫主义传统题材，其视角和处理手法却往往前卫，常常与抽象表现主义绘画有异曲同工之处。例如，阿什贝利也十分重视诗歌的乐感；他曾说，"关于音乐，我喜欢它的说服力，它能够成功地将一个论点进行到底，尽管这个论点的语言表达始终是一些未知数。剩下来的是结构、论点的构建、场景或故事。我想在诗歌中做到这一点"。另外,他还致力于在诗歌中营造一种梦幻般的效果。他想要通过诗歌"复制梦幻所具有的那种魔力",即:梦幻"使你相信某个事件有一种缺乏逻辑联系的意义,或者毫无关联的事物之间有一种潜在的关联"。令人出乎意料的并置、自相矛盾的叙述、松散的因果关联以及多重意象与观点的恣意冲撞使得他的某些作品显得晦涩难懂,而这些技巧所制造的"陌生化"效果却使其极具现实穿透力。

阿什贝利既受实验派艺术家推崇,又能得到学院派批评家认可,这在现当代诗人中是不多见的。他至今已出版诗集二十余部,作品获奖无数,其诗集《凸面镜中的自画像》(*Self-Portrait in a Convex Mirror*, 1975)曾获国家图书奖、普利策奖和全美图书批评界奖等三项大奖。著名批评家布鲁姆夸赞诗人"把包括惠特曼、迪金森、史蒂文斯、哈特·克兰的美国的严肃性连接起来,从而实现了爱默生对于美国文学自治的幻想的预言"(《二十世纪外国诗人如是说》,王家新等编,河南人民出版社,1992年,第559页)。

What Is Poetry

The medieval town, with frieze①
Of boy scouts from Nagoya? The snow

That came when we wanted it to snow?②
Beautiful images? Trying to avoid

Ideas, as in this poem? But we
Go back to them as to a wife, leaving

The mistress we desire?③ Now they④
Will have to believe it

---

① frieze: *n.* (在墙顶与天花板间起装饰作用的)横条,饰带。此处形容大批日本童子军的队列。
② The snow/That came when we wanted it to snow?:人类控制自然的企图。诗人通过语言达到控制自然现象的目的,比如象征主义表现手法。
③ But we/Go back to them as to a wife, leaving/The mistress we desire?:此句探讨的是诗歌创作原则。诗人将思想(ideas)比作妻子,将美丽的意象(beautiful images)比作情妇。
④ Now they/Will have to believe it/As we believed it:他们现在相信我们过去相信的东西。"It"指代诗歌传统;"他们"指代不明,根据上下文可以理解为年轻一代。古老的诗歌传统代代相传,创新成为无稽之谈。

As we believed it. In school
All the thought got combed out①:

What was left was like a field.
Shut your eyes, and you can feel it for miles around.

Now open them on a thin vertical path.②
It might give us—what?—some flowers soon?③

  《什么是诗歌》是体现阿什贝利诗歌创作思想的重要诗作。该诗以"什么是诗歌"为标题,提出了有关诗歌本质与诗歌创作的一连串重大问题。其中的核心问题是:在诗歌中,思想与意象,孰重孰轻?传统的延续是否会扼杀诗歌的原创性?问题最终悬而未决,但是这首诗本身对思想与意象的处理方式、对现实的不确定性的直观体现却为读者留下极大的思考与阐释空间,引导读者回顾并反思阿什贝利以及"纽约派"诗人对诗歌创作传统的颠覆与创新。

  在一次访谈中,阿什贝利面对"诗歌中有没有可能避免思想"的提问时,答曰:"当一个人直奔思想的时候,比方说带上锤子和钳子,思想往往会在诗歌里躲避他。我觉得只有在一个人假装对它们不经意时才会重现,就像一只猫蹭你的腿一样。"在谈论《什么是诗歌》这首诗的创作过程时,阿什贝利明确宣称,他的诗歌创作方法基本上就是自由联想(free associating),而且不肯拘泥于形式。他反对以个人经验为主的就事论事的传统创作方法,采取回避主题的迂回策略进行创作,以"欲擒故纵"之道达到"旁敲侧击"的美学效果。比如,中世纪小镇上来自名古屋的童子军是一个颇为独特的意象,这一意象代表了充满华丽矫饰、异域风情或复杂叙事情节的传统诗歌。在一次访谈中,阿什贝利声称这个诗句是自由联想的结果:在英格兰切斯特镇参观城墙时见到的大批外国童子军、在帝国大厦的电梯里遇到的佩带不同城徽的日本童子军(其中有一个来自名古屋)等零散事件在想像中产生了奇特的关联。又如最后一行诗句:阿什贝利在访谈中称这行诗其实来自于他在一家书店里无意听到的一对情侣之间的对话,对旁人来说本无意义,但引述于此处却与上下文产生了很大的关联。

  总之,如同许多现代派画家,阿什贝利对现实的处理方式不是简单模仿,而是通过独立事件的拼接与组合、时空的转换与嫁接等各种手段重新组织细节,对现实进行再创造,颠覆人与自然、社会环境、与神之间的传统关系,以充分彰显诗歌的原创性和诗人的创造力。

---

① comb out:清除,梳理。该句包含着对学校教育扼杀学生创造力的批评。
② Now open them on a thin vertical path:睁开眼睛后看到的是一条狭窄的垂直小径,用来比喻狭窄的视野。这个田地与小径的意象强调了想像力因受限制而变得贫瘠、枯竭。
③ It might give us—what?—some flowers soon?:该句表达了怀疑和很大的不确定性:这条小径能给我们什么?难道无生命力的小径会产生代表生命力的花儿吗?此问颇具反讽色彩。

思考题

1. What images does the poet adopt in this poem? What do they stand for respectively?
2. What is the poet's view of the relationship between images and ideas? Please compare it with that of another poet, say, Wallace Stevens, William Carlos Williams, etc.
3. What does the poem say about poetic imagination and artistic creativity? In what ways are the ideas conveyed?

And Ut Pictura Poesis① Is Her Name

You can't say it that way anymore.
Bothered about beauty you have to
Come out into the open, into a clearing,
And rest. Certainly whatever funny happens to you
Is OK. To demand more than this would be strange
Of you, you who have so many lovers,
People who look up to you and are willing
To do things for you, but you think
It's not right, that if they really knew you...
So much for self-analysis②. Now,
About what to put in your poem-painting:
Flowers are always nice, particularly delphinium③.
Names of boys you once knew and their sleds,
Skyrockets④ are good—do they still exist?
There are a lot of other things of the same quality

---

① Ut Pictura Poesis：拉丁文，u.p.p., "as is painting so is poetry"（Horace, Ars Poetica）。公元前一世纪罗马著名诗人贺拉斯在《诗论》中提出的"诗歌绘画性"概念。
② self-analysis：*n.* 自我分析，这里指的是诗中称呼的"你"，应为带给诗人创作灵感的缪斯女神。
③ delphinium：*n.* 飞燕草，翠雀花，在这里取其读音，并无特别意义。
④ skyrocket：*n.* 流星焰火。

As those I've mentioned. Now one must
Find a few important words, and a lot of low-keyed,
Dull-sounding ones. She approached me
About buying her desk. Suddenly the street was
Bananas and the clangor of Japanese instruments.
Humdrum testaments were scattered around. His head
Locked into mine. We were a seesaw. Something
Ought to be written about how this① affects
You when you write poetry:
The extreme austerity of an almost empty mind
Colliding with the lush, Rousseau-like foliage② of its desire to
communicate
Something between breaths, if only for the sake
Of others and their desire to understand you and desert you
For other centers of communication③, so that understanding
May begin, and in doing so be undone.

作品赏析

该诗选自阿什贝利的一部重要诗集《休闲日》(又译作《船屋的日子》,*Houseboat Days,* 1977)。与前一首诗相似,这首诗同样集中体现了诗人对诗歌创作原则的反思。

本诗开篇提出的问题是:在现代语境下,"诗歌绘画性"的古典主义诗歌理念已变得不再适用。首先,在题材上,诗歌需要开诚布公地讲述日常发生的趣事,一贯受人仰视的缪斯女神不得不走下神坛,其凡性得到强化。其次,作为传统诗歌要素的浪漫意象遭到质疑,日常生活的平凡事件和琐碎细节被纳入诗歌创作中。另外,在语言上,低调、沉闷的词语多于华丽的词藻,诗歌风格变得朴素平实。但是,极其空洞平淡的头脑与内涵丰富的交流欲望之间产生了强烈的反差。最后四行诗句表达了诗人在当下语境中的尴尬处境:诗人具有强烈的倾诉欲望,为了得到他人的理解并且满足他人了解自己的愿望,可是,一旦理解,对方就会弃之而去。在这个互动过程中,理解与消解几乎同时发生,其中暗含了对当时盛行的解构主义思潮的应和。

宇宙的多变性(mutability)以及人类自我意识的多元流动性作为英国文艺复兴和美国超验主义时期的中心主题,也是阿什贝利在诗歌创作中反复思考的一个问题。对他来说,现实是充满变数的意识碎片之组合,而非切实固定的整体,因此,其诗作也就相应地

---

① 这里"this"一词指的是上述所有这些日常生活的琐碎细节,诗人在此提出的问题是:它们是如何影响诗歌创作的。
② lush: *a.* 繁茂的,郁郁葱葱的;foliage: *n.* 树叶。该意象在此与空虚乏味的头脑形成对照,用来比喻强烈的交流欲望。
Rousseau:皮埃尔·卢梭(1812—1867),法国风景画家,巴比松画派主要人物之一,该画派诞生于巴黎南郊约50公里处紧挨着枫丹白露森林的一个村落,活跃于19世纪30—40年代,主张描绘具有民族特色的法国农村自然风景。
③ other centers of communication: 其他交流中心,指具有不同特性的其他意识主体。

折射出关于这种现实的记忆、印象、欲望碎片及其流动多变性。有评论说"在阅读阿什贝利的作品时,你偶然在这里那里抓住一些清晰的意义,但它们很快就转变成别的陌生的东西,或者迅速消失、融化。"线性时间模式的破坏、传统认知秩序的颠覆、意义的随机性、反讽语气等特点都是造成阿什贝利的诗歌晦涩难懂的原因,这些特点可在本诗中窥见一斑,值得深刻探讨。

思考题

1. The poet sets in contrast two kinds of artistic ideals in this poem. What are they?
2. In illustrating the contemporary poetic practices, who is the speaker addressing the audience? What kind of tone is conveyed, didactic or ironic or whatsoever?
3. What do you make of the last four lines?

作品

Paradoxes① and Oxymorons②

This poem is concerned with language on a very plain level.
Look at it talking to you. You look out a window
Or pretend to fidget. You have it but you don't have it.
You miss it, it misses you. You miss each other.③

The poem is sad because it wants to be yours, and cannot.
What's a plain level? It is that and other things,
Bringing a system of them into play. Play?
Well, actually, yes, but I consider play to be

A deeper outside thing, a dreamed role-pattern,

---

① paradox: n. 悖论,似非而是的隽语。即:有悖于常理、看似自相矛盾却包含真理的话语。该诗第三行中的"You have it but you don't have it"(你有它但你没有它)就是一个典型的例子。
② oxymoron: n. 逆喻,矛盾修辞法。即:在名词前加上一个与之反义的形容词,比如诗中第九行的"A deeper outside thing" (一种更深刻的外在事物)等。这是悖论的一种类型。
③ You miss it, it misses you. You miss each other.: miss 一词具有双关语义,一方面可理解为"想念",另一方面也可理解为"错过,未觉察"。

As in the division of grace these long August days①
Without proof. Open-ended. And before you know
It gets lost in the stream and chatter of typewriters.

It has been played once more. I think you exist only
To tease me into doing it, on your level, and then you aren't there
Or have adopted a different attitude. And the poem
Has set me softly down beside you. The poem is you.

  《悖论与逆喻》创作于 1979 年 3 至 10 月间，最早见于《泰晤士报文学副刊》(*Times Literary Supplement*, 1902 年作为伦敦《泰晤士报》副刊出版，1914 年独立发行)，后来收入被评论界比作"十四行诗系列" (sonnet sequence) 并获美国图书奖提名的《影子列车》(*Shadow Train*, 1981)。它探讨了诗歌创作与接受中的边界划分问题上，涉及到诗歌与读者、诗人与语言、诗人与读者、语言与身份等多重复杂关系的悖论，再现了诗歌从写作到阅读的过程中语言、诗人、读者是如何共同参与意义生产的，代表着后现代诗歌的创作理念。

  首先是诗歌与读者之间的关系。该诗一开篇便摆出一副直接与读者对话的姿态来，声明"这首诗只关心非常普通层面上的语言"，试图通过诗人的屈尊与读者建立起一种平等关系。而接下来的三行诗句则表现了读者在阅读过程中的不安和费解。读者与诗歌的关系如同一对貌合神离的恋人，一方"装作烦躁不安"的样子，最终却因未解其意而不能真正拥有对方。诗歌"感到悲哀"，因为它没有得到理解，所以不能属于读者。

  其次是诗人与语言之间的关系。诗人为了迎合普通读者，尽量使用平实的大众话语，却无意间触到了诗歌与戏剧之间的界线。事实上，戏剧更具系统性 (system)，是更外在的东西，"一种人们想扮演的角色模式"；相比之下，诗歌则散乱而没有结论，意义存在极大的不确定性——"在打字机的咔嚓声中烟消云散"。看来，平实的语言并不十分适用于诗歌。

  此外还有诗人与诗歌、读者之间的关系。最后一小节声明诗人其实是为了心目中的"理想读者"而写作的，诗人的意图是使诗歌面向读者——"我觉得你存在着就是 / 为了引诱我去做它，在你的层面上"。可是，"真实读者"似乎并不领情——"然后你又不在那儿了 / 或者态度又不一样了"。诗人将完成的作品交给"真实读者"，宣布"The poem is you"(这首诗就是你)；也就是说，诗歌一旦完成便摆脱了作者意图的羁绊，完全交由读者来阐释，不同的读者会有不同的阐释。值得注意的是，此句绝不等同于"The poem is yours"(这首诗是你的)，可以理解为：读者的身份决定语言的意义发生，是读者最终成就了诗歌，赋予它独立的生命。

  如同阿什贝利的其他代表作一样，读者的注意力往往更多被引向作品的语言层面。

---

① As in the division of grace these long August days/Without proof：就像处在优美分界线的这些八月的漫长白天 / 无需证明。八月是夏秋的分界线，用来比喻戏剧所规定的角色模式自然而分明，有着外在参照物，使得语言自成系统。

标题的"悖论与逆喻"本身就同诗中标榜的"普通层面上的语言"形成了一个自相矛盾的悖论,全诗也不乏悖论、逆喻以及比喻、类比、拟人等修辞法的实例,同时这首诗还兼具抽象性、跳跃性、自身和互文指涉等后现代诗歌的典型特色。可以说,其形式上的规律性(如:六步格、抑扬重音、尾韵等)在一定程度上掩盖了内容所包含的自我解构性,而后者对浪漫主义诗学的命题(如:自我与外部世界、诗歌与主体性等)构成了深刻质疑。

思考题

1. Do you agree with the speaker's claim that "This poem is concerned with language on a very plain level"? Why or why not?
2. Like Ashbery, many modern and contemporary poets see poetry primarily as a form of play. Please define the term "play" according to your own understanding, and then discuss how you see "Paradoxes and Oxymorons" as an illustration or not an illustration of play.
3. What are the paradoxes and oxymorons contained in this poem? Please talk about the (paradoxical) relation between self and language and also how words and meaning relate.

作品

Novelty Love Trot①

  I enjoy biographies and bibliographies,
  and cultural studies. As for music, my tastes
  run to Liszt's Consolations②, especially the flatter ones,
  though I've never been consoled
  by them. Well, once maybe.

  As for religion, it's about going to hell,
  isn't it? I read that 30% of Americans believe in hell,

---

① trot: n. 流行于日本、韩国和中国台湾的一种大众音乐形式,从日本"演歌"演变而成的韩式固有的老式曲风,是由5个音阶构成,2/4节拍或4/4节拍的音乐形态,曲调悲伤感人,独具韵味。标题"Novelty Love Trot"(新奇旧式恋曲)是一个逆喻修辞。
② Liszt's Consolations: 匈牙利作曲家、钢琴家、指挥家和音乐活动家弗伦兹·李斯特(1811—1886)的《安慰曲》。

though only one percent thinks they'll end up there,
which says a lot about us, and about the other religions.
Nobody believes in heaven. Hell is what gets them fired up.
I'm probably the only American

who thinks he's going to heaven, though my reasons
would be hard to explain. I enjoy seasons
and picnicking. A waft from a tree branch
and I'm in heaven, though not literally.①
For that one must await the steep decline
into a declivity, and shouts from companions
who are not far off.②

In the end it matters little what things we enjoy.
We list them, and barely have we begun
when the listener's attention has turned to something else.
"Did you see that? The way that guy cut him off?"
Darlings, we'll all be known for some detail,
some nick in the chiseled brow③, but it won't weigh much
in the scale's careening pan. What others think
of us is the only thing that matters,
to us and to them. You are stuffing squash blossoms
with porcini mushrooms④. I am somewhere else, alone as usual.

I must get back to my elegy.

这首诗选自阿什贝利2005年出版的诗集《我将在哪里游荡》(*Where Shall I Wander*)，读来很像是自传或回忆录的戏仿，其中包含了对宗教、死亡、回忆等严肃问题的反思，也不乏幽默的调侃成分。自由联想的充分发挥、话题转化的突兀性、口语化的表达方式等都很好地体现了阿什贝利的诗歌创作特色。

---

① and I'm in heaven, though not literally：我在天堂，却不是字面意义上的天堂。这里取天堂一词的比喻义，表示生活幸福。
② For that one must await the steep decline/into a declivity, and shouts from companions/who are not far off：that 指的是去往实际的天堂，此句描述了死亡的场景：诗人将死亡比作一次迅速滑落的过程，身边还有亲友陪伴哭喊。
③ some nick in the chiseled brow：刀刻般眉毛上的缺口，代表让人容易识别、记住的小细节。
④ stuffing squash blossoms/with porcini mushrooms：把牛肝菌塞进南瓜花里，此指烹饪一道菜。

第十九单元

正如一幅性格自画像,叙述者(诗人本人?)从兴趣爱好谈起,一一列举了自己在学术、音乐、宗教信仰、业余活动方面的爱好,字里行间渗透出一位暮年之人对死亡的思考。比如,第一小节中提到了李斯特的《安慰曲》,第二小节谈论了死后上天堂还是下地狱的问题,第三小节包含了一个对真实死亡场景的描述。接下来的诗句便彻底偏离了自我介绍的轨道,话题转向了记忆与永生问题,在一定程度上对前面的叙述进行了解构:列举兴趣爱好根本无济于事,说者兴致勃勃,听者却心不在焉,或许一些小细节会令人难忘,但是他人的看法于人于己才是唯一重要。不幸的是,"你"忙于自己的事情,"我"依旧孤独如初——双方其实难以达成沟通交流。

在形式上,该诗采取了与读者直接对话的方式,似在回答友人的问题,又似自问自答、自说自话,语气轻松随意。标题名为"Novelty Love Trot"(新奇旧式恋曲,旧曲新唱),却与内容没有直接的关联,显得名不副实。而结尾一句"I must get back to my elegy"(我必须回到我的挽歌上去)中的"elegy"一词则在内容和形式上起到了双重效果,成为理解全诗的一个关键。首先,这个词突现了全诗的死亡主题,使得散见于诗行中与死亡相关的暗示都跃然前景(foreground),获得了相对连贯的意义。其次,该词一锤定音,似为全诗定性,令读者不禁回过头重新审视此前的诗句而发现:"我"本来要为自己写挽歌,却因自由联想而离题千里。这里面也蕴含了诗人对传统的挽歌诗体的反讽:为自己写的挽歌都要包括些什么?挽歌的意义何在?读者感兴趣的会有几许?这又是一个阿什贝利式的开放结尾,发人深思。

思考题

1. What does the title mean? What kind of poem is it supposed to be?
2. What do you learn about the poet's view of death from this poem?
3. Why does the speaker declare that "I must get back to my elegy" at the end of the poem? How does it make sense in terms of the whole poem?

1. *The Painter (1956)*
2. *Self-Portrait in a Convex Mirror (1975)*
3. *Chinese Whispers: Poems (2002)*

参考书目

1. Herd, David. *John Ashbery & American Poetry*. New York: Farrar, Straus, and Giroux, 2001.
2. Lehman, David. *Beyond amazement: new essays on John Ashbery*. Ithaca, NY: Cornell University Press, 1980.
3. Shapiro, D. *John Ashbery: an introduction to the poetry*. New York: Columbia UP, 1979.

第二十单元

Adrienne Rich (1929—　)
艾德里安娜·里奇

作者简介

艾德里安娜·里奇生于美国马里兰州巴尔的摩的一个上中层家庭。她的父亲有犹太人血统,等待多年也得不到约翰·霍普金斯大学的教授职位;祖父留下的遗物包括一支象牙长笛、一只金怀表和一本希伯莱语的祷告书。这些背景都在里奇的自白性诗歌里有所反映。1951年,里奇毕业于拉德克利夫学院,同年凭诗集《世事一沧桑》(*A Change of World*)获得耶鲁年轻诗人奖。作为评委之一的"现代派"诗人W.H.奥顿(W.H. Auden)在为其诗集所写的序言中评论道:"呈现在读者面前的这些诗有着整洁谦逊的衣着,言说从容平静而不含混,尊重长辈而不畏缩,并且没有谎言:这对于第一部诗集来说,已经相当不俗了"。字里行间多少暴露了男性轻视女性的文化沙文主义心态。

1953年,里奇不顾家人的反对与哈佛大学经济学教授、德系东正教教徒阿尔弗雷德·康拉德结婚,随后生了三个儿子,完全沦为家庭主妇。继1955年发表第二部诗集《钻石切割者》(*The Diamond Cutters*)之后,经过八年之久的沉默,她于1963年出版了诗集《儿媳妇的快照》(*Snapshots of a Daughter-in-Law*),倾诉了具有创造力的女性受到压抑的愤懑,其女权主义立场初见端倪。1966年,里奇与全家迁居纽约后便开始积极参与民权、反战运动,1966年、1969年和1971年分别出版诗集《生命必需品》(*Necessities of Life*)、《传单》(*Leaflets: Poems 1965—1968*)和《改变的意志》(*The Will to Change: Poems 1968—1970*)。1969年,里奇婚姻解体,次年丈夫自杀。

自20世纪70年代初期,里奇全身心投入女权主义运动,后于1976年公开了同性恋身份。她在诗歌和散文中反映了女性以及女同性恋者在父权社会的成长经历和自我意识觉醒过程,并且将艺术创作与政治行动有效地结合起来,成为了20世纪美国激进女性主义的艺术代言人。里奇最出色的诗集

《潜入沉船》(Diving into the Wreck, 1973)承载了女性主义者对美国社会的激进批评立场，著名论文《当我们死人醒来时：作为再修正的写作》(When We Dead Awaken: Writing as Re-Vision, 1971)和《强制的异性恋与同性恋的经验》(Compulsory Heterosexuality and Lesbian Existence, 1978)可谓当代女性主义思想的宣言书。创作于1974—1976年间的组诗《二十一首情诗》(Twenty-One Love Poems)以她与米雪儿·克利芙(Michelle Cliff)之间从隐秘走向公开的同性恋情为主题，是里奇转变为女性主义/同性恋诗人的标志性作品。

八九十年代的作品则在主题上更具多样性，比如：《你的故土、你的生活》(Your Native Land, Your Life, 1986)、《血、面包与诗歌》(Blood, Bread and Poetry, 1986)和《时间的力量》(Time's Power, 1988)、《艰难世界的地图集》(An Atlas of the Difficult World, 1991)等所表现的贫困、暴力和种族主义主题，《那里找到了什么》(What Is Found There, 1993)对美国社会、生态、政治危机的大背景下诗歌与政治文化之间的关系所作的深刻思考，《共和国的黑土地》(Dark Fields of the Republic, 1995)所反思的美国梦以及阶级、性别、种族冲突，等等。

作为美国当代最著名的诗人之一，里奇尤以其鲜明的政治立场引人注目。她的诗歌作品曾多次获奖，几乎囊括了美国诗歌的所有奖项。除了激进的政治主张以外，她在诗歌创作中所关注的还有语言与历史之间的张力、权力关系、诗歌的意识形态功用等问题。同时，里奇也十分注重诗歌语言的创新：抒情性与音韵技巧、自由诗体与正式用语的完美结合带来了一种颇具个性与力度的独特诗风。如她在文集《谎言、秘密与沉默》(Lies, Secrets, and Silences)中所说，"诗歌首先是一种语言的批评。最重要的是，诗歌是语言的力量的集中体现，这种力量也就是我们与宇宙万物之间的终极关系的力量。"

Aunt Jennifer's Tigers

Aunt Jennifer's tigers prance across a screen①,
Bright topaz denizens of a world of green.

---

① screen：屏风，绣屏。第三小节的 panel 为"屏面"，所指相同。

They do not fear the men beneath the tree;
They pace in sleek chivalric certainty.①

Aunt Jennifer's fingers fluttering② through her wool
Find even the ivory needle hard to pull.
The massive weight of Uncle's wedding band
Sits heavily upon Aunt Jennifer's hand.

When Aunt is dead, her terrified hands③ will lie
Still ringed with ordeals④ she was mastered by.
The tigers in the panel that she made
Will go on prancing, proud and unafraid.

《詹尼弗姨妈的老虎》发表于1951年,是里奇的一首早期诗歌代表作。诗人通过绣屏上生气勃勃的老虎形象表达了一位家庭主妇的内心叛逆和抗争愿望,同时也反映了富于创造力的女性艺术家在男权社会中所遭受压抑与遏制的境遇。

该诗在形式上主要采用了象征主义的表现手法。詹尼弗姨妈手上的婚戒至死也未能脱下,它象征了虽不在场却无处不在的丈夫及其代表的强大的夫权统治,暗示着女性在男权体制下无从逃脱的现实宿命;婚戒的沉重给刺绣带来了障碍,这表明了男权体制对女性艺术天分的压制。姨妈颤抖的手指所传达的胆怯、压抑与这双手绣出的老虎所表现的力量、勇气、高贵形成了巨大的反差;绣屏上的老虎傲然无畏与女人对比强烈,前者的昂扬姿态衬托出了后者作为男性附属品的缺乏自信和独立性的生活状态。同时,绣品的大气恢弘也体现了姨妈对自由的向往以及出色的艺术潜质。诗歌形式虽然传统简洁,但足以承载了里奇早期的女性主义思想萌芽——即,在社会现实层面上对父权体制的强烈谴责和在艺术想像层面上对女性理想世界、自由国度的构建。可以说,艺术超越现实的能力在这首诗歌里得到了充分体现。

与此同时,不少评论家注意到这首小诗不乏意义含混与暧昧的成分。其一,老虎形象的传统内涵是男性力量和权威乃至帝国霸权的象征,如18世纪英国诗人威廉·布莱克(William Blake)的《老虎》(*The Tiger*),而诗人却选取了老虎作为女性自由理想的载体。这在一定程度上可以理解为反讽:女性在构建乌托邦时仍旧难以摆脱男性思维模式,致使女性特质未得彰显;借用后殖民主义的批评术语,也就是,叛逆者用以表达叛逆

---

① They pace in sleek chivalric certainty: 它们皮毛光滑,带着骑士般的自信悠然地踱步。
② fingers fluttering: 手指颤动,flutter一词形象地勾勒出刺绣者穿针引线时的笨拙、迟疑。
③ her terrified hands: 这里采纳的是"移就"(transferred epithet)修辞法,整日诚惶诚恐的不是双手,而是手的主人,只是双手能够通过颤抖来表达主人的内心。
④ Still ringed with ordeals: 女人死后仍然戴着象征着枷锁的婚戒。

的恰是压迫者的语言,因而意义具有自行消解的潜质,叛逆便显得苍白无力。其二,作为女性的代表,詹尼弗姨妈的身份显示出一定的局限性。此诗虽未提供太多的社会文化语境,但有评论家根据主人公活动的范围狭小、与世隔绝的"私人领域"(家庭)推断出詹尼弗姨妈的中产阶级白人女性身份,认为基本上符合20世纪五六十年代美国社会所推崇的"家庭天使"形象,故而其经历与理念的普适性受到了深刻的质疑。以上两个问题从不同角度为这首看似简单的诗歌增添了复杂性,颇值得读者深思。

思考题

1. Please delineate the tigers' image on the screen. What does it symbolize?
2. What kind of a woman is Aunt Jennifer, according to the descriptions?
3. How does the poet bring out the contrast between the tigers and Aunt Jennifer? And what does the contrast signify?

作品

Orion①

Far back when I went zig-zagging
through tamarack pastures
you were my genius, you
my cast-iron Viking②, my helmed
lion-heart king in prison.
Years later now you're young

---

① orion:猎户星座。在希腊罗马神话中,猎户星座为海神尼普顿的儿子奥里翁所变。他是一名英俊而神力无比的巨人猎手,父亲传授给他在海底潜水和海面上行走的本领。奥里翁与开奥斯岛国王俄诺皮翁的女儿墨罗佩的恋爱受挫,俄诺皮翁弄瞎了他的双眼。受到日神救助后,狄安娜爱上他并打算与他成婚,其兄阿波罗在不满之下诱骗她射杀了爱人。痛苦而无奈的狄安娜只好把奥里翁放到天上的星宿中间。猎户星座酷似巨人,系着腰带,佩着宝剑,披着狮皮,拿着大棒,猎犬西利乌斯紧随身后。

② my cast-iron Viking:我那铁铸的北欧海盗,与下一行"我那因禁中的、戴头盔的狮心国王"同指在松林中为诗人引路的猎户星座。后者包含着"狮心王"理查一世(英格兰国王1189—1199)的历史典故;作为英格兰金雀花王朝第二任国王,理查一世是历史上有名的"战神国王",在10年国王生涯中,有9年零2个月的时间在国外征战。他即位后将内政交给坎特伯雷大主教,自己参加了第三次十字军东征,一度在阿卡和雅法等战役中打败了"伊斯兰守护神"萨拉丁的军队,虽因国内出现变故而未能攻下耶路撒冷,临走前与萨拉丁达成了协议,由十字军控制巴勒斯坦沿海地区,穆斯林控制圣城和巴勒斯坦内陆地区,基督徒可自由往返耶路撒冷进行朝拜。但是,他在回国途中被奥地利公爵俘虏,最后缴纳了15万马克才得以释放。

my fierce half-brother①, staring
down from that simplified west②
your breast open, your belt dragged down
by an oldfashioned thing, a sword
the last bravado③ you won't give over
though it weighs you down as you stride

and the stars in it are dim
and maybe have stopped burning.
But you burn, and I know it;
as I throw back my head to take you in④
an old transfusion⑤ happens again:
divine astronomy is nothing to it.

Indoors I bruise and blunder,⑥
break faith, leave ill enough
alone, a dead child born in the dark.
Night cracks up over the chimney,
pieces of time, frozen geodes
come showering down in the grate.⑦

A man reaches behind my eyes
and finds them empty
a woman's head turns away
from my head in the mirror
children are dying my death
and eating crumbs of my life.

---

① my fierce half-brother：我那凶猛的同胞兄弟。half-brother 确切是指同父异母或同母异父的兄弟，表达了诗人在其内在自我与猎户星座之间建立的情感关联。《当我们死人醒来时：作为再修正的写作》一文为此提供了详细背景：里奇将活跃的（生活）原则、旺盛的想像力称作自己的同胞兄弟，并且多年来将其比做猎户星座。

② that simplified west：简化的西天。太阳落山后，猎户星座在余晖落尽的西天边显现。

③ ravado：n. 虚张声势，唬人的把戏。这里指猎户星座在形状上酷似佩带一把华丽而无用的宝剑。

④ as I throw back my head to take you in：当我向后仰头，把你尽收眼底。

⑤ an old transfusion：transfusion 意为"输血，液体倾注"，此处指等同于一次醍醐灌顶的顿悟，昔日曾经有过类似经历，此时再次发生。

⑥ Indoors I bruise and blunder：在室内，我跌跌撞撞，伤痕累累。此句暗指被囚禁于内室的女性冲破家庭牢笼的努力。本诗节以及下一诗节提供了若干细节：违背婚姻誓言、任由生病的孩子因缺乏照料而死去、忽略丈夫和孩子们的需要。

⑦ frozen geodes/come showering down in the grate：从炉排片中斜落的冻结晶簇，用来比喻时间的碎片。

美国 诗歌 选读

Pity is not your forte.
Calmly you ache up there
pinned aloft in your crow's nest,①
my speechless pirate!
You take it all for granted
and when I look you back

it's with a starlike eye
shooting its cold and egotistical spear②
where it can so least damage.
Breathe deep! No hurt, no pardon
out here in the cold with you
you with your back to the wall.

《猎户星座》选自里奇出版于1969年的诗集《传单》(*Leaflets*)，是诗人朝向明确的女性主义立场转变的过渡期代表作。这个时期的作品表达了一种迟疑的越界冲动，诗人对牺牲女性想像力来实现传统性别角色分工的社会规范提出了质疑，寻回失去的自我(身体、灵魂)的尝试为下一阶段的女性本能释放、直接挑战父权等主题做了充分铺垫。

事实上，20世纪60年代晚期，该诗创作时也是里奇与丈夫的婚姻陷入危机之时，诗人开始重新审视自我并反思往昔的生活模式。时隔两年，里奇后来在《当我们死人醒来时：作为再修正的写作》一文中宣称，《猎户星座》是"同我感到正在失去的一部分自我，即活跃的(生活)原则、旺盛的想像力，重新建立关联的一首诗歌"。她认为自己必须在两种非此即彼的价值观之间作出选择："在爱——女人的、母性的、利他的爱——由整个文化的分量来界定和规范的一种爱——和自我主义——由男人转化为创造、成就、雄心的一种力量，通常是以牺牲他人为代价的，但却有正当的理由。"尽管里奇"现在(1971年)知道其他选择都是不真实的——还有，'爱'这个字眼本身需要修改，"但是，在强调创造力的男性价值观与注重关联的女性价值观之间，在诗人与女性两种看似不可调和的身份之间，里奇当时所作的选择显然是前者，即：以放弃"女性特质"、母性枯竭为代价的诗人身份。

顿悟一刻，在"猎户星座"面前，"神圣的天文学"变得毫无意义；在艺术想像力面前，生物解剖学也同样一钱不值。里奇指出，"冷酷"和"自我本位"这两个形容词其实是她的自我写照。诗中的女性叙述者把自我完全托付给了"猎户星座"，全身心投入艺术事业，留给丈夫的是"空洞的双眼"，给予孩子们的是"生命的残渣"，她唯一能够做到的也只有

---

① crow's nest：乌鸦巢；(航海术语)桅斗，桅杆瞭望台。
② egotistical：自我本位的，任性的。its cold and egotistical spear 指猎户星座向人间射出的冷漠、超然的星光，像长矛一般形状却毫无杀伤力而言，可谓"事不关己，高高挂起"。

把"冷酷自私"带给他人的伤害减低到最小程度,字里行间不无歉疚之意。这充分体现了里奇过渡时期的两难困境和矛盾心理。

思考题

1. The Orion is addressed directly in the poem. How is it addressed? What can you infer from the appellations about its symbolic role here?
2. The third stanza includes the line "as I throw back my head to take you in/an old transfusion happens again." How do you understand the "old transfusion"?
3. The line "Indoors I bruise and blunder" reveals something about the narrator's life. What kind of life is it? What can you infer about the narrator's identity?

作品

Diving into the Wreck

First having read the book of myths,
and loaded the camera,
and checked the edge of the knife-blade,
I put on
the body-armor of black rubber
the absurd flippers
the grave and awkward mask①.
I am having to do this
not like Cousteau② with his
assiduous team
aboard the sun-flooded schooner
but here alone.

There is a ladder.
The ladder is always there

---

① the body-armor of black rubber/the grave and awkward mask/the absurd flippers: 黑橡胶的盔甲、脚蹼和面罩构成了全套的潜水用品。
② Cousteau: 科斯特,指雅克·科斯特(1910—),法国水下探险家、作家。

hanging innocently
close to the side of the schooner.
We know what it is for,
we who have used it.
Otherwise
it is a piece of maritime floss
some sundry equipment.

I go down.
Rung after rung and still
the oxygen immerses me
the blue light
the clear atoms
of our human air.
I go down.
My flippers cripple me,
I crawl like an insect down the ladder
and there is no one
to tell me when the ocean
will begin.

First the air is blue and then
it is bluer and then green and then
black I am blacking out and yet
my mask is powerful
it pumps my blood with power
the sea is another story
the sea is not a question of power
I have to learn alone
to turn my body without force
in the deep element①.

And now: it is easy to forget
what I came for

---

① element：自然环境，此处指海洋。

among so many who have always
lived here
swaying their crenellated① fans
between the reefs
and besides
you breathe differently down here.

I came to explore the wreck.
The words are purposes.
The words are maps.
I came to see the damage that was done
and the treasures that prevail.
I stroke the beam of my lamp
slowly along the flank
of something more permanent
than fish or weed

the thing I came for:
the wreck and not the story of the wreck
the thing itself and not the myth
the drowned face always staring
toward the sun
the evidence of damage
worn by salt and sway into this threadbare beauty
the ribs of the disaster
curving their assertion
among the tentative haunters.②

This is the place.
And I am here, the mermaid whose dark hair
streams black, the merman in his armored body.③
We circle silently

---

① crenellated: 锯齿状的。
② the ribs of the disaster/curving their assertion/among the tentative haunters: 灾难的肋骨/在暂时的逗留者中/弯曲地倾诉着。
③ mermaid、merman: 美人鱼、雄人鱼,此指男女遇难者的尸体,前者长发飘扬,后者遍身盔甲。

about the wreck
we dive into the hold.
I am she: I am he

whose drowned face sleeps with open eyes
whose breasts still bear the stress
whose silver, copper, vermeil cargo lies
obscurely inside barrels
half-wedged and left to rot
we are the half-destroyed instruments
that once held to a course
the water-eaten log
the fouled compass

We are, I am, you are
by cowardice or courage
the one who find our way
back to this scene
carrying a knife, a camera
a book of myths
in which
our names do not appear.

这首诗是里奇20世纪70年代诗歌代表作,也是她作为女性主义诗人的身份确立的标志。她凭借1973年出版的同名诗集《潜入沉船》(*Diving into the Wreck*)与金斯堡(Allen Ginsberg,1926—1997)分享1974年的美国全国图书奖。作品表现了她在这个阶段把"雌雄同体(androgyny)"看作父权制社会中两性关系调和的理想状态的女性主义思想。

《潜入沉船》表达了诗人对女性命运的历史观照。首先,如玛格丽特·阿特伍德所说,"沉船"意象象征着"为世人遗忘的神话,特别是关于男女两性的神话"的残骸。诗歌开篇,"我"有备而来,带着一本神话书,而在诗歌结尾处,诗人指出,这是"一本没有我们名字的神话书"。值得注意的是,与男性探险家科斯特不同,"我"没有群体的协助,而是独自一人踏上这段充满未知的旅程:"那里无人告诉我/海洋何时/开始";"我必须独自学习/在深沉的海洋中/不费力地转身"。同时,"我"也是抱着特定目标而来,即:亲自搜集证据,以期发现事情的真相——尽管"词语是我的目标/词语是地图","我"却并不迷信文字,因为"我为它而来:/是沉船而非沉船的故事/是事物本身而非神话"。结果,"我"看到了死去的同类,与他们相融合,从而获得了跨越时空的群体归属感和历史观。

从诗人特有的女性主义立场出发,"沉船"的意象承载了父权社会中被埋没的女性史。相应地,"潜入沉船"是一个象征性行动,集中体现了整个诗集的"探寻"(quest)主题。在一定程度上,潜水的过程正是女性个体发掘历史,唤醒沉睡的自我的过程。至此,里奇已走出过渡时期的困惑坚定地信奉诗歌改变生活乃至带来社会变革的功用,而该诗恰好代表了20世纪六七十年代女性主义者发掘湮没的妇女史、女性文学史的积极行动倡议和艺术创作理念。

思考题

1. What does the wreck symbolize? And what about the act of diving?
2. What message do the lines "the thing I came for:/the wreck and not the story of the wreck/the thing itself and not the myth" communicate?
3. Why do "I" identify with the mermaid and the merman at once? Who do you think "we" are toward the end of the poem?

作品

Transit①

When I meet the skier she is always
walking, skis and poles shouldered, toward the mountain
free-swinging in worn boots
over the path new-sifted with fresh snow
her greying dark hair almost hidden by
a cap of many colors
her fifty-year-old, strong, impatient body
dressed for cold and speed
her eyes level with mine

And when we pass each other I look into her face
wondering what we have in common
where our minds converge

---

① Transit:根据词义,诗歌标题可以有两种理解:交错经过,擦肩而过;转变。

for we do not pass each other, she passes me
as I halt beside the fence tangled in snow,
she passes me as I shall never pass her
in this life①

Yet I remember us together
climbing Chocorua②, summer nineteen-forty-five
details of vegetation beyond the timberline
lichens, wildflowers, birds,
amazement when the trail broke out onto the granite ledge③
sloped over blue lakes, green pines, giddy air④
like dreams of flying

When sisters separate they haunt each other⑤
as she, who I might once have been, haunts me⑥
or is it I who do the haunting
halting and watching her on the path
how she appears again through lightly-blowing
crystals⑦, how her strong knees carry her,
how unaware she is, how simple
this is for her, how without let or hindrance⑧
she travels in her body
until the point of passing, where the skier
and the cripple must decide
to recognize each other?

---

① she passes me as I shall never pass her/in this life：她经过我的身旁，而此生我将不会从她身边经过。此句读来意义含混，指向了这个诗节所制造的一个朦胧悬念。诗人似乎在刻意强调我和她之间存在的某种不平等：我们并不是擦肩而过。二者的反差在于：她大步前行，而我静止伫立；她从我眼前走过，而我此生不会经过她的身旁。其中似有某种暗示，谜底将在诗歌结尾处揭开。
② Chocorua：沙科拉瓦峰，美国新罕布什尔州白山山脉。
③ when the trail broke out onto the granite ledge：当小径陡然通到花岗岩礁石上。broke out 一词表示"出其不意，突兀"。
④ giddy air：令人晕眩的高空。暗示着从悬崖坠落。
⑤ When sisters separate they haunt each other：当姊妹分离时，她们仍彼此魂牵梦绕。往昔的记忆在两位女子之间建立起一种如影随形的关联，共同的经历会通过记忆而跨越时空，将彼此联结在一起。
⑥ she, who I might once have been, haunts me：我对她念念不忘，那也许就是旧日曾经的我。意思是：往昔的记忆将我和她联系在一起，她使我想起自己的旧日模样。
⑦ through lightly-blowing crystals：透过轻飘飘的冰晶，亦即：轻舞飞扬的雪花。
⑧ without let or hindrance：没有迟疑、障碍。作为名词，let 取 delay 之意。

作品赏析

《转变》是里奇发表于1980年代初期的作品。诗歌的标题意味深长。事实上,自推出惊世骇俗的《二十一首情诗》以来,里奇在60年代中期开始了她向同性恋女性主义诗人的公开转变,到1980年发表那篇引发争议的理论文章《强制的异性恋与同性恋的经验》为止,该身份已完全确立。与前期作品相比,《转变》这首诗的关注点从两性之间的情感纠葛转向了女性之间,记录了又一个带来"顿悟"般心灵震撼的瞬间,似在言说一种建立于苦难记忆之上的"姐妹情谊"(sisterhood)。

首先,这是一个怎样的瞬间呢?从表层叙事来看,一个落雪的日子,一位年届五十的滑雪女子从"我"的眼前经过,"我"有种似曾相识的感觉,猛然想起30年前共攀山峰的一次经历;对方一开始并未注意到"我"的目光,直到交错的那一刻,两个人必须决定是否相认。这个瞬间发生的事情很简单;然而,简单的表象下涌动着令人不安的潜流。叙事者似乎故意留下了一连串的缺口,使得全诗的意义变得异常含混,从而制造了一个又一个悬念。读者不禁渐次产生这样的疑问:"我"为何要强调她经过"我"身旁而反之不成立?1945年到底发生了什么而致使"姊妹"分离?"我"又为何对她念念不忘,一直到再次偶遇?这次偶遇怎么会让"我"产生如此复杂的感触?谜底其实全部在于倒数第二行的"cripple"一词。在"我"的身份真相揭开之时,不仅上述疑问全都有了确定的答案,而且诗中一些原先看似无意义的细节铺陈一下子变得意义丰富起来。比如,一、四诗节分别包含了对滑雪女子外表的描述,其中"我"刻意强调的是对方的身体状态,即,意气风发的形象和充满活力的步态,特别是第一小节中"她五十岁的身体强壮而跃跃欲试,衣着适应御寒和高速运动"以及第四小节中"强健双膝支撑着她"、"她毫无察觉,这对她来说有多么简单"、"身体行动起来毫无迟疑障碍"等措词。这些恰恰反衬了一个跛者的缺憾。此时,全诗以双方在擦身而过的一瞬间"必须决定是否相认"结尾,"必须"一词再次将前面诗节所构建的悬念推给了读者。

如评论家彼得·贝利(Peter Berry)所说,这首诗最主要的特点是充满矛盾、自相抵触的叙事。矛盾修辞法的例子比比皆是:第一小节的"graying dark hair"(斑白的深色头发)和"fifty-year old, strong impatient body"(强健而跃跃欲试的50岁的身体);第二小节中的"when we pass each other"(当我们经过彼此身旁)和"we do not pass each other"(我们没有经过彼此身旁)。同时,用词本身的歧义造成了意义含混。例如,第九行的"level"一词作为形容词暗示着双方的身高相似,作为动词则表明双方保持目光接触,难以移开视线;第五小节中的"she, who I might once have been"指向了两者的关系之谜,可以作多种解释:"she, whom I once had the potential to become or to be like","she whom I might have been like, had I chosen to be"(她是我曾经有可能成为的模样),或者"she, who I perhaps once was (or once was like)"(她可能就是我的昔日模样);最后一句,不仅"must"一词奇特地暗示着一种没有选择余地的义务,而且"the cripple"也可以有身体和精神的两种可能性。另外,该诗的叙事情节也存在诸多漏洞。叙事者对滑雪女子的描述使其身份变得扑朔迷离,具有很大的不确定性:开篇明明作为陌生人出现,"我"却能确定她藏在帽子下的头发颜色和年龄;第三小节她被确认为旧日相识,而到了最后一节"she appears again through lightly blowing/ crystals"却又赋予她幽灵般的特性,疑似自我的投射。

　　归根结底,是否跛者因为多年前致残的一次爬山经历耿耿于怀,从而迁怒于同行的姐妹,多年以后的偶遇时刻要作一个恩怨了断?抑或跛者非跛,而是存在某种心理障碍,此时必须要与昔日自我达成和解?总之,该诗给读者留下了丰富的想象空间,滑雪女子与跛者之间的关系成为理解该诗的一个焦点,而语义含混和叙事跳跃性在很大程度上为这一阅读过程增加了难度。

思考题

1. About the image of the woman skier, which aspect is highlighted in her portrayal? For what purpose(s)?
2. What can be inferred about the relationship between the skier and "me"?
3. How is it possible to read the poem in terms of Rich's construction of "sisterhood" since mid-1970s?

推荐作品

1. *On Lies, Secrets and Silence: Selected Prose, 1966—1978* (1979)
2. *Blood, Bread and Poetry: Selected Prose, 1979—1986* (1986)
3. *What Is Found There: Notebooks on Poetry and Politics* (1993)
4. *The Fact of a Doorframe: Poems Selected and New, 1950—2001* (2002)

参考书目

1. Cooper, Jane Roberta, ed. *Reading Adrienne Rich: Reviews and Re-Visions, 1951—1981.* Ann Arbor: U of Michigan P, 1984.
2. Gelpi, Barbara Charlesworth, & Albert Gelpi, eds. *Adrienne Rich's Poetry and Prose.* New York & London: W.W. Norton, 1993.
3. Werner, Craig. *Adrienne Rich: The Poet and Her Critics.* Chicago: American Library Assoc.,1988.

第二十一单元

Gary Snyder (1930—)
加里·斯奈德

作者简介

加里·斯奈德,诗人、作家、环保活动家,生于旧金山,在华盛顿州和俄勒冈州的小农场长大,童年时家境贫寒。1947年进入里德学院(Reed College)攻读文学和人类学,大学期间曾当过水手,参加过温哥华堡垒的考古挖掘,并在学生刊物上发表诗歌。1951年获得学士学位后,夏季曾作为森林测量员到印第安部落保留地工作(这一经历成为他早期发表的《浆果盛宴》["A Berry Feast"]等诗歌的素材),秋季进入印第安纳大学学习人类学,但一学期后便退学,回到旧金山打零工。斯奈德对东方文化极其神往,阅读铃木大拙的书是他从印第安纳大学退学的原因之一;1953年他进入加州大学伯克利分校学习东方语言、哲学和文化;1954年翻译《寒山诗》(Cold Mountain Poems);1956年获得中国古典文学学位后到日本习禅,此后,他多次往返于日美之间,对佛教禅宗进行了深入的研究;1968年,他回到美国加州西部山区定居,栽树养蜂,过着躬耕田园、沉思默想的俭朴生活;1970年,斯奈德夫妇组织了一个地方性的佛学团体,定期举行坐禅、讲经活动。1984年,斯奈德随美国作家代表团访问中国。他在思想和生活方式上受东方哲学影响深刻,借鉴中国和日本的古诗词的意境和手法进行诗歌创作,赋禅机佛理于诗,取得了公认的成就。斯奈德常被认为是"垮掉的一代"的骨干,因为他同金斯堡(Allen Ginsberg)、凯鲁亚克(Jack Kerouac)等人有过交往。1955年10月7日,在著名的旧金山"六画廊(Six Gallery)诗歌朗诵会"(被认为是"旧金山文艺复兴"的开始)上,金斯堡朗诵了《嚎叫》,斯奈德朗诵了《浆果盛宴》,正式融入"垮掉的一代",之后,他和凯鲁亚克到磨坊谷简易房同住,这一段时光被后者写进《达摩流浪者》(The Dharma Bums, 1958,又译《法丐》),斯奈德就是书中Japhy Ryder的原型。斯奈德还是一位出色的生态诗人,他追求人类与自然的统一,关心文明和进步造成的生态不平衡问题。他1959年发表的第一部诗集《砌石》(Riprap)就是根据他从事环保工作的经历创作的;他的其他诗集,如《神话与文本》(Myths & Texts, 1960),《无尽山川》(Mountains and Rivers Without End, 1965)、《遥远的山村》(The Back Country, 1968)、《观浪》(Regarding Wave, 1969)、《龟岛》(Turtle Island, 1974,1975年获普利策奖)、《自然无存》(No Nature: New and Selected Poems, 1992)等都在不同程度上关注生态问题。斯奈德把美国本土历史同广袤的自然以及东方哲学思想融合在一起,诗作领域宽阔,语言清晰,感情真挚,蕴涵丰富,在20世纪60年代末70年代初产生过巨大的影响。他1997年获得伯林根诗歌奖(Bollingen Poetry Prize),已经出版20余部诗文集,退休前在加州大学戴维斯分校讲授文学和"荒野思想"。

Mid-August at Sourdough Mountain Lookout

Down valley a smoke haze
Three days heat, after five days rain
Pitch① glows on the fir-cones②
Across rocks and meadows
Swarms of new flies.

I cannot remember things I once read
A few friends, but they are in cities.
Drinking cold snow-water from a tin cup
Looking down for miles
Through high still air.

《八月中旬于苏窦山守望台》选自斯奈德根据自己在喀斯喀特山脉和内华达山脉当护林员、铺路工的经历而作的第一部诗集《砌石》。该诗为诗集的开篇作,其立意和取材颇得中国古典诗歌之神韵。第一阙里,一组朴实无华的自然画卷慢慢展开,烟雾、树脂、冷杉果、岩石、草地、蝇群等具体意象构成一幅远离尘嚣的自然风光,诗人(观望者)隐退其后,其感知

---

① pitch: 树脂。
② fir-cones: 冷杉果。

以无我的方式出现,不仅突出了意象的自我表现力,而且也使个体经验具有普遍意义,使读者身临其境,感受意象创造出来的美,让人想起"碧涧泉水清,寒山月华白"、"明月松间照,清泉石上流"等诗句。第二阙里,诗人走到前台,于不经意间说出自然旖旎瑰丽到令他忘却尘世("I cannot remember things I once read")的地步。的确,在炎热的夏季"喝着锡杯里冰冷的雪水","穿越高旷宁静的空气","俯瞰千里",与蒙蒙的山雾融为一体,飘飘欲仙,虽无李白"吾将囊括大块,浩然与溟涬同科"之豪放,也足以睥睨"城里"的朋友!

思考题

1. What impresses you more, techniques in poem composition or the situation the poem creates?
2. By what means does the poem convey a sense of serenity and solemnity?
3. What similarities can you find between this poem and some classical Chinese poems?

Riprap①

  Lay down these words
  Before your mind like rocks.
      placed solid, by hands
  In choice of place, set
  Before the body of the mind
      in space and time:
  Solidity of bark, leaf, or wall
      riprap of things:
  Cobble of milky way,
      straying planets,
  These poems, people,
      lost ponies with

---

① 斯奈德自己解释说:Riprap 是"铺在山里陡峭而光滑岩石上为马垫脚用的大卵石。"("a cobble of stone laid on steep slick rock to make a trail for horses in the mountains.")

Dragging saddles—
        and rocky sure-foot trails.
The worlds like an endless
        four-dimensional
Game of *Go*①.
        ants and pebbles
In the thin loam②, each rock a word
        a creek-washed stone
Granite③: ingrained
        with torment of fire and weight
Crystal and sediment④ linked hot
        all change, in thoughts,
As well as things.

《砌石》是斯奈德第同名诗集中的压轴作。诗人结合他在内华达山脉铺路队工作的经历阐述了自己的诗歌艺术观，告诉读者如何理解其诗作。在他看来，诗歌欣赏和诗歌创作同"砌石"有许多相似之处。正如铺路工在光滑岩石上铺上大卵石为马垫脚，使马可以稳步登高一样，诗人用文字这种石块般实在的形式在人们的大脑设置台阶和抓手，在时间和空间上为人们通往更高境界（"milky way"）搭建道路（"sure-foot trails"）；诗人还像修路工那样精心选材用料，让每一个词发挥其应有的作用，像围棋一样变化多端，蚂蚁与银河并存的包罗万象的世界浓缩成诗，使读者能看"岩石"和"文字"、"思想"和"事物"之间的瞬息万变的关系。诗文排列错落有致，形如云梯，句子结构中省略了传统英语诗歌中被认为是不可或缺的成分，用意象和形式勾画出有形的轮廓和变幻不定的意义。

 思考题

1. What is the analogy between words and rocks?
2. What are the "worlds" mentioned in line 15?
3. How does the poetic structure relate words, things and thoughts?

---

① game of Go：围棋。
② loam：壤土；沃土。
③ granite：花岗岩。
④ sediment：沉积（物）。

Pine Tree Tops

In the blue night
frost haze, the sky glows
with the moon
pine tree tops
bend snow-blue, fade
into sky, frost, starlight.
The creak of boots.
Rabbit tracks, deer tracks,
what do we know.

《松树冠》选自《龟岛》，是诗人最为得意之作。诗歌用清朗恬淡的意象连缀成优美画面，表现出自然的诡秘神奇和与之相对的人类的浅薄，景中有情，以景托情，情景交融。前六行写景，意象多而不乱，从蓝色的夜空到缥缈的雾气，从朦胧的月亮到低垂的树冠，再从树冠上的霜晶到淡蓝色的星空，由上及下，再由下至上，天地相连，相互映照，勾勒出一幅幽静朦胧、空廓虚无，宛如太古之境的画面。然而，月夜的松林并非静默死寂。第七行写声："靴声嘎嘎"而至，似乎打破了月夜的静谧。但是，这来自人类的响声只是局部的、暂时的，相对星月霜雾，人类的活动微不足道。月夜野外的几声靴响，愈见旷野之静谧，就像在"空山"闻得"人语响"一样。君不见，松林里留下的是兔和鹿的足迹，而不是人的行踪！诗眼随即自然地跟出：在空灵玄寂的自然之中，人类到底懂得什么（"what do we know"）？这是诗人对人类状况的思索，或者说是让人警醒的提示，前面所描绘的具体意象都是为了托衬这一情感。

思考题

1. It has been argued that Snyder advocates peaceful co-existence between man and animals by placing "[t]he creak of boots" parallel with "[r]abbit tracks, deer tracks". Do you find the interpretation reasonable?

2. Does the title have any special meaning? If it is changed to "Pine Forest in Moonlight", will the poem be affected?

3. Here is Snyder's translation of a poem by Hanshan. What do you think of the translation?

美国 诗歌选读

登徒寒山道
寒 山

登徒寒山道，
寒山路不穷。
溪长石磊磊，
涧阔草蒙蒙。
苔滑非关雨，
松鸣不假风。
谁能超世累，
共坐白云中。

Clambering Up Cold Mountain Path
Hanshan (Tang)

Clambering up the Cold Mountain path,
The Cold Mountain trail goes on and on.
The long gorge choked with scree and boulders,
The wide creek
the mist-blurred grass.
The moss is slipprey
though there's been no rain,
The pine sings
but there's no wind.
Who can leap the world's ties,
And sit with me among the white clouds?

Three Deer One Coyote① Running in the Snow

First three deer bounding②
and then coyote streaks③ right after
        tail   flat out

I stand dumb a while   two seconds
blankly black-and-white of trees and snow

       Coyote's back!
    good coat, fluffy tail,
sees me: quickly gone.

      Later:
I walk through where they ran
to study how that news all got put down.

---

① coyote：郊狼。
② bound：跳跃着跑。
③ streak：飞跑，疾驰。

作品赏析　哈佛大学从事生态文学研究的布鲁斯·库克(Bruce Cook)教授把斯奈德比喻成"垮掉的一代"的梭罗。《砌石》里,"Cobble of milky way"很有梭罗(《我生活的地方;我的生活方式》)在时间的长河钓鱼、钓星星、钓月亮的韵味。这首《三头鹿一头郊狼在雪地上奔跑》则更像《访客》和《冬天的动物》中描绘的人兽为邻、和谐共处的情景。诗歌用平实内敛的语句,带有寓言色彩的故事,描绘了诗人在纯净的大自然里阅读、寻找自然与内心的诗篇时见到体壮毛亮 ("good coat, fluffy tail") 的郊狼重返他生活的地方时的惊奇 ("I stand dumb a while")兴奋和喜悦("Coyote's back!")。这种失而复得的强烈感受既是旧友重逢的激动,又是对生态环境改善的欣慰。然而,曾经受过伤害的郊狼则对人心存芥蒂,看到"我"后马上跑开了。对于郊狼捕猎鹿的行为,诗人吸取美洲印第安人的泛灵论的观念,认为个体为了获得生存的能量,难免会杀生,不浪费生命的杀生是大自然的一部分,所以郊狼并没有因为(企图)捕杀鹿而让诗人厌恶或反感。诗歌最后通过诗人阅读郊狼在雪地上留下的诗篇/新闻("news")再次强化人和其他动物之间的平等伙伴关系。诗歌文字清晰优雅,蕴含无限的张力和广阔的思想空间。

思考题

1. How do you account for the unusual spacing in lines 3, 4, 5 and 8? And why is the space in the middle of line 8 the largest?
2. Why do you think the poet primarily uses the present tense in the poem?
3. What kind of mood do you think the poet is in when he begins "to study how that news all got put down"?

参考资料

1. Dean, Tim. *Gary Snyder and the American Unconscious: Inhabiting the Ground*. New York: St. Martin's Press, 1991.
2. Molesworth, Charles. *Gary Snyder's Vision: Poetry and the Real Work*. Columbia: U of Missouri P, 1983.
3. Murphy, Patrick D., ed. *Critical essays on Gary Snyder*. Boston: G.K. Hall, 1990. ...*Understanding Gary Snyder*. Columbia: U of South Carolina P, 1992.

第二十二单元

Sylvia Plath (1932—1963)
西尔维亚·普拉斯

作者简介

西尔维亚·普拉斯(Sylvia Plath, 1932—1963),美国女诗人,与同时代诗人罗伯特·洛威尔(Robert Lowell, 1917—1977,1947 年和 1974 年两度普利策奖得主)、安妮·塞克斯顿(Anne Sexton, 1928—1974,1967 年获普利策奖)等人并称"自白派"(confessional poets)。

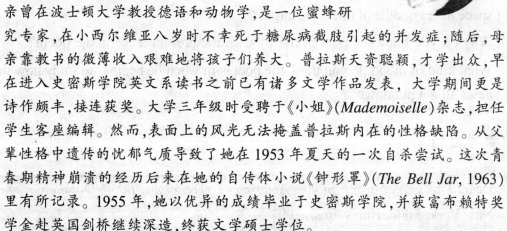

普拉斯生于马萨诸塞州的一个中产阶级家庭。父亲曾在波士顿大学教授德语和动物学,是一位蜜蜂研究专家,在小西尔维亚八岁时不幸死于糖尿病截肢引起的并发症;随后,母亲靠教书的微薄收入艰难地将孩子们养大。普拉斯天资聪颖,才学出众,早在进入史密斯学院英文系读书之前已有诸多文学作品发表,大学期间更是诗作颇丰,接连获奖。大学三年级时受聘于《小姐》(Mademoiselle)杂志,担任学生客座编辑。然而,表面上的风光无法掩盖普拉斯内在的性格缺陷。从父辈性格中遗传的忧郁气质导致了她在 1953 年夏天的一次自杀尝试。这次青春期精神崩溃的经历后来在她的自传体小说《钟形罩》(The Bell Jar, 1963)里有所记录。1955 年,她以优异的成绩毕业于史密斯学院,并获富布赖特奖学金赴英国剑桥继续深造,终获文学硕士学位。

1956 年,普拉斯与日后成为英国桂冠诗人的泰德·休斯(Ted Hughes, 1930—1998)结婚,次年一同回到美国,普拉斯在史密斯学院任教,1959 年底两人又一同返回英国,安家于德文郡的一个小乡村。三年间,普拉斯生下一儿一女,出版了首部诗集《巨神像及其他诗歌》(The Colossus and Other Poems, 1960),后因丈夫的婚外恋情而分居,独自带着孩子栖身于伦敦的一间小公寓房里,靠写作来维持生计。1963 年 2 月 11 日,《钟形罩》出版后数周,生活贫困、精神抑郁的普拉斯走投无路,在寓所中打开煤气自杀身亡。两年后,诗集《爱丽儿》(Ariel, 1965)出版,《渡河》(Crossing the Water)和《冬树》(Winter Trees)也于1971年面世,其中收录了她临终前的诗作。1981年,由休斯编辑的《诗全集》(Collected Poems)出版,次年荣获普利策奖。

  普拉斯自始至终关注的是女性的生命历程与苦痛情感,其诗作以个人内心体验的深度探索为主要特征,多半充斥着愤怒、反抗与黑色幽默,彰显了渐趋鲜明的女性自我意识与个性化声音,并体现出诗人对女性多重社会角色的深刻理解。与主题内容相得益彰,反传统的诗歌形式表达了一种近乎病态却不无节制的神经质激情,不寻常的隐喻、扭曲更迭的意象、跳跃激荡的节奏、语气的突兀变换等手法构成了休斯所谓"噼啪作响的文字能量"(crackling verbal energy)。这里选取的《爹爹》和《拉撒路夫人》是诗人60年代初期代表作。相比之下,普拉斯的临终诗作激情消退,语气内敛,趋于冷峻肃穆,一种神秘主义倾向初见端倪。《词语》便是一例。

Daddy

You do not do, you do not do
Any more, black shoe
In which I have lived like a foot
For thirty years, poor and white,
Barely daring to breathe or Achoo①.

Daddy, I have had to kill you.
You died before I had time—
Marble-heavy, a bag full of God,
Ghastly statue with one gray toe
Big as a Frisco seal②

And a head in the freakish Atlantic
Where it pours bean green over blue

---

① Achoo:啊啾,打喷嚏发出的声音。
② a Frisco seal:实为"San Francisco Seal Rocks",是指位于旧金山湾的太平洋上的海豹岩。
③ Nauset:马萨诸塞州科德角/鳕鱼角(Cape Cod)瑙塞特滩。

In the waters off beautiful Nauset③.
I used to pray to recover you.
Ach, du.①

In the German tongue, in the Polish town
Scraped flat by the roller
Of wars, wars, wars.
But the name of the town is common.
My Polack friend②

Say there are a dozen or two.
So I never could tell where you
Put your foot, your root,
I never could talk to you.
The tongue stuck in my jaw.

It stuck in a barb wire snare.
Ich, ich, ich, ich,③
I could hardly speak.
I thought every German was you.
And the language obscene

An engine, an engine
Chuffing me off like a Jew.④
A jew to Dachau, Auschwitz, Belsen.⑤
I began to talk like a Jew.
I think I may well be a Jew.

The snows of the Tyrol⑥, the clear beer of Vienna
Are not very pure or true.
With my gipsy ancestress and my weird luck

---

① "Ach, du"：德语感叹词，"Ah, you"。
② Polack：n. <美俚>波兰人，波兰血统的家伙，有贬低轻蔑之含意。
③ Ich：德语，第一人称单数"我"。
④ Chuffing me off like a Jew：chuff,（引擎）发出噗噗声；chuff off,这里指粗暴地发落,如同二战中纳粹对待犹太人一样。
⑤ Dachau, Auschwitz, Belsen：达豪、达斯威兹、倍尔森，均为二战时期的纳粹集中营。
⑥ the Tyrol：提洛尔，指奥地利阿尔卑斯山区。

And my Taroc① pack and my Taroc pack
I may be a bit of a Jew.

I have always been scared of *you*,
With your Luftwaffe, your gobbledygoo.②
And your neat moustache
And your Aryan eye, bright blue.③
Panzer-man, panzer-man, O You—④

Not God but a swastika⑤
So black no sky could squeak through.
Every woman adores a Fascist,
The boot in the face, the brute
Brute heart of a brute like you.

You stand at the blackboard, daddy,
In the picture I have of you,
A cleft in your chin instead of your foot
But no less a devil for that, no not
Any less the black man who

Bit my pretty red heart in two.
I was ten when they buried you.
At twenty I tried to die⑥
And get back, back, back to you.
I thought even the bones would do.

But they pulled me out of the sack.
And they stuck me together with glue.
And then I knew what to do.
I made a model of you.

---

① Taroc：算命用的塔罗牌（或译"泰洛牌"）。
② Luftwaffe：德语，二战中的纳粹德国空军；gobbledygook：官样文章，这里指军腔。
③ Aryan：*a.* 亚利安人种的，指的是在纳粹德国指犹太人以外的白种人，尤其是北欧的。
④ panzer-man：*n.* 装甲兵。
⑤ swastika：*n.* 纳粹党所用的十字记号卍。
⑥ At twenty I tried to die：暗指诗人自己在大学三年级暑假里的自杀经历。

A man in black with a Meinkampf look①

And a love of the rack—and the screw.②
And I said I do, I do.
So daddy, I'm finally through.
The black telephone's off at the root,
The voices just can't worm through.

If I've killed one man, I've killed two—
The vampire who said he was you
And drank my blood for a year,
Seven years, if you want to know.
Daddy, you can lie back now.

There's a stake in your fat black heart③
And the villagers never liked you.
They are dancing and stamping on you.
They always *knew* it was you.
Daddy, daddy, you bastard, I'm through.

作品赏析 这首诗是普拉斯最著名的诗篇之一，写在与丈夫的感情破裂之后。普拉斯成长于20世纪50年代的美国，一方面仍深受女性"相夫教子、纯洁忠贞"的传统性别观影响，另一方面却强烈认同现代女性对个人事业和性自由的追求，这一冲突给她的人生观乃至婚姻生活带来了很大困扰。诗人对性别角色与性别关系的困惑在这首以父亲为题材的诗作当中得以充分体现。

首先，此诗淋漓尽致地表达了普拉斯对父亲/男性爱恨交织的心情，成为诗人的自我意识与女性视角的巧妙载体。事实上，父亲的德国血统和过早辞世是笼罩在普拉斯心头挥之不去的阴影，对亡父的怨恨和内疚感交织，折磨了她一生。本诗直接抒发了这种复杂感情，如第二、三小节。同时，诗中反复出现的德国纳粹与犹太人形象构成了父女/两性关系的一个独特隐喻。诗人反复强调父亲是纳粹分子和法西斯分子，一如魔鬼般残暴的父权统治者形象；她则把自己与受迫害的犹太人联系在一起。与之相呼应的是诗中的密集得令人窒息的暴力意象。开篇的女性像只脚一样被关在鞋子里面，贯穿全诗的是

---

① a Meinkampf look：长相像希特勒。Meinkampf，希特勒的自传《我的奋斗》，指代希特勒本人。
② the rack—and the screw：两种刑具，老虎凳与拇指夹。
③ There's a stake in your fat black heart：传说中对付吸血鬼的一种方法是将一根尖桩钉入他的心脏，以达到彻底杀死他的目的。

纳粹战争机器的暴力工具和行动(压路机、带铁刺的陷阱、老虎凳、拇指夹以及碾压、卡住、踩踏、杀戮等),结尾则推出与吸血鬼同归于尽的意象,全诗在狂怒的诅咒和深深的幻灭中结束。

然而,诗作运用儿歌的韵律,自始至终反复出现同一韵脚(do,you,blue,Jew),从整体上形成一种抚慰的语气。

思考题

1. What kind of father image is constructed in this poem? Please describe it.
2. What complex feeling(s) does the poet express over the father figure? Which lines reveal the poet's own relationship with her late father?
3. What are the dominant images and metaphors the poet adopts to convey her views about father-daughter relationship and gender relationship in general?

Lady Lazarus

I have done it again.①
One year in every ten
I manage it—

A sort of walking miracle, my skin
Bright as a Nazi lampshade,
My right foot

A paperweight,
My face a featureless, fine
Jew linen.

Peel off the napkin
O my enemy.
Do I terrify?—

---

① I have done it again: 指自杀行为。

The nose, the eye pits, the full set of teeth?
The sour breath
Will vanish in a day.

Soon, soon the flesh
The grave cave ate will be
At home on me①

And I a smiling woman.
I am only thirty.
And like the cat I have nine times to die.

This is Number Three.
What a trash
to annihilate each decade.

What a million filaments.②
The peanut-crunching crowd
Shoves in to see

Them unwrap me hand and foot—
The big strip tease.③
Gentlemen, ladies,

These are my hands
My knees.
I may be skin and bone,

Nevertheless, I am the same, identical woman.
The first time it happened I was ten.④
It was an accident.

---

① The grave cave ate will be/At home on me：(被墓穴吞吃的肉体)会回到我身上。
② C3. filament：*n.* 纤维；细丝。
③ strip tease：脱衣舞会。
④ The first time it happened：指叙述者的第一次自杀尝试。

The second time I meant
To last it out and not come back at all.
I rocked shut

As a seashell.
They had to call and call
And pick the worms off me like sticky pearls.

Dying
Is an art, like everything else,
I do it exceptionally well.

I do it so it feels like hell.
I do it so it feels real.
I guess you could say I've a call.①

It's easy enough to do it in a cell.
It's easy enough to do it and stay put.②
It's the theatrical

Comeback in broad day
To the same place, the same face, the same brute
Amused shout:

"A miracle!"
That knocks me out.③
There is a charge

For the eyeing of my scars, there is a charge
For the hearing of my heart—
It really goes.

And there is a charge, a very large charge,

---

① (I've a) call: 天职, 义务, 使命。
② stay put: 保持一动不动的姿态。
③ That knocks me out: (拳击用语)打垮, 挫败。

For a word or a touch
Or a bit of blood

Or a piece of my hair or my clothes.
So, so, Herr Doktor.①
So, Herr Enemy.

I am your opus,②
I am your valuable,
The pure gold baby

That melts to a shriek.
I turn and burn.
Do not think I underestimate your great concern.

Ash, ash—
You poke and stir.
Flesh, bone, there is nothing there—

A cake of soap,
A wedding ring,
A gold filling.③

Herr God, Herr Lucifer,
Beware
Beware.

Out of the ash
I rise with my red hair
And I eat men like air.

---

① Herr Doktor：德语，Mr. Doctor。
② opus：n. 艺术作品。
③ "A cake of soap,/A wedding ring,/A gold filling."：这些意象暗指二战时期纳粹焚烧犹太人时留下的残骸。

作为普拉斯所有"死亡书写"中最为鲜明、直白的诗篇,《拉撒路夫人》(另译为"女拉撒路")是对死亡经验的深度探索。

拉撒路(Lazarus)是圣经中一个关于死亡与复活的故事,出自《约翰福音》第11章。拉撒路是耶稣的一位好友,有一天得了非常严重的病,有人去通知耶稣,希望他快来医治拉撒路,可是,耶稣在拉撒路死后第四天才到达。耶稣来到拉撒路的坟墓前,叫众人打开墓穴,大声呼唤拉撒路出来,死去多日的拉撒路竟然奇迹般地从棺木中走了出来。普拉斯在诗中赋予拉撒路女性的身份,以一种戏剧性的极端方式探讨了死亡与复活的主题,借以对女性生命体验进行反讽式检视。这首私人化的自白式诗作既可看作普拉丝对死亡的戏弄,也可看作对复活的渴求。在叙述者"我"看来,死亡已然成为一种行为艺术,她可以公然地轻易做到;亦如一项使命,她感到反复为之的必要。普拉斯游戏般地穿越了生与死、阴与阳的界线,表现出一种独特的死亡观。

与主题呼应,诗中交替出现的是死亡与复活的种种意象。关于二战中德国纳粹对犹太人进行大屠杀的隐喻颇具深意,结尾处的吸血鬼意象带有明显的女性主义内涵。

思考题

1. What is the confessional dimension of this poem? What does the poet have in common with Lady Lazarus?
2. What kind of feminist ideas does the poet convey through the image of Lady Lazarus?
3. Please find out the images of death and resurrection.

Words

    Axes
    After whose stroke the wood rings,①
    And the echoes!
    Echoes traveling
    Off from the center like horses.

---

① After whose stroke the wood rings:定语从句,whose指代斧头的,斧头的敲击过后树木发出回响。

The sap
Wells like tears, like the①
Water striving
To re-establish its mirror②
Over the rock

That drops and turns,
A white skull,
Eaten by weedy greens.③
Years later I
Encounter them on the road—

Words dry and riderless,④
The indefatigable hoof-taps.⑤
While
From the bottom of the pool, fixed stars
Govern a life.

　　这是普拉斯去世前的遗作,表现的是激情消退后的平静以及日常生活的平静表象掩盖下的绝望。此诗包含着不同于普拉斯以往诗作的丰富意象,颇具神秘主义色彩,从整体上代表了普拉斯辞世前的作品风格。

　　斧头击砍树木,回声迅速消散;汁液涌出,表面立刻平滑如初,恰似投石入水后的情形;石子像一颗白色颅骨,在杂草丛中湮没。时隔许久,词语已然失去往日的激情,干枯无主,一如单调的马蹄声不绝于耳。统辖生活的则是池底冷冰冰的恒星所代表的恒久不变的秩序。这些意象交替传达了激情的涨消、秩序的打破与恢复;最后一个小节的"池底恒星"意象指向了广袤宇宙间的冷漠秩序,似乎蕴含着一种平静中的深切绝望,成就了全诗的哲性基调。

　　从效果上看,与前两首诗直接表达的痛苦相比,此诗字里行间流露出的平静下的绝望更加让人感到毛骨悚然。普拉斯一向相信词语的力量,以词语表露心迹,如今却发现词语苍白无力,激情消散殆尽。考虑到普拉斯的诗作多半都从个人经历出发,诗人的抑郁心境走向这般极致,此后不久的自杀之举便在情理之中了。

---

① Wells like tears: 如泪水般涌出。well: *vi.* 涌出。
② mirror: 此处指镜面般的水面。
③ A white skull,/Eaten by weedy greens: 一颗白色颅骨,在这里与上一小节的石子并置,表示同位语之间的比喻关系。
④ riderless: *a.* (马)没有骑手的,无主的。
⑤ The indefatigable hoof-taps: 不知疲倦的马蹄声声。

思考题

1. Which images signify passion as well as the disturbance of normal order?
2. How does the poem convey the loss of passion and the restoration of order?
3. Wherein lies the philosophical and mystic implication of the poem?

1. *The Colossus (1960)*
2. *Ariel (1965)*
3. *Fever 103° (1965)*

参考书目

1. Bloom, Harold, ed. *Sylvia Plath: Comprehensive Research and Study Guide* (Bloom's Major Poets). New York: Chelsea, 2001.
2. Levy, Pat. *A Guide To: Poems of Sylvia Plath.* London: Hodder & Stoughton, 1999.
3. Wisker, Gina. *Sylvia Plath: A Beginner's Guide.* Vermont: Trafalgar Square, 2001.
4. *York Notes on the Selected Works of Sylvia Plath.* UK: York, 1991.

第二十三单元

N. Scott Momaday (1934—)
斯科特·莫马戴

作者简介

斯科特·莫马戴，美国当代著名印第安裔诗人、小说家和画家。莫马戴身上有一半印第安血统，母亲是白人，父亲是印第安人，属于现居住在俄克拉何马州一带的基奥瓦印第安部落。莫马戴从小生活在印第安领地，1960年和1963年获斯坦福大学硕士和博士学位。后曾任教于加州大学伯克力分校和圣·芭芭拉分校、斯坦福大学以及新墨西哥州立大学，在英语系教授文学。现为亚利桑那大学教授。

莫马戴的写作和诗歌表明了其与印第安文化和传统的一种心心相印的关联。他曾提到在印第安领地内长大时，看到了印地安人深深浸淫在传统中的生活，传统的记忆流淌在他们的血液中，在他们身上，他看到了一种力量和美，而这正是现代人所缺乏的。赞颂印第安文化传统以及在当代社会状况下所面临的困境成为了莫马戴写作的一个主要内容。1968年出版第一部小说《黎明做成的屋子》(The House Made of Dawn)，描写一个从二战回来的印第安人寻找自我身份的艰难过程，次年这部小说获普利策奖。莫马戴说过他主要是一个诗人，即使在小说中，用的也是一种诗的语言。他的写作是从诗歌开始的。莫马戴非常注重印第安口语传统，有些诗歌采用了说话体的方式，接近口语，语言简练但不乏深意。如同他的小说一样，莫马戴的诗歌在很大程度上表现了对印第安历史、文化和传统的思考和挖掘，为读者了解印第安文化提供了不可多得的文本。

New World

1	2	3	4
First Man, behold: the earth glitters with leaves; the sky glistens with rain. Pollen is borne on winds that low and lean upon mountains. Cedars blacken the slopes— and pines.	At dawn eagles hie and hover① above The plain where light gathers in pools. Grasses shimmer and shine. Shadows withdraw and lie away like smoke	At noon turtles enter slowly into the warm dark loam.② Bees hold the swarm.③ Meadows recede through planes of heat and pure distance.	At dusk the gray foxes stiffen in cold; blackbirds④ are fixed in the branches. Rivers follow the moon, the long white track of the

　　天色犹黑，大地已开始苏醒，细雨蒙蒙，微风中飘来一阵花香；天破晓，几只苍鹰在空中急急盘旋，晨曦中，青草微微闪光。天终于亮了，夜色散去，像一缕烟冉冉地隐入光亮之中。午时，三两只乌龟徐徐爬来，黑土地的温暖侵入它们的肌肤，还有蜜蜂，蜂巢里成群成群的蜜蜂。热浪，正午的热浪在草地上留下一片蔫草，长长的像是一条通道。傍晚，冷风吹过，灰狐

---

① hie and hover：急行、盘旋。
② loam：土壤。
③ swarm：蜂群。
④ blackbirds：黑鸟，乌鸦。

狸禁不住打起了寒战,黑鸟、乌鸦上了树,一动不动。水流循着月亮流去,倒映出一个完整的月亮的白色轮廓。这是一幅何其美妙的自然之画!莫马戴本人就是一个画家,为他自己的诗集做插图。在这首诗中,诗人用简洁的词语描述了自然界的一些特征,目光敏锐,就像画家在随意的泼墨之中记录下了美的真谛,虽是寥寥几笔,却惟妙惟肖。身为印第安后裔,对自然的感受自然会不同一般。值得注意的是,诗人在传达大自然的静谧、美妙的同时,也使读者感到一种冷峻的氤氲在诗中蔓延。相比于唐朝诗人王维的"我心素已闲,清川淡如此"(《青溪》)或"即此羡闲逸,怅然吟式微"(《渭川田家》)这种充满人间关怀的田园情怀,莫马戴描述的大自然似乎是远离了人间,突出了自然的纯粹,应是"人之初"(First Man)看到的景观,而这与其从中汲取的印第安文化传统应是吻合的。

The Horse That Died of Shame

Once there was a man who owned a fine hunting
horse. It was black and fast and afraid of nothing.
When it was turned upon an enemy it charged in a
straight line and struck at full speed; the man
need have no hand upon the rein①. But, you know,
that man knew fear. Once during a charge he turned
that animal from its course. That was a bad thing.
The hunting horse died of shame.
　　　　　—from The Way to Rainy Mountain

In the one color of the horse there were many colors.
And that evening it wheeled, riderless, and broke
away into the long distance, running at full speed.
　　And so it does again and again in my dreaming. It
　seems to concentrate all color and light into the
　final moment of its life, until it streaks② the
　vision plane③ and is indefinite, and shines vaguely
　like the gathering of March light to a storm.

---

① the man... rein:骑手用不着控制缰绳。
② streak:疾驶,闪过。
③ vision plane:视野。

Prayer

Darkness,
You are forever.
 Aho.
You are before the light.
 Aho
You stain the long ledge above the seep
  at Leaning Walss.
 Aho
You are the smoke of silence buring.
 Aho.
Above, below, beyond, among the glittering things.
  you are.
 Aho.
The days descend in you,
  yesterday,
  today,
  the day to die.
Aho.
Aho.
Aho.
Aho.

  这里选择的两首小诗表明了莫马戴记录印第安传统的努力。第一首诗由两部分组成,引子和正文。引子讲述的是一个流传在印地安人中间关于一匹神马的故事,这个故事本身源自莫马戴1969年出版的记录基奥瓦印第安历史和传统的书:《通向雨山之路》。神武英勇的马与怯懦胆小的主人形成了鲜明的对照,人可以在死亡面前选择逃避,但是马却做出了另一种选择,为了荣誉,毋宁死,以此捍卫自己的品格。在正文中,莫马戴集中描述了神马在冲向敌人的瞬间的英勇表现:转身、冲锋、义无反顾,直至消失在天边。值得注意的是,在引子故事里,神马在羞耻中死去,在正文里,摆脱了主人的神马却是野性勃发,一展其不屈至死的神勇,而这样的描摹是通过莫马戴的想象来表现的,则更表明了诗人在现代状况下对印第安传统的怀念。

  这种怀念情绪同样也弥漫在第二首诗中。如同题目"祈祷"所表示的那样,这首诗是对一个名叫"Aho"的印第安老年妇女做祈祷的回忆。"Aho"其实就是莫马戴的祖母。诗人在他的小说《黎明做成的屋子》里,借用叙述者的角度,讲述了他祖母的故事:她诞生

美国 诗歌 选读

于 19 世纪中叶最后一批基奥瓦印第安人被美国军队打败的时刻,她也是基奥瓦印第安人的文化和宗教传统,"太阳舞"的最后一批传承者之一。因此,在诗人眼中,"Aho"是基奥瓦印第安人的象征,而他只能在记忆中追忆其祖母的形象。下面一段摘自小说中的文字可以帮助理解这首诗的含意:"我记得她常常做祈祷……最后一次我看到她时,她在黑夜中靠着墙站着祈祷,腰部以上全裸,煤油灯的光亮在黑夜的皮肤上跳跃……我通常不明白她的祈祷,……她的声音中有一种深深的悲凉……。""悲凉"源自于诗人对基奥瓦印第安人命运的感叹,但是另一方面,诗人也在"Aho"身上看到了一种永恒的存在,透过闪烁的光亮,诗人让我们联想到了印第安人的过去、现在和永远——一个身体可以消失,但记忆永远不会磨灭的时刻。这或许正是诗人回忆祖母得到的启迪。

思考题

1. How is the concept of nature represented in the poem "New World" and what does the title imply?
2. What is the conspicuous language style of this poem?
3. What causes the horse to die of shame in the second poem?
4. In the main body of the poem, the word "color" is mentioned several times, what does it mean?
5. What is the function of remembering for the poet in the poem "Prayer"?

推荐作品

1. *The Bear*
2. *The Burning*
3. *Four Charms*

参考书目

1. Maddox, Lucy. "Native American Poetry." *The Columbia History of American Poetry*. Eds. Jay Parini and Brett C. Miller. New York: Columbia UP, 1993. 728—749.
2. Schubnell, Matthias. *N. Scott Momaday: The Cultural and Literary Background*. Norman: U of Oklahoma P, 1985.

第二十四单元

Robert Pinsky (1940—   )
罗伯特·平斯基

作者简介

罗伯特·平斯基生于美国新泽西州，在斯坦福大学获硕士、博士学位。平斯基的写作风格凝聚了古典和现代的写作特征,语言清晰典雅、节奏明快匀称,主题含义深刻。他认为,诗歌是存储记忆的一种技术手段。《悲伤与欢愉》(*Sadness and Happiness*, 1975) 勾勒出美国寻常百姓生活的各个侧面,象征"美国诗歌步入充满信心的新时代"。长诗《对美国的一种解释》(*An Explanation of America*, 1980) 回顾了美国的历史进程。《我的心史》(*History of My Heart*, 1985) 以诗人回忆全家欢度圣诞节为开端,用冷峻的目光审视家庭所经历的酸甜苦辣,并融入他对政治、社会与哲学等问题的思考。该诗获威廉·卡洛斯·威廉斯奖。1996年出版的《想象中的车轮:新旧诗选》(又译《花车巨轮》,*The Figured Wheel: New and Collected Poems 1966—1996*),用丰富的想象力展现遍及美国城乡、贫富阶级、男女老少、各色人种的"车轮",再次突出平斯基作为诗人兼评论家的创新与深邃,1997年获普里策诗歌奖提名。1997年至2000年,平斯基成为美国历史上第一次连任三届的桂冠诗人。在此期间,平斯基与人合编《美国最受欢迎的诗歌:最受欢迎的诗歌项目选集》(*Americans' Favorite Poems: The Favorite Poem Project Anthology*, 1999),通过摄像和录音记录了美国人对他们最喜爱的诗歌的阐释,平斯基认为它"记录了我们的现在,为未来的教育树立了典范,并见证了人们或许忽略现有文化的这一事实。"2000年出版的诗集《泽西雨》(*Jersey Rain*)汇集平斯基对各种科技发明的感悟与思考。译作《但丁的地狱》(*The Inferno of Dante*)获美国诗歌学会的诗歌翻译奖。现担任网络周刊 *Slate* 的诗歌编辑,并在波士顿大学讲授研究生文学创作课程。平斯基的诗歌反映出他对现代技术与诗歌创作关系的关注,对平凡人生的思考,以及对诗歌语言的革新。

美国诗歌选读

To Television

Not a "window on the world"
But as we call you,
A box a **tube**①

Terrarium② of dreams and wonders.
Coffer③ of shades, **ordained**
Cotillion of phosphors
Or liquid crystal

Raster dance,
Quick one, little thief, escort
Of the dying and comfort of the sick,   In a blue glow my father
and little sister sat
Snuggled④ in one chair watching you
Their wife and mother was sick in the head
I scorned you and them as I scorned so much
Homey miracle, tub
Of acquiescence, vein of defiance.
Your patron in the **pantheon**⑤ would be **Hermes**

Now I like you best in a hotel room,
Maybe minutes
Before I have to face an audience: behind
The doors of the **armoire**⑥, box

---

① tube：(美俚)电视。
② terrarium：陆栖小动物饲养箱。
③ coffer：保险箱。ordain：注定。cotillion：法国花式舞；早期法国交谊舞。phosphor：磷光体。raster：(电)光栅。
④ snuggle：偎依。
⑤ Pantheon：罗马万神殿。Hermes：(希神)赫尔墨斯(众神的使者，并为掌管疆界、道路、商业以及科学发明、辨才、幸运、灵巧之神，也是盗贼、赌徒的保护神)。
⑥ armoire：大型衣橱。

Within a box—**Tom & Jerry**①, or also brilliant
And reassuring, **Oprah Winfrey**②.

Thank you, for I watched, I watched
Sid Caesar③ speaking French and Japanese not
Through knowledge but imagination,
His quickness, and Thank You, I watched live
Jackie Robinson④ stealing

Home, the image—O strung shell—enduring
Fleeter than light like these words we
Remember in, they too winged
At the helmet and ankles.

　　"致电视"选自《泽西雨》,是诗人关注科技发明与诗歌创作之间关系的一个例证。诗人对电视的态度似难以捉摸:富有哲理的话语让读者领略到电视具有白衣天使的功效,"陪伴垂危的人,安抚卧榻的病人"("escort of the dying and comfort of the sick")。然而,电视作为人类生活不可或缺的一部分,固然能改善人类生活,但它是否可以展示生活的真谛,诗人对此表示怀疑。诗中,诗人把电视与古希腊的神话人物联系了起来。电视的传播速度之快,范围之广,堪称古罗马神话中的信神赫尔墨斯。一方面使读者意识到高科技的迅猛发展使昔日的神话成为现实,另一方面又暗示大众对电视的顶礼膜拜。电视为广大观众提供各种层次的娱乐节目,人们在享受愉悦的同时不可避免地成为电视的俘虏。接着,电视媒体被巧妙地切换到文字媒介,从而有力地突出了诗的核心:诗的语言犹如头盔和双脚都长有双翼、象征科学与发明的赫尔墨斯信神,与电视节目相比,诗歌会真正深入人心,将流芳千古。1999年平斯基在斯坦福大学毕业典礼上讲道,"诗歌的媒介就是人的声音。按照这种媒介的本质,诗歌就要与大众艺术保持平衡。""致电视"借助电视这一娱乐媒介抒发了诗人希望在社会普及诗歌这一心愿,也恰恰印证了诗人藉助网络技术倡导美国大众阅读并赏析诗歌这一事实。

---

① Tom & Jerry:美国《猫和老鼠》动画片。
② Oprah Winfrey:美国脱口秀著名黑人女主持人。
③ Sid Caesar:美国著名喜剧家,擅长模仿外国语言。
④ Jackie Robinson:美国著名黑人棒球明星。

美国诗歌选读

思考题

1. What does "a window on the world" suggest about the television?
2. How can the television be the "escort of the dying and the comfort of the sick"?
3. What relevance does the television bear to Hermes?

作品

The Figured① Wheel

The figured wheel rolls through shopping malls and prisons,
Over farms, small and immense, and the rotten little downtowns.
Covered with symbols, it mills everything alive and grinds
The remains of the dead in the cemeteries, in unmarked graves and oceans.

Sluiced by salt water and fresh, by pure and contaminated rivers,
By snow and sand, it separates and recombines all droplets and grains.
Even the infinite sub-atomic particles crushed under the illustrated,
Varying treads of its wide circumferential track.

Spraying flecks of tar and molten rock it rumbles
Through the Antarctic station of American sailors and technicians,
And shakes the floors and windows of whorehouses for diggers and smelters
From Bethany, Pennsylvania to a practically nameless, semi-penal② New Town

In the mineral-rich tundra of the Soviet northernmost settlements.
Artists illuminate it with pictures and incised mottoes
Taken from the Ten-Thousand Stories and the Register of True Dramas.
They hang it with colored ribbons and with bells of many pitches.

---

① figured: 想象中的。
② semi-penal: 半带有处罚性的(场所)。

With paints and chisels and moving lights they record
On its rotating surface the elegant and terrifying doings
Of the inhabitants of the Hundred Pantheons of major Gods
Disposed in iconographic stations at hub, spoke and concentric bands.

And also the grotesque demi-Gods, Hopi gargoyles[①] and Ibo dryads[②].
They cover it with wind-chimes and electronic instruments
That vibrate as it rolls to make an all-but-unthinkable music,
So that the wheel hums and rings as it turns through the births of stars

And through the dead-world of bomb, fireblast and fallout
Where only a few doomed races of insects fumble in the smoking grasses.
It is Jesus oblivious to hurt turning to give words to the unrighteous,
And is also Gogol's feeding pig that without knowing it eats a baby chick[③]

And goes on feeding. It is the empty armor of My Cid[④], clattering
Into the arrows of the credulous unbelievers, a metal suit
Like the lost astronaut revolving with his useless umbilicus,
Through the cold streams, neither energy nor matter, that agitate

The cold, cyclical dark, turning and returning.
Even in the scorched and frozen world of the dead after the holocaust
The wheel as it turns goes on accreting ornaments.
Scientists and artists festoon it from the grave with brilliant

Toys and messages, jokes and zodiacs, tragedies conceived
From among the dreams of the unemployed and the pampered,
The listless and the tortured. It is hung with devices
By dead masters who have survived by reducing themselves magically

To tiny organisms, to wisps of matter, crumbs of soil,
Bits of dry skin, microscopic flakes, which is why they are called "great,"

---

① Hopi gargoyles：亚利桑那州东北部印第安人的一个部落所雕刻的怪兽画。
② Ibo dryads：西非尼日利亚东部的居民所信奉的树神。
③ Gogol's feeding pig that without knowing it eats a baby chick：见果戈里的《死魂灵》第一部分第三章，女主人家中的母猪吞吃了一只小鸡，却毫无察觉，继续啃吃西瓜皮。
④ My Cid：El Cid，十一世纪西班牙将领，死后身着盔甲，被拴在马后，人们相信他可以继续率兵战斗。

美国 诗歌 选读

In their humility that goes on celebrating the turning
Of the wheel as it rolls unrelentingly over

A cow plodding through car-traffic on a street in Iasi①
And over the haunts of Robert Pinsky's mother and father
And wife and children and his sweet self
Which he hereby unwillingly and inexpertly gives up, because it is

There, figured and pre-figured in the nothing-transfiguring wheel.

贯穿全诗的意象为想象中的车轮,它无异于岁月的流逝,时空的转变给世间万物留下痕迹。自然的力量不可抗拒,它波及城市、乡村、生者、死者、海洋、陆地、天空等,车轮的威力远远胜于所谓的超级大国,因为试图粉饰民族文化的种种努力终将无法逃脱车轮的旋转与碾压。诗中流露出自然主义的倾向,诗人对缺乏信仰、充满暴力与血腥的当今社会忧心忡忡。想象中的车轮使读者联想到英国诗人叶芝的《第二次来临》(*The Second Coming*),不断吞噬一切的旋转着的车轮与不断旋转、不断扩大的"螺旋"不谋而合,尤其是第七节的第三、四行与叶芝的"The best lack all conviction, while the worst/Are full of passionate intensity"共同体现了邪恶与正直的较量,邪恶势力的强大似乎无可阻挡,人们的灵魂正处于麻木不仁的危机状态。假如不正视这一危机,个人利益将极端膨胀,追逐名利的人们不仅会葬送他们的生命,而且会带来一种精神幻灭感。在这种悲观主义的笼罩下,诗人通过自己的行为警醒读者,尽管自我非常"甜美"("sweet"),但想象中的车轮预示着虚无和幻灭,自我终会被无情地碾碎和遗忘。放弃自我对名利的追求是明智之举,但同时也难以企及。诗人的"不情愿"("unwillingly")以及"不完美"("inexpertly")流露出诗人的现实主义世界观:理智与欲望、理想与现实之间毕竟存在分歧。

思考题

1. What do you think is Pinsky's view of religion after reading the poem?
2. Why do you think the quotation marks are used for "great"?
3. There is only one line in the last stanza. Why is it arranged this way?

---

① Iasi:罗马尼亚的一个城市。

ABC

Any body can die, evidently. Few
Go happily, irradiating joy.

Knowledge, love. Many
Need oblivion①, painkillers②,
Quickest respite.

Sweet time unafflicted,
Various world:

X= your zenith.

　　全诗简明扼要，用英文26个字母作为诗句中每个单词的第一个字母，象征着人生的全部内容，也巧妙传达出人生处世的智慧。人生的理想与现实之间存在着不可逾越的差距，这似乎是痛苦的根源。事实上，人们对真理与真爱缺乏完整和清醒的认识。真理与真爱本身隐含无尽的痛苦，在追求真理的过程中，人们注定要付出努力，遭致误解。同样，在追求真爱的路途上，由于人们所秉信的价值观有所不同，因此也必然面临不同价值观的挑战。由此可见，一个人是否能够获得快乐、真理和真爱，很大程度上取决于他对这三种因素的理解。既然个人对人生的认识是变量，并且同一个人在他生活中的不同阶段对人生的领悟也同样不恒定，那么个人的成功指数与幸福指数也注定是未知数。这首短诗以一个近似数学公式收尾，X= your zenith，简明扼要地传达出人具有巨大潜力这一事实。

思考题

1. What is the symbolic meaning of the title "ABC"?
2. How do you interpret the contrast of "few" and "many" across the first two stanzas?
3. What does the poet mean by "various world"?

---

① oblivion：与上一行中的 knowledge 相对，构成人们渴求真理与希望忘却真理之间的对比。
② painkillers：与上一行中的 love 相对，反映出人们在追求真爱过程中所受到的无限伤害。

美国诗歌选读

推荐作品
1. *The Questions* (1987)
2. *The Uncreation* (1990)
3. *The Haunted Ruin* (2000)

参考书目

1. Pinsky, Robert. *The Situation of Poetry: Contemporary Poetry and Its Traditions.* Princeton, N. J.: Princeton U P, 1976.
2. ——. *Democracy, Culture and the Voice of Poetry.* Princeton, N. J.: Princeton UP, 2002.

第二十五单元

Gary Soto (1952—)
加里·索托

作者简介

加里·索托,美籍墨西哥人后裔,出生在富饶的加利福尼亚州圣约魁谷弗雷斯诺市的一个工人阶级家庭,早年受过良好的教育,受到普利策奖诗人菲利普·莱文(Philip Levine)的影响对文学产生兴趣,1973年在《爱荷华评论》(*Iowa Review*) 上发表首篇诗作,1977年出版首部诗集《圣约魁谷要素》(*The Elements of San Joaquin*),同年开始任教于加州大学伯克利分校,至今获得过包括古根海姆奖和美国诗人协会奖在内的多个重要诗歌奖项,是入选《诺顿现代诗选》的诗人中最年轻的一位。1995年,索托凭诗集《新诗精选》(*New and Selected Poems*)获得《洛杉矶时报》图书奖和美国国家图书奖两项提名奖。

索托诗风平易朴实,创作中往往以童年时代所熟悉的场所和少数族裔的生活经历为素材,加州弗雷斯诺的街道和他自己的家庭成员经常出现在作品中。"失去"(loss)被看作记忆的一个必不可少的成分。虽然索托笔下的墨西哥裔美国家庭多半经济拮据窘迫,面临诸多生活难题,但是,他仅仅着眼于问题及其解决方法,并非表达怨天尤人的消极情绪。其作品集中反映丰富多彩的民族文化,强调以家庭为核心的价值观,有助于美国社会消除历史上墨西哥人懒惰的负面形象,树立健康积极的少数族裔形象,并且为后殖民主义研究提供了颇为有效的文本参照。

美国诗歌选读

作品

Mexicans Begin Jogging

At the factory I worked
In the fleck of rubber①, under the press②
Of an oven yellow with flame,
Until the border patrol③ opened
Their vans and my boss waved for us to run.
"Over the fence④, Soto," he shouted,
And I shouted that I was American.
"No time for lies," he said, and pressed
A dollar in my palm, hurrying me
Through the back door.

Since I was on his time,⑤ I ran
And became the wag to a short tail of Mexicans—⑥
Ran past the amazed crowds that lined
The street and blurred like photographs, in rain.
I ran from that industrial road to the soft
Houses where people paled at the turn of an autumn sky.⑦
What could I do but yell *vivas*⑧
To baseball, milkshakes, and those sociologists
Who would clock me⑨

---

① fleck of rubber：橡胶颗粒。
② press：*n.* 熨烫。
③ border patrol：边境巡逻队，专门负责追查遣返非法越界人员。
④ over the fence：跳过栅栏。
⑤ since I was on his time：在他的工作时间里。由于"我"是受雇于老板，所以只好奉命开始奔跑。
⑥ the wag to a short tail of Mexicans：在美国的白人主流社会中，作为少数族裔的墨西哥移民（合法或非法）被边缘化，诗人在这里将其比作动物躯干以外的一条短短的尾巴，"我"这个个体则在奔跑中引起了这条短尾的摆动。
⑦ the soft/Houses where people paled at the turn of an autumn sky：这里指贫民住宅区。按照字面的意思，房屋在雨中变得松软，人们在秋凉的天气中变得面色苍白。诗人通过这两个意象暗示了少数族裔贫民住居条件的恶劣和生活的窘迫。
⑧ viva：*n.* 意大利、西班牙语中"万岁"的欢呼，欢呼声。
⑨ baseball, milkshakes, and those sociologists/Who would clock me：棒球和奶昔都是美国中产阶级大众文化的代表；更具讽刺意味的是，那些社会学家理应对少数族裔的现状了如指掌，却无力改变，只能一味用计时等方法采集数据。

As I jog into the next century
On the power of a great, silly grin.①

How Things Work

Today it's going to cost us twenty dollars
To live. Five for a softball②. Four for a book,
A handful of ones for coffee and two sweet rolls③,
Bus fare, rosin④ for your mother's violin.
We're completing our task. The tip I left
For the waitress filters down⑤
Like rain, wetting the new roots of a child⑥,
Perhaps, a belligerent cat⑦ that won't let go
Of a balled sock⑧ until there's chicken to eat.
As far as I can tell, daughter, it works like this:
You buy bread from a grocery, a bag of apples
From a fruit stand, and what coins
Are passed on helps others buy pencils, glue,
Tickets to a movie in which laughter
Is thrown into their faces.⑨
If we buy goldfish, someone tries on a hat.
If we buy crayons, someone walks home with a broom.

---

① On the power of a great, silly grin：傻乎乎地咧嘴大笑，表示一种处事态度。意思是，促使"我"继续奔跑前行的力量惟有装傻充愣，自欺欺人。
② softball：n. 垒球。这里指一场垒球比赛。
③ sweet rolls：甜面包卷。
④ rosin：n. 松香。
⑤ filter down：逐渐渗透。此处采用"陌生化"技巧，将付小费与细雨的意象联系起来，表示尽管微不足道，却由于连绵不断而产生累积效应，达到"润物细无声"的效果。对于付者来说，累计起来，这会是一笔不小的开支。
⑥ wetting the new roots of a child：打湿一个孩子新生的毛发。暗指小费的去向：一方付出的小费很可能会帮助对方养育一个孩子。
⑦ a belligerent cat：执拗的猫。
⑧ a balled sock：卷成一团的袜子。
⑨ Tickets to a movie in which laughter/Is thrown into their faces：在电影中，人们享受到难得的欢笑。这里的动词"抛撒"代表了诗人对商业化社会娱乐活动的一种讽刺态度，花钱买到的快乐被轻率而粗暴地掷向人们的脸上去。

美国诗歌选读

A tip, a small purchase① here and there,
And things just keep going. I guess.

作品赏析

与其家庭背景和成长经历相对应,索托的诗歌创作有两个主要特征:

其一是鲜明的自传体特性,尤其是他的种族和群体意识。诗人的工人阶级出身和少数族裔身份赋予了他独特的文化视角以及对边缘群体所处困境的敏锐感知力和为受压迫人群代言的强烈责任感。他曾这样明确表述过自己的政治立场:"我信奉穷人的文化。"

可以说,这个特征在前一首诗里得以集中体现。开篇三行诗句交代了"我"身处的恶劣工作环境:空气中悬浮着橡胶颗粒,炉火烧得正旺,热浪逼人。随后,边境巡逻人员的到来打断了单调的工作,老板招呼工人们赶快逃跑,以免这些人被作为非法移民抓获而给自身带来麻烦。"我"也在其中,老板不理会"我"是合法公民的辩解,硬塞给"我"一美元,命令"我"跑。在雨中,"我"从工业区一直穿越少数族裔贫民窟,心中苦楚,却只能依靠傻乎乎咧嘴大笑的力量活下去。

其二则是生动的日常生活题材和朴素的生活口语。诗人擅长从熟悉的日常生活场景中提炼素材,具有将司空见惯的庸常事件化入诗歌语境的高超技巧。这里所选的两首短诗分别集中体现了上述特征。特别值得注意的是,与美国诗歌传统相符,诗中的主要意象多半取自于自然;然而,与经典主流诗风相异,自然意象并非旨在营造超脱尘世的美感,而是为了强化生活艰辛的主题。

后一首短诗借助于日常生活场景,采用了口语体语言,读来通俗平实,琅琅上口。开篇所直接称呼的"我们"以及第四行所指的"你"到第十行才得到具体化处理:该诗是一名父亲对女儿所讲的心里话。随之,语境也得以具体化,即父亲带年幼的女儿一起出发去逛街购物,前五行相当于列举了当天的开销预算清单(看球赛、买书、喝咖啡、吃甜点,乘坐公共汽车、买母亲拉小提琴用的松香,总共二十美元),从中可以推知这是一个普通的美国中产阶级家庭。诗句通过可以为孩童所接受的一连串具体而浅显的实例解释了消费社会人类生存链条的运作方式,这其中体现了人际间紧密的相互依存关系,颇具朴素的哲理性。

思考题

1. What is the Mexican immigrants' situation in the American context? How is ethnic identity constructed in the first poem?

2. What kind of attitude toward life does "a great, silly grin" indicate? What does the first poem imply about the illegal immigrants' pursuit of the American dream?

---

① a small purchase:购物的小笔开支。

3. Describe the specific view of human life and relationship the father imparts to his daughter in the second poem.

Saturday at the Canal

I was hoping to be happy by seventeen.
School was a sharp check mark in the roll book①,
An obnoxious tuba② playing at noon because our team
Was going to win at night. The teachers were
Too close to dying to understand. The hallways
Stank of poor grades and unwashed hair. Thus,
A friend and I sat watching the water on Saturday,
Neither of us talking much, just warming ourselves③
By hurling large rocks at the dusty ground
And feeling awful because San Francisco④ was a postcard
On a bedroom wall. We wanted to go there,
Hitchhike⑤ under the last migrating birds⑥
And be with people who knew more than three chords⑦
On a guitar. We didn't drink or smoke,
But our hair was shoulder length, wild when
The wind picked up⑧ and the shadows of
This loneliness gripped loose dirt⑨. By bus or car,
By the sway of train over a long bridge,
We wanted to get out. The years froze⑩

---

① check mark：对勾，复选标记；roll book：考勤簿，点名册。
② an obnoxious tuba：【音】大号；(簧风琴的)低音大号音栓。
③ warm oneself：晒太阳，取暖。
④ San Francisco：圣弗朗西斯科，亦称旧金山，位于美国加州，西部沿海主要城市之一。
⑤ hitchhike：沿途搭便车，搭顺风车。
⑥ under the last migrating birds：候鸟迁徙即将结束之时，深秋初冬时节。
⑦ chord：和弦。
⑧ The wind picked up：起风。
⑨ loose dirt：飘浮的粉尘。
⑩ The years froze：岁月凝固，时间静止。

美国诗歌选读

As we sat on the bank. Our eyes followed the water,
White-tipped but dark underneath①, racing out of town.

《运河边的星期六》这首诗选自索托新近出版的诗集《我手中的火》(*A Fire in My Hands*, 2006),诗中表达了一种为生活所困而渴望逃离的强烈感受。该诗最突出的特点是丰富的意象表征。

叙事者是一名青少年在校学生,他已年过十七,为了未能实现的梦想而怅然感怀。他厌恶枯燥乏味、毫无生机的学校生活。把上学比做点名册中的一个尖锐的对勾,表明学校教育泯灭个性,学生也只是将课堂看作一种空洞的形式、一种心不在焉的状态而已。学校里的一切——无聊的球赛、死气沉沉的老师、邋遢的同学、可怜的分数——全都索然无味。同样,小镇上的生活也犹如死水一潭,卧室墙上的旧金山图片代表了一个遥不可及的美梦,与现实生活形成了鲜明的对照。两名水边静坐无语的少年心中油然而生的是难以排解的无边绝望。

诗中的意象表现了静与动之间的力量对比。平静的水面、灰尘覆盖的地面、静坐无言的少年构成了一幅孤寂苍凉的静物画,而少年不时投掷石块的动作、乍起的风吹乱的长发和卷起的尘土、水面泛起的水花则打破了令人绝望的平静,折射出少年内心兴起的波澜和躁动的欲望。时光凝滞,运河经年不息地朝向未知的远方奔涌而去,追随渴求的目光承载着少年们不灭的梦想。

这首诗沿袭了索托诗歌创作中一贯的日常生活题材和口语化风格。同时,该诗虽取材于诗人在加州中央河谷(Central Valley)度过的青少年时代的切身体验,但典型化场景的隐喻内涵超越了个体与种族特殊经历的局限,直面普遍人性的深层情感体验,能够引起不同身份读者的共鸣。

思考题

1. This poem is dominated by vivid imagery. Could you please pick out some dominant images of motion/activity and stillness/stagnation and tell the meanings they each convey?

2. The poem begins with the line "I was hoping to be happy by seventeen." In fact, the theme of unfulfilled adolescent dreams is a popular literary motif in American literature. How is it developed in this poem? Please name one or two literary works with similar thematic concerns.

3. What kind of reaction to life does this poem display? Is desire available in this situation? How universal is the schoolboys' emotional experience? Can you relate to it in real life?

---

① White-tipped but dark underneath:水面泛起白色的水花,水下却幽深晦暗。

推荐作品

1. *Braly Street* (1977)
2. *Kearney Park* (1985)
3. *A Simple Plan* (2007)

参考书目

1. The Official Gary Soto Website. http://www.garysoto.com/.
2. Gary Soto; A Teacher Resource File. http://falcon.jmu.edu/~ramseyil/soto.htm.
3. Orr, Tamra. *Gary Soto*. New York: Rosen Publishing Group, 2005.